Spiritual Architecture and *Paradise Regained*

Medieval & Renaissance Literary Studies

SPIRITUAL

ARCHITECTURE

and

PARADISE

REGAINED

Milton's Literary Ecclesiology

KEN SIMPSON

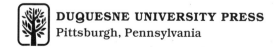

DUQUESNE UNIVERSITY PRESS
Pittsburgh, Pennsylvania

Published in the United States of America by

Duquesne University Press
600 Forbes Avenue
Pittsburgh, Pennsylvania 15282

Library of Congress Cataloging in Publication Data

Simpson, Ken (Kenneth R.), 1957–
Spiritual architecture and Paradise regained : Milton's literary ecclesiology /
    Ken Simpson.
        p. cm. — (Medieval & Renaissance literary studies)
        Summary: "Examines the literary ecclesiology of Paradise Regained,
    arguing that there Milton continues his critique of the English
    Reformation and also continues to develop the consistent theology of the
    church that preoccupied him in his prose during the Civil War" —
    Provided by publisher.
        Includes bibliographical references and index.
        ISBN-13: 978–0–8207–0391–6 (hardcover : alk. paper)
        ISBN-10: 0–8207–0391–5 (hardcover : alk. paper)
        1. Milton, John 1608–1674. Paradise regained. 2. Milton, John,
    1608–1674 — Religion. 3. Religion and literature — England — History —
    17th century. 4. Christian poetry, English — Early modern, 1500–1700 —
    History and criticism. 5. Protestantism and literature — History — 17th
    century. 6. Great Britain — History — Civil War, 1642–1649 — Literature
    and the war. 7. Reformation — England. 8. Theology in literature. I. Title.
        PR3565.S56 2007
        821'.4—dc22   2007019644

∞ Printed on acid-free paper.

CONTENTS

ACKNOWLEDGMENTS

This book has benefited from so much help that a list of people who have contributed to it would fill pages. For those not mentioned here, it will have to suffice that you know who you are and that you know how much I have appreciated your guidance. I should begin, however, by thanking Thompson Rivers University and the Social Sciences and Humanities Research Council of Canada for their financial assistance.

I am also grateful to Albert C. Labriola, Susan Wadsworth-Booth, and everyone at Duquesne University Press for their insightful advice. Many other journals and presses should be noted, too, especially those who have granted permission to reprint altered versions of my work: *Studies in Philology*, the University of Pittsburgh Press, Medieval and Renaissance Texts and Studies, Benwell-Atkins Press, and Cambridge University Press.

Lee Johnson, Dennis Danielson, Mark Vessey, Merv Nicholson, Connie Brim, Alex Forbes, Rod Michell, and David Gay are prominent among the many colleagues who have contributed to my work at different stages and in a variety of ways, from their penetrating remarks at conferences and helpful suggestions at libraries across the globe to the art and wit of their scholarly conversation. Paul Stanwood, however, deserves special acknowledgment. Without Paul's good humor, unwavering encouragement, and sound judgment, as a teacher, scholar, and supervisor, this project simply would not have been possible.

Finally, I am indebted to my friends and family for their support over the years. I am grateful to Chris Speropoulos, Cheryl Matthews, and Des Price for their hospitality during many trips to Vancouver. My mother and father, Jean Fenerty and Ken Simpson, have been remarkably patient, while John and Anne, my son and daughter, have always kept me honest. I owe my deepest thanks, however, to Joanne, who has been there from the beginning.

PREFACE

This study examines the literary ecclesiology of *Paradise Regained*.[1] Milton's ecclesiology or theology of the church is literary not only because it takes poetic form, but also because of the important roles that humanist literary, textual, and rhetorical categories and practices play in his writing of the church. This formulation differs from previous accounts of Milton's relationship to the church in two key ways. First, the interplay between humanist textual and literary goals and Protestant theology, familiar to cultural historians of the Reformation, has not been acknowledged in discussions of Milton's ecclesiology, resulting in disciplinary boundaries that didn't exist for him.[2] Humanist reading and writing practices paved the way for the emergence of Scripture as the Word of God in Protestant theology, which, in turn, became both a foundational metaphor guiding literary activity and the cornerstone of the church.[3] Theology was not a set of abstract propositions to which all discourses referred; rather, it was one of several overlapping discourse fields, including poetry, polemics, and hermeneutics, that offered different opportunities to fulfill the religious imperative to build the church. It was through literary activity — primarily reading and writing in response to Scripture, but also singing, speaking and hearing the Word — that the church came to be and continued to be reformed, its "spiritual architecture" providing an imaginative space for all participants. In Milton's case, then, the church is inseparable from the writing of the church, a view that is not served well by attaching denominational labels to the writer based on confessional statements in his work. Indeed, Milton has not fared well in the denominational approach to his ecclesiology: he is often portrayed as devolving from Presbyterianism to Independency to a "church of one" after the Restoration, isolated, defeated, and quietist, writing his poetry for all time, unconcerned about the church. This brings us to the second way my description of Milton's ecclesiology differs from many previous accounts.

My view of the church coming to be in writing carries forward Milton's ecclesiological concerns not only into his poetry, but also into the Restoration, and particularly into *Paradise Regained*. According to Fredric Jameson, *Paradise Regained* is marked "very explicitly by the emphasis on personal, private salvation" and the "failure of hope following upon the failure of revolution."[4] Similarly, Andrew Milner maintains that the theme of quietism in *Paradise Regained* "is itself an indication of a general fatigue in the revolutionary movement" even if Milton's quietism is "tactical" as he prepares for "that future time when 'doing' rather than 'suffering' will be the order of the day."[5] Both Jameson and Milner, by reducing Milton's religious views to a function of his apparently diminished political aspirations, underestimate the extent to which Milton's ecclesiology continued to be a source of radical opposition in *Paradise Regained*.[6] In this study, *Paradise Regained* is a literary form of spiritual architecture arising from a religious imperative, not power politics or rhetorical self-fashioning.

Other readers, less willing to dismiss the importance of his commitment to Nonconformity after the Restoration, conclude that in *Paradise Regained* Milton remains as engaged as ever in reforming the church and state, despite the conditions of censorship and persecution, the generic demands of the brief epic, and the subtle, restrained tone of the poem. Most recent works refine details of or expand upon the most comprehensive and learned study to date: Barbara Lewalski's *Milton's Brief Epic*.[7] Joan Bennett reminds readers of the religious and political implications of Milton's radical Christian humanism, although she concentrates on the tradition of philosophical rather than textual humanism, which is the emphasis here.[8] Careful attention has also been paid to the poem's relationship to the religious politics of the Restoration.[9] Gary Hamilton presents Jesus as a "nonconformist hero" whose interiority provides an example for persecuted dissenters exiled to worship in private houses by the Conventicle Act of 1664 and 1670.[10] Ashraf Rushdy concludes that *Paradise Regained* is a "stridently anti-monarchist tract" while Laura Knoppers suggests that "the construction of the self-disciplined subject is a model for dissenters of the 1660s and 1670s."[11] In this study, I argue that in *Paradise Regained* Milton not only continues his critique of the English Reformation by confronting the failures of the Restoration settlement, but also continues to develop the consistent theology of the church that preoccupied him in his prose during the civil war and Interregnum. The battle between Jesus and Satan is not simply a solitary, ethical struggle; it is also a contest between the true and false church, Jesus' victory standing as an ecclesiological ideal for persecuted Nonconformists of the 1670s, and as a strident warning for the established church.

The literary, rhetorical, and humanist emphasis in Milton's ecclesiology is unique among theologies of the church in the seventeenth century.[12] God's revelation is profoundly literary and rhetorical as the divine author speaks his Word in Scripture and in the incarnate Word, Jesus. Each individual has the authority of the Holy Spirit to read Scripture to determine what God's revelation is, turning the church into a textual community unified by Christian liberty in reading, celebrating, and interpreting the Word, and in writing works arising from the scriptural encounter.[13] The details of Milton's ecclesiology are also shaped by literary humanist categories and practices. I have mentioned that revelation is primarily rhetorical in structure for Milton, but the Lord's Supper and baptism are redefined by verbal models as well. Church discipline refers to self-discipline achieved by reading and applying classical texts, in addition to the Scriptures. Ministry and liturgy are reshaped in literary terms: ministry includes inspired writers and liturgy is enacted in the repetitions of biblical models and tropes during verbal performance. In many ways, Christian literary activity is a verbal sacrament in which the visible kingdom of the church is transformed into a textual community progressively unfolding the Word over time and space, a *convivium religiosum* made possible by the agency of the book. Of course, Milton does not offer an explicit argument about the church in *Paradise Regained* as he does in his prose, nor does he offer a systematic allegory. Nevertheless, in the course of Satan's temptation of Jesus, and in the metaphors, structural parallels, scriptural allusions, and characterizations of the poem, the embattled but eventually triumphant church that so inspired Milton in his earlier work emerges as a significant presence in the poem. Readers aware of the religious controversies of the age, as many of Milton's readers were, can appreciate the depth of his hope for the church in connotations, resonances, and brief flashes of allusiveness.

Even though the authority, ministry, liturgy, and visibility of the church are examined separately here, it should be kept in mind that these are also closely connected. Since every reader has the authority to interpret God's revelation, all believers belong to the priesthood and have the potential to enact the discipline and liturgy of the visible church until the truth and the invisible community of the elect known only by God are revealed at the end of time. Chapter 1 outlines this ecclesiology as it was gradually unfolded prior to the publication of *Paradise Regained*, primarily in *Areopagitica* and *De*

Doctrina Christiana. Chapter 2 explores Milton's theology of representation as it appears in the interplay between silence and the Word in *Paradise Regained*. The authority of the church derives from each individual's reading of Scripture, but Scripture brings into play both silence and the Word, allowing for the progressive revelation of truth with the guidance of the Holy Spirit until the Second Coming. Ministry, revealed primarily in Jesus' confrontation with Satan, the false teacher, is discussed in chapter 3. During his preparation for his vocation as the preacher of the kingdom, Jesus displays the qualities of a true minister — knowledge of the Word and care for his flock — as he suffers persecution for the sake of the church. Jesus' actions also suggest that the order and government of the church as a whole are inseparable from classical and humanist ideals of moderation and self-control when he responds obediently to God through scriptural interpretation and rational dialogue. Milton alludes to the nature of liturgy in *Paradise Regained* as well: chapter 4 shows that silent prayer, songs of praise, and good works, among other forms of worship in the poem, are important features of public worship in Milton's ecclesiological thought. Finally, the content of the lesson that Jesus must learn throughout the temptations — the meaning of the kingdom he has come to proclaim — is the central theme of the poem and of chapter 5. Jesus learns about the birth, growth, and glorification of his church, but Milton also suggests through apocalyptic and astrological allusions that the kingdom should not be confused with the state. Unlike Presbyterian, Anglican, and Independent apologists, Milton maintains that only Christ, through his Word interpreted by the Holy Spirit in the heart of each believer, rules the church. It is a visible kingdom of the Word besieged by Satan until the Apocalypse when the invisible church will be disclosed once and for all. Milton elaborated the literary ecclesiology that informs *Paradise Regained* prior to 1671, however, so it is necessary to outline its main features before discussing its importance in the poem.

ONE

Writing the Church

That Milton continued his critique of the English Reformation in *Paradise Regained* should not be surprising given his interest in the church prior to 1671. Destined as a child for a life in the church, supported in his literary aspirations by his parents, and convinced by biblical and classical models of the poet's divine purpose, Milton never really separated his religious and poetic vocations.[1] As a young man he commemorated important church figures such as Bishop Andrewes, celebrated the victory of the true church in the Gunpowder Plot, acknowledged events in the church calendar, and responded to the beauty of church architecture, windows, and music.[2] Among his earliest compositions are metrical psalms, a poetic form he returns to in 1648, possibly to contribute to a new psalter.[3] In the Nativity Ode he portrays himself as a sacred poet, offering his poem as a gift of worship to the infant Christ, and in *Lycidas* he condemns the false shepherds of the English church, later adding that the poem "foretels the ruine of our corrupted Clergy." *A Mask* (*Comus*) has also been read as an allegory of the battle between the true and false church, the Lady, like the Protestant church, remaining pure and steadfast in the wilderness.[4] Although these early indications of Milton's interest in the church and of his religious calling as a poet are somewhat conventional, his passionate devotion to the community of faith and to his exalted place in it are unmistakable.

It is unclear whether he decided not to take holy orders in the Church of England to devote himself exclusively to his religious calling in poetry, or whether the actions of the "corrupt Clergy" made it impossible for him to enter the ministry in good conscience. What is clear, however, is that by the late 1630s and early 1640s, Milton found himself devoted to the church but without a public role in it. From 1641 onward, his religious and priestly calling would be fulfilled in writing, offering his prose, in one example, as a "plain ungarnish't" "thanke-offering" to the Son while looking forward to singing him "an elaborate Song to Generations" when he "hast settl'd peace in the Church" (*Animadversions, CPW* 1:706). His poetic ambitions on hold, with the exception of the metrical psalms and the sonnets, many of which also address church reformation, Milton served the church through prose controversy over the next 20 years.

As a result of writing in the genre of prose controversy, Milton's ecclesiology became more clear and detailed than was possible in the early poetry. The same exalted purpose for the church persists, but because the established clergy resists reform, denying the church its biblical form, Milton's passionate devotion becomes vituperative polemic, hermeneutic argument, and prophetic condemnation. In the antiepiscopal tracts of 1641–42, the "seeds of a sufficient determining" (*Tetrachordon, CPW* 2:679) that will grow into the mature ecclesiology of *De Doctrina Christiana* and the late poems are planted for the first time. The authority of the Word over tradition, presbyters over bishops, toleration over persecution, the independent, apostolic church over the state-sponsored church introduced by Constantine, worship over idolatry, the upright heart over formal observance — all of these ideas, introduced with varying degrees of emphasis in 1641–42, were called out of Milton by the events of the civil war and Interregnum and refined by him as circumstances arose. They are also variations on two essential principles of Christian liberty: that the Bible is God's Word and that each Christian is free to interpret it to determine what to believe and how to worship.

This is not to say that Milton began an ecclesiological program in 1641 that remained consistent and unchanged until his death. Positions intuited in the 1640s emerged more fully when circumstances forced him to define his views more carefully according to the two "canons" of Christian liberty. Milton's ecclesiology, then, is not a series of disconnected responses to Laudian Anglicanism, Presbyterianism, and state Independency as Barker suggests.[5] Nor does it evolve "toward something like a vanishing point" until nothing is left but the "church of one man," in which Milton is a victim of his own "self-isolating conviction" and the "archetypal encounter of idealism and realpolitik," as Fixler argues. Milton, according to Fixler, is not interested in the "particular church but the universal one within which he and his ideal readers . . . communed on that level of Christian understanding that came to serve him as the surrogate for the congregational communion of the church of visible saints."[6] The word "surrogate" also reveals Fixler's conviction that Milton's view of church unity is a substitute for the real thing rather than part of a coherent ecclesiology in itself. Although it is true that Milton often does address the universal Protestant church rather than a particular one, he also addresses specific concerns of Nonconformists, especially during the Restoration. Recognizing the continuity of Milton's ecclesiology while acknowledging the local and specific occasions of its formulations also avoids reducing Milton's views to rhetorical strategies or cynical postures designed to manipulate an audience and imposing a postmodern sense of decentered selfhood onto early modern texts.[7] Of course Milton uses rhetorical methods, but they are used for a purpose and by a person that both change and remain consistent over time. From 1641 until his death, Milton's view of the church as a textual community united by the textual practice of Christian liberty remained consistent even though he adapted the external form of the church and all "things indifferent" to a variety of historical conditions in order to secure a visible presence for the church.

Thus, while supporting the Presbyterian position on church government in the antiepiscopal tracts (1641–42), he argues against them and with the Independents for the toleration of the sects, an argument that emerges more fully in *Areopagitica*. He also denounces the "ignoble Hucsterage of pidling Tithes" (*Of Reformation, CPW* 1:613), an argument made later against both Presbyterians and Independents in *Considerations Touching the Likeliest Means to Remove Hirelings Out of the Church* (1659). While he supports the Independents on toleration in the antiepiscopal tracts and *Areopagitica*, in *A Treatise of Civil Power in Ecclesiastical Causes* (1659) Milton insists on the further separation of church and state and a more comprehensive toleration of Protestants based on the authority of the Holy Spirit in each sincere reader of Scripture. This view of the nature of scriptural hermeneutics was approximated earlier in *Of Reformation*, where he imagines each Christian "searching, trying, examining all things, and by the Spirit discerning that which is good" (*CPW* 1:566). The latest and most detailed prose account of his ecclesiology before the publication of the late poems, however, occurs in *De Doctrina Christiana*, the theological treatise that Milton seems to have been patching together for many years and probably was still emending at the time of his death.[8] Arguments about the church appearing in earlier prose works are extended, refined, and often pushed to their logical and radical conclusions. The authority of the ministry, in particular, is diminished on almost every front: anyone with appropriate gifts can preach, the head of the household can administer the Lord's

Supper, and the clergy are elected, supporting themselves by learning a trade or by accepting the congregation's donations. The coherence of Milton's theology of ministry and of other ecclesiological details in the treatise and in earlier prose works only emerges when the textual basis of the church in Christian liberty is kept in mind.

Even if we set aside *Of True Religion* (1673), published after *Paradise Regained*, and the growing number of excellent studies of *Paradise Lost* and *Samson Agonistes* that acknowledge Milton's interest in the Restoration church, the preceding outline is enough to argue that Milton's commitment to the English Reformation did not disappear in 1660.[9] In fact, given the depth of Milton's commitment, it would be unusual if, finally returning to his sacred calling as a poet after so many years, he abandoned the church in the late poems and particularly in *Paradise Regained*. His subject is the temptation of Christ, "the head of the body" (Col. 1:18) and "the chief corner stone" (Eph. 2:20) of the church.[10] His hero is "our Morning Star then in his rise" (*PR* 1.294), an allusion to Revelation 22:16 and the promise of resurrection but also of the Second Coming, an allusion and promise echoed in Nathanael Homes's *The Resurrection Revealed, or, The Dawning of the Day-Star, About to rise and radiate a visible incomparable Glory, far beyond any, since the Creation, upon the Universal Church on Earth . . .* (1654). His hero distinguishes himself in debate and dialogue, preeminent forms of humanist discourse, but also forms highlighted in Simon Patrick's *A Friendly Debate between a Conformist and a Non-conformist* (1669) and Roger L'Estrange's *Toleration Discuss'd, in Two Dialogues. 1. Betwixt a Conformist and a Non-conformist. 2. Betwixt a Presbyterian and an Independent* (1670), both of which condemn Nonconformity. Like Thomas Vincent, author of *God's Terrible Voice in the City of London*, a tract that went through 13 editions between 1666 and 1671, his hero is also called upon to read the providential meaning of historical events, but unlike

Vincent, he does so with restraint, humility, and deference to God's will. Milton's restrained, vigorous blank verse, his plain diction, and his sparing use of classical allusions or elaborate figures, coupled with a tightly wound, often highly schematic syntax that demands sustained intellectual agility from readers, create the kind of aesthetic that Milton hopes to promote in the church. The style of the poem celebrates a simple, unassuming, but cultivated aesthetic surface while recreating the centripetal force and calm inwardness of rigorous spiritual attention that is such an important feature of Protestant spirituality generally. Finally, Milton's genre is the brief epic, a suitable genre for the depiction of struggle and spiritual warfare, precisely the kind of conflict faced by post-Restoration Nonconformists. All of these implied engagements with the church and its immediate conflicts do not suggest quietism or indifference.

In the epistolary preface to *De Doctrina Christiana*, a work he addressed to the universal, visible church (*CPW* 6:117; *CE* 14:1), Milton refers to the two ideas upon which Christian liberty and his ecclesiology are based: the Bible is "God's self-revelation" and all Christians are "free not only to sift and winnow any doctrine, but also to give their opinion of it and even to write about it" (*CPW* 6:118, 122; *CE* 14:4, 12). The first principle concerns revelation and the authority of the church, while the second leads to Milton's view of the visible church as a textual community unified by the common pursuit of Christian truth through literary activity, especially reading, writing, singing, and speaking in response to the Word of God. The nature of the Word of God, and the rhetorical theology of revelation which follows from it, will be discussed as it is explored in *De Doctrina Christiana*, while the notion of Christian liberty in reading and writing will be discussed as it is expressed in *Areopagitica*, where Milton's vision of the church as a textual community is represented most powerfully.[11]

With the first principle, Milton is on solid ground, for the noun phrase, "the word of God" (*"debhar yhvh"*) — the most common expression used throughout the Bible to describe "God's self-revelation" — occurs over 200 times in the Old Testament. When variants are also considered, in which God speaks to Israel generally or to a specific prophet (*"dibber yhvh"*; Isa. 8:5; Amos 3:8), the biblical basis for a rhetorical doctrine of revelation and church authority can be seen clearly.[12] Indeed, "in the most varied literary contexts the OT says of God: '*dibber*,' 'he speaks.'"[13]

God's self-revelation through the Word is also emphasized by the New Testament writers, but their experience is transformed by the Word made flesh and the effort to extend Jesus' presence in time through the church. Like the prophets, the apostles are inspired (2 Tim. 3:15) and continue to proclaim God's word in their ministry, but the prophetic formula "the word of God," is now applied to the Gospels (Mark 2:2) and to preaching the gospel in the church (2 Cor. 4:5; Titus 1:3). This is possible because, according to the canonical Gospel writers, the words of the prophets have been fulfilled in the words (John 8:43, 55; 17:8) and person (John 1:1–14) of Jesus. The Son's preexistent unity with the Father gives him fuller divinity and, therefore, more authority than the prophets, and his incarnate nature, as the Word made flesh, fulfills the merely spoken words of Old Testament writers (Matt. 5:17). In the New Testament, the salvational content of the Word is not the law, which leads to sin (Rom. 3:20), but the grace of God in Jesus, and in the indwelling word of the Holy Spirit, which is written upon the heart (2 Cor. 3:3–6; James 1:21). Moreover, the creative activity of the Old Testament Word is fulfilled in the new creation, the new beginning in the Word. The prologue of the fourth Gospel deliberately echoes Genesis 1:1, while the efficacy of the creative word is emphasized in the way the word grows (Acts 19:20), resounds (1 Thess. 1:8), runs (2 Thess. 3:1), pierces and discerns (Heb. 4:12), and judges (Rev. 19:13–16). For Milton, the consequence of God having "adjusted his word to our understanding" in the Scriptures (*Christian Doctrine, CPW* 6:136; *CE* 14:37) is that each Christian is capable of receiving "the word or message of God" by being "scrupulously faithful to the text" (*CPW* 6:132, 120; *CE* 14:31, 7). The translation of "word," however, was far from straightforward, as Erasmus's translation of the Greek *logos* into the Latin *sermo* in John 1:1 showed. Milton's acceptance of Erasmus's translation helped to shape the rhetorical theology of revelation and church authority that underlies his literary ecclesiology.

Even Erasmus, no stranger to controversy, must have been surprised by the uproar caused by the publication of the second edition of his New Testament translation in 1519.[14] In particular, as Marjorie O'Rourke Boyle notes, the word which his enemies seized "to crystallize ecclesiastical opposition" was *sermo*.[15] In England, Henry Standish, bishop of St. Astaph, denounced Erasmus in a sermon outside St. Paul's, at a court banquet, and before the king and queen, arguing that Erasmus, in presuming to correct the Vulgate, was undermining the authority of Scripture.[16] Although Erasmus saw attacks like these as efforts of entrenched clergymen and theological faculties to rouse opinion against the reforming humanists, there was more at stake than professional jealousy and infighting. As the detailed commentary in *Annotationes in Novum Testamentum*, the polemical defence in *Apologia De In Principio Erat Sermo*, and the eloquent, theological reflections of *Paraphrasis In Evangelium Joannis* testify, Erasmus's revision of Jerome's Vulgate translation of John 1:1 from "*In principio erat verbum*" to "*In principio erat sermo*" reveals both his theological method and his doctrinal emphasis.

Over and over again Erasmus reminds his readers that there is only a grammatical, not a doctrinal, difference between *verbum* and *sermo* as renderings of the Greek *logos* in the New Testament. It implies speech as a whole rather than a single word; it is masculine rather than neutral (*verbum*) or feminine (*oratio*) and, therefore, suits the Son of God; and finally, it is preferred by the majority of Latin authors as well as patristic authorities.[17] Erasmus's rhetorical strategy is astute here since his opponents cannot attack him without condemning themselves. He also demonstrates his theological method; since the Son as *sermo* is the eloquence of God speaking to Christians through the sacred text, philology and rhetoric must be joined to theology. Despite his disclaimers, Erasmus's view of the *logos* as "the revealing discourse [*sermo*] of the Father" did have doctrinal implications, especially for the Trinity, and his attempts to align his translation with doctrinal orthodoxy are not always convincing.[18] Forseeing that the *sermo* analogy might lead to anti-trinitarianism because the speaker precedes the speech in time, he argues that those who "think that the word of God is secondary to him who produces it, as with us intention is prior to utterance," are mistaken; this word is not created in time but begotten from eternity, "the eternal word of the eternal mind, whereby the Father forever speaks."[19] By opting for the philologically correct though theologically suspect *sermo* over the doctrinally safe *verbum*, Erasmus compromises orthodoxy for textual rigour and substitutes a hierarchy of understanding for a hierarchy of tradition, despite his insistence that *sermo* altered nothing in church doctrine.

When Milton translated *logos* as *sermo* rather than *verbum* in his discussion of the Word of God in *De Doctrina Christiana*, the controversy surrounding Erasmus had long subsided. However, the influence of the rhetorical theology promoted by Erasmus, of which *sermo* was the flash point, extended far beyond this occasion.[20] Applying techniques learned in their study of ancient literature to Scripture, such diverse figures as Ficino, Erasmus, Luther, and Calvin guaranteed the rhetorical structure of theology and the textual conditions that made such a theology viable.[21] Freed of textual corruptions, scholastic glosses, and poor Latin, the biblical text, as God's *sermo* (conversation, speech), could speak plainly and directly to readers, moving them to embrace the Christian life. God's self-revelation through the Word in its preexistent, incarnate, and scriptural forms is especially clear in Erasmus's *Lingua* (1525). For Erasmus, *sermo* plays an important role in the construction of revelation as a series of divine disclosures mediated by speech, viewed as a mirror of the speaker's mind: "God the Father spoke once and gave birth to his Eternal Word. He spoke again and with his almighty word created the entire fabric of the universe. And again he spoke through his prophets, by whom he entrusted to us his Holy Writ. . . . Finally he sent his Son, that is the Word clothed in flesh . . . compressing everything, as it were, into an epilogue."[22]

Milton's relationship to rhetorical theology has not been explored in any detail; understandably, scholars have been interested in patristic or Reformed sources of *De Doctrina Christiana,* and more recently, the authorship of the manuscript itself.[23] Readers who do note Milton's use of *sermo* assume that he simply transcribes the Junius-Tremellius Bible without giving much thought to the implications of the translation, but such indifference is unlikely given his precise attention to philology and etymology throughout both his prose and poetry.[24] Milton's use of *sermo* underlies his antitrinitarian theology: Father and Son are related as speaker to speech, author to text, and intention to representation. These analogies are used throughout Scripture to describe God's revelations and were used by rhetorical theologians to authorize their own literary activities. According to Erasmus, "the tongue was given to men so that by its agency as messenger one man might know the mind and intention of another. So it is fitting that the copy should match the original, as mirrors honestly reflect the image of the object before them. . . . For this reason the Son of God, who came to earth so that we might know God's will through him, wished to be called the Word [*Sermo*] of God."[25] Just as speech mediates the self and the Son mediates the

Father in the rhetorical theology of Erasmus, so the Son mediates the revelation of the Father in Milton's view of the Trinity. For Milton, however, the essence or intention of the Father is never fully revealed in his Son any more than an author's intention is fully revealed in a speech or text. It is the work of the Holy Spirit to bring together speech and author in the understanding of the reader.

Before he discusses the Son's generation as God's first act of external efficiency, Milton has prepared his argument in the first four chapters of *De Doctrina Christiana:* the self-existent, ineffable Creator transcends both human understanding and the Word through which the author is revealed. "God's decree, or intention," Milton writes, corresponds to "that idea of all things which, to speak in human terms, he had in mind before he decreed anything" (*CPW* 6:154; *CE* 14:64). As Sidney explained in a different context, "the skill of each artificer standeth in that idea, or foreconceit of the work and not in the work itself."[26] When he turns to his interpretation of John 1.1 (*Christian Doctrine, CPW* 6:206; *CE* 14:180), the scriptural basis of the orthodox view of the Son's generation from eternity, Milton's translation of the Greek *logos* into the Latin *sermo* builds upon his notion of God as an author and reveals the rhetorical nature of the Father's relationship to the Son. They are related as a speaker is to speech, as the author is to the Word and, as Milton argued in his discussion of the Father, the speech is subordinate to the speaker.[27] Except on three occasions, Milton adopts *sermo* whenever he cites the preexistent Word; moreover, he demonstrates that his view of the Son's subordinate divinity is a result of the rational explication of the metaphor of God's speech so prominent in the Bible. "*The Word* [Sermo]" Milton argues, "must be audible, but God is inaudible just as he is invisible, John v. 37; therefore the Word is not of the same essence as God" (*CPW* 6:238–39; *CE* 14:252). The generation, or more precisely, the creation of the Word within the limits of time following God's internal decree is the logical consequence of Milton's construction of revelation as a speech act, the Word emerging from the silent presence of God's fullness. When he explains the precise way in which the Father and Son are one, Milton again uses the metaphor of speech: they "are one in that they speak and act as one" (*CPW* 6:220; *CE* 14:210).

As I've shown, Erasmus argued that *sermo* had no doctrinal implications. In the *Paraphrasis In Evangelium Joannis* he outlines the possible heresies related to *sermo*, including Milton's — that the Word follows the Father in time and is, therefore, not equal to him in essence — but insists that his translation is compatible with the eternal generation of the Son.[28] Milton, however, follows the logical implications of the *sermo* metaphor, insisting that the temporal difference between author and text cannot be ignored.

When Milton turns to the relationship of the Word to the Spirit, he repeats that Jesus is the medium of revelation. The difference in divinity between the Son and Spirit is crystallized in his translations. The Holy Spirit, sometimes called "voice, or word [*verbum*]," is "sent from above, either through Christ, who is the Word of God [*qui Dei sermo est*], or through some other channel" (*CPW* 6:284; *CE* 14:366). To show that the inequality of the Son and Spirit is based on the same principle as the inequality of the Son and Father, Milton reiterates the earlier argument, using the same metaphor of speech: "for the Word [*sermo*] is both Son and *Christ* . . . and as he is the image, as it were, by which God becomes visible, so he is the word [*sermo*] by which God is audible. Since this is what he is like he cannot be one in essence with an invisible and inaudible God. The same thing has been proven above about the Spirit . . ." (*CPW* 6:297; *CE* 14:400). In Milton's account of the generation of the Son and his relationship to the Father and the Spirit before creation, then, revelation is constructed as a rhetorical act. God speaks the Word and the world into existence, for it is through expressions like "through the Word of

God [*per Dei sermonem*]," which describe how God created
the world, that the Son derived his "title of the Word [*sermo
dicitur*]" (*CPW* 6:301; *CE* 15:6).

To emphasize the incarnational nature of the Word and
Jesus' redemptive office of preaching, Milton adopts the same
translation of *logos* in John 1:14 as he did in John 1:1: "*et
sermo factus est caro*" (*CPW* 6:418; *CE* 15:258). In the words
of the Word, God speaks clearly and Jesus takes on material
form. Jesus' divine and human natures are identified in his office
as the prophet of the Word in words. Milton consistently uses
sermo to refer to the Gospels and to the "preached word" of
the apostles. Moreover, the incarnate Word who proclaims God's
Word in human speech is the same preexistent Word who was
with God in the beginning, giving Jesus' preaching ministry
divine authority. Jesus is "primarily and properly, the Word of
God [*sermo Dei*], and the Prophet of the Church" (*CPW* 6:285;
CE 15:368). It is an office that includes the external revelation
of divine truth, subsequently written down by the church, and
the internal illumination of the mind, both of which form the
double scripture of the Word and Spirit. The incarnate Word
will continue to be revealed in the scriptural Word by the
Spirit who writes the inner Word on the hearts of believers.

The words of Christ are the last forms of revelation that began
when the Word was spoken and then used to create the universe. To be accommodated to human limitations, the Word
had to become words as well as flesh. This act of divine rhetorical decorum, in which the Father adjusts his speech to the scope
and understanding of a human audience, underlies Milton's
view of the scriptural Word, the primary means, with the Spirit,
by which God continues to be revealed to the church after
the Ascension.[29] Each reader is capable of receiving "the word
[*verbo*] of God" — that is, the textual presence of the absent
Jesus — by being "scrupulously faithful to the text" (*CPW*
6:120; *CE* 14:6). Even though God is "always described or outlined not as he really is, . . . they understand best what God is

like who adjust their understanding to the word of God [*Dei verbo*], for he has adjusted his word [*verbo*] to our understanding, and has shown what kind of an idea of him he wishes us to have" (*CPW* 6:133, 136; *CE* 14:30, 36). The text itself, then, cannot be identified with the author of the text, words with the Word, any more than the preexistent or incarnate Word can be. Milton might have chosen the less rhetorically emphatic "*verbo*" to emphasize the difference between the material Scripture and the Spirit needed to interpret it. Not only is Scripture an accommodated text and human understanding fallible, but no "indisputable word of God [*Dei verbo*]," no autograph copy of the New Testament, exists (*CPW* 6:589; *CE* 15:278).

Illumination by the Holy Spirit enables the external Scripture to become the Word of God in the act of reading and transforms the individual reader into the foundation of the church. Milton assigns many names to the unwritten Word — the "internal scripture" (*CPW* 6:587; *CE* 16:272), the "ingrafted word [*insititium sermonem*]" (*CPW* 6:524; *CE* 16:118), the "indwelling word [*sermo Christi inhabitet*]," and the "internal law" (*CPW* 6:478, 536; *CE* 16:6, 148) are all used at different times — but each expression conveys the authority of each individual in the reading of Scripture. As long as a doctrine or discipline is in the spirit of Scripture, Christians "should tolerate each other until God reveals the truth to all" (*CPW* 6:584; *CE* 16:266). The difference between the Father and Son, the author and the text, which results from Milton's rational explication of God's speech, is reiterated in the doctrine of the inner Word. The Father is not identical to the Word and the Word is not identical to the words of Scripture, but the Spirit encourages the unity of Father and Son, not in personhood or essence, but in divine utterance as the Father speaks through his Word to believers who return the gift in words with the guidance of the Holy Spirit, leading to the Christian liberty of the church.

Milton's rhetorical theology is evident in his use of *sermo* to account for the preexistent, incarnate, scriptural, and indwelling Word and in his structuring of revelation as a rhetorical relationship between author, speech, and audience. Literary and textual practices shape his theological thinking as much as his theology informs his poetry and prose. In keeping with his doctrine of scriptural accommodation, Milton presents the biblical God as an author and creator who reveals infinite goodness by speaking the Word in the creation of the Son, the Scriptures, and the incarnate Word. God's unity parallels the self-presence of a speaker since, when the Father speaks in Scripture, he speaks as one character, not three at the same time. His internal decrees correspond to the internal ideas that precede speech, limiting the extent to which the speech ever conveys the complete intentions of the author.

The texts themselves also reflect a rhetorical structure. The Son is not equal to the Father because the Word is temporally and essentially subordinate to the speaker. Scripture, although a more reliable form of God's self-revelation than the created world, is not identical to the Word, given that the Son sits at the right hand of the Father. Nor should the text be identified with the author; God's transcendent nature needs to be accommodated to the limited capacities of human beings. Finally, the incarnate Word, although fulfilling the words of the prophets, is limited in divinity. He must take on human syllables and letters to express the unlimited glory of the author of the Word. In each case, the textual absence and presence of the Father authorizes the continuing, progressive revelation of the Word in the literary activities of the church.

Thus, despite Erasmus's attempts to control its scope of reference by insisting on its orthodoxy, *sermo* appears to have had a metaphoric life of its own. For a radical like Milton, the logical outcome of the rhetorical relationship between Father and Son implied in *sermo* is not only the inequality of Father and Son, whether we want to call the doctrine Arian or not, but also a church transformed into a textual community progressively unfolding the Word. In 1522 Erasmus retracted his suggestion in the *Paraclesis* of the first edition of his New Testament (1516) that every plowman could interpret Scripture because the Word speaks there with power, but Milton was not so cautious. For him, if God speaks in the Word, the sacerdotal function and hierarchy of the priesthood are dispensable. Instead, the Holy Spirit in Milton's literary Trinity illuminates and persuades readers according to their gifts, progressively revealing truths to the church. The clarity and sufficiency of God's self-revelation, then, led Milton to the conclusion that all Christians illuminated by the Holy Spirit are authorized by God not only to "sift and winnow any doctrine but also openly to give their opinions of it" (*CPW* 6:122; *CE* 14:11). Everyone is fallible, each person possessing only part of the spirit of Truth; to enforce an interpretation is to "yoke the Spirit" and to abrogate God's authority. Each believer can receive Christ and participate in the church through the vernacular Bible, in which God speaks clearly and sufficiently to readers about all necessary matters of salvation. This position underlies Milton's vision of the church as a textual body and community of believers united in the production and reception of the Word.

The coexistence of presence and absence in Milton's view of God's *sermo*, a structure implicit in the preexistent, incarnate, scriptural and indwelling Word in *De Doctrina Christiana*, underwrites the ongoing interpretive activity of the church as well. God's revelation is a text or "speech-event" that discloses as much of his presence as is necessary for salvation in the literal sense of the Word, making each reader an equal member of the priesthood of believers, provided that talents are also equal. Such individualism profoundly shifted the foundations of church unity. "Free discussion and enquiry," once associated only with "academic circles" (*CPW* 6:121; *CE* 14:9), are now the essence of the Gospels and the foundation of the church. Heresy refers only to willful contradictions of Scripture, and all ideas, as unconventional as they might appear, should be openly debated and tolerated as long as they are derived from the Scriptures in good faith. Such debate will fill the church with "the daily increase of the light of truth" (*CPW* 6:121; *CE* 14:9). *De Doctrina Christiana* is provisional, even polemical in the way that many of Milton's texts are. Miltonic textuality, inseparable from his theology of the church, implies a dynamic textual community gathered at a great religious feast across the ages to discover and unfold the Word of God. Not only is the Word the only visible mode of Christ's presence available to Christians since the Ascension, but the visible church is unified by Christian literary production, whether oral or written. Nowhere is this vision of the church more powerfully depicted than in *Areopagitica*, Milton's defence of Christian liberty as a textual activity in which "considerat builders" construct the "spiritual architecture" of the church in "free writing and free speaking" (*Areopagitica*, *CPW* 2:555, 558) until the Second Coming of Christ.

Areopagitica has been justly praised as a superb example of English humanist oratory.[30] Its structure and style, as well as the allusion to Isocrates's oration to the Athenian assembly in its title, reflect Milton's high opinion of the rhetorical tradition in which he was educated. The arguments of the tract have also been effectively related to the Licensing Order of 1643 and the various contexts of radicalism that were emerging during the early stages of the civil war.[31] At the same time, however, Milton's *sermo* to Parliament — he himself calls it a "homily" and imagines it as an oral performance — often reflects a religious purpose. Two metaphors derived from Pauline ecclesiology — the church as a building and as a body — are especially important. The tract's title recalls St. Paul's sermon at the Areopagus in Acts 17:19–31, and its theme is not only the freedom of each individual to choose what he or she wants to read, but also the nature of the church as it was being formulated and debated in the Westminster Assembly. Many of the allusions and images in *Areopagitica* refer to biblical and ecclesiastical figures and events, both ancient and contemporary, while Milton's prophetic ethos conveys the authority of one "whom God has fitted for special use with ample gifts" (*CPW* 2:567). Despite his use of classical form, then, Milton reinvents his model to present his vision of the church grounded on the inner Word granted to each believer in the doctrine of Christian liberty and manifested in the "disputing, reasoning, reading, inventing, [and] discoursing" (*CPW* 2:557) of a nation of prophets. *Areopagitica* is the closest Milton ever came to systematic ecclesiology in his early prose. It is no accident that his argument against pre-publication censorship is the immediate occasion for its publication, for it is primarily in reading and writing that the visible church consists.

Milton transforms the occasion of his address — the demand for the enforcement of Parliament's Licensing Order of June 1643 calling for the censorship of works before they were published — into an issue of solemn importance for the church. Certainly he had more than enough personal and political motivation for associating his Presbyterian enemies with such unpopular precedents as the Council of Trent and the episcopal hierarchy (*CPW* 2:512, 529, 539, 493). Herbert Palmer, a Presbyterian, denounced his *The Doctrine and Discipline of Divorce* (1643, 1644) in Parliament just three months before *Areopagitica* was published. Milton's association of the Presbyterian clergy with the episcopal hierarchy also may have been calculated to sway Erastian members of Parliament, many of whom resented the intrusion of the clergy in state affairs (*CPW* 2:163).[32] The Presbyterians who condemned the Laudian church for silencing the preaching of God's Word and for imposing external conformity on unwilling consciences (*CPW* 2:539) are now doing the same things. The parish minister has now been "exalted Archbishop over a large dioces of books" (*CPW* 2:540), the ecclesiastical imagery linking the false authority of the two churches while emphasizing the living presence of books in the life of the church. The immediate occasions of Milton's prose works, however, often lead to more general considerations, and *Areopagitica* is no exception.

Milton alludes to St. Paul in his discussion, suggesting that if there are differences of opinion regarding doctrine or discipline that are not openly blasphemous, it is better to tolerate those differences in the *"unity of the Spirit"* than to compel conformity (Eph. 4:3; *CPW* 2:565). Milton extends the argument against his opponents by associating them with the Pharisees, identified with external conformity to the letter of the law, and by associating himself with "Christian liberty which *Paul* so often boasts of" (*CPW* 2:563). Paul argued that Christians will be saved by faith, not by observing dietary laws, which were matters of Christian liberty and left to each individual's conscience and the "gift of reason" to determine (*CPW* 2:513, 514). Thus, Milton's argument is simply an extension of his belief in salvation by faith and Scripture alone. As God's Word, the Bible contains everything necessary for salvation. The Word does not include prescriptions against specific books, so each individual is free to decide what to read and write, by the inner Word and the external Scripture that God has provided. To deny books to church members is to deny God's gift of the inner Word, to deny the Holy Spirit who could be speaking in those books, and to deny the unity of the church as a community dependent upon literary activity for its existence.

By treating books as things indifferent to salvation and, at the same time, emphasizing each person's freedom to search them for truth, Milton forces his audience to examine the nature of the church itself. His vision of the nation as a "mansion house of liberty" inhabited by prophets "reading, trying all things, [and] assenting to the force of reason and convincement" (*CPW* 2:554) is more than just hyperbole. Its echoes of Peter's Pentecostal sermon in Acts 2:17–18 indicate that the Holy Spirit, rather than ecclesiastical law, is the source of church unity. Against the charge that liberty encourages schism, Milton uses the metaphor of temple building, drawing on the image of the church as a building with Jesus as the cornerstone (Eph. 2:20–22) to show that "much arguing, [and] much writing" is only mistaken for disunity (1 Kings 6:7; *CPW* 2:554). Milton claims that it is irrational, even impossible, to expect perfect symmetry in all parts of the house of God and perfect agreement on all matters of doctrine and discipline among all members of the church. It is irrational because such a variety of people with such different gifts are involved in building the church, "some cutting, some squaring the marble, others hewing the cedars." "Many dissections," or what his opponents call schisms, are an inevitable condition of human freedom. Perfect conformity is impossible because symmetry among all the parts of the building, and all the members of the church, is "not of this world." Every stone of the building, though each one rests on the cornerstone of Christ, "cannot be united into a continuity, it can but be contiguous in this world." The unity of the church, "the gracefull symmetry that commends the whole pile and structure," arises not from unity imposed upon the diversity of individuals within it, but from "moderat varieties and brotherly dissimilitudes," from the unity of the Spirit in the diversity of believers. What the church needs for its "spiritual architecture," then, is not more outward conformity but more "considerat builders" (*CPW* 2:555).

Milton goes on to reassure his readers that, despite his defence of the "dividing of one visible congregation from another" that occurs in Independent ecclesiology, he does not "think well of every light separation." Unlike leaders of the gathered churches, who believe "that all in a Church is to be expected *gold and silver and pretious stones*" and who "sever the wheat from the tares, the good fish from the other frie" by admitting only the saints in their membership, Milton believes this identification of visible saints with the body of the church is "the Angels Ministery at the end of mortall things" (*CPW* 2:569–70). Assurance of salvation and signs of membership in the invisible, mystical church cannot be criteria for membership in the visible church any more than external conformity to predetermined standards or doctrines can be, for both assume the infallibility of a believer's grasp of truth.

Truth, Milton suggests in the most memorable passage in *Areopagitica*, is beyond human comprehension until the Second Coming. The allegory of Truth is based on Plutarch's rendering of the Egyptian myth of Osiris, whose corporeal body was dismembered and whose figurative, textual body was scattered by Typhon and his associates, leaving Isis to gather and reassemble the sacred *corpus* (*CPW* 2:549). In Milton's version of the myth, Truth and the early apostolic church are nearly identical, especially if we keep in mind that, in Greek myth, Typhon was a ferocious, hundred-headed dragon covered in serpents. The apostolic church, like Truth, was incarnate, "a perfect shape most glorious to look on." After Jesus' Ascension and the death of the apostles, it became apostate at the hands of Satan and the clergy or, in allegorical terms, it was cut to pieces by Typhon and his "wicked race of deceivers." Those devoted to Truth and the church are then left to gather the pieces of Truth's body by reading and writing until the Second Coming, when Jesus "shall bring together every joynt and member, and shall mould them into an immortall feature of loveliness and perfection" as parts of the revealed body of the invisible church.

Many readers have commented on Milton's use of the Osiris myth as a figure of progressive revelation, but few have noted the references to the church and the Word of God in this passage.[33] As in Revelation 12:6 and the allegory of the Song of Songs, the church, like truth in *Areopagitica*, is represented as a woman; more particularly, the true church is often the virgin bride of Christ, as in Revelation 19:7–9, *Of Reformation*

(*CPW* 1:557), *The Reason of Church Government* (*CPW* 1:756), and perhaps even the Lady in *A Mask*. Truth's birth at the same time as Jesus and her dismemberment after the apostolic age parallel the history of Scripture and the church in *Paradise Lost* (12.502–14, 535) and roughly parallel the growth of the church from purity to apostasy after the apostolic age sketched in *The Reason of Church Government* (*CPW* 1:827).[34] The Gospel is called "the word of truth" (2 Cor. 6:7) while Jesus calls himself "the way, the truth, and the life" (John 14:6). Milton's image of knowledge as a process of gathering also looks forward to his own method of seeking "tirelessly after truth" by "collecting together, as it were, into a single book texts which are scattered here and there throughout the Bible" (*Christian Doctrine, CPW* 6:119). Finally, the female figure of Wisdom in Proverbs 8:22–23 was often associated with the *Logos* of John 1:1 in early Christian literature since she existed with God in the beginning and was instrumental in creating the world. It would have been a short, imaginative leap for Milton to turn from the image of Wisdom in Proverbs, to her assimilation by early theologians of the *Logos,* to a combination of the two views in his figure of Truth.

In the New Testament and in Milton's earlier prose, the church itself is often described as a body as well (*Of Reformation, CPW* 1:519; *Reason of Church Government, CPW* 1:756). Ephesians 1:22–23 and Colossians 1:18 explain the hierarchical relationship between Jesus and the church. What the head is to the body, Jesus is to the church. More importantly, other uses of the body metaphor emphasize the relationship between members within the church, especially the unity of the church in the Spirit and the necessity of welcoming diverse spiritual gifts, the very principles that Milton defends in *Areopagitica*. In 1 Corinthians 12:12–31 and Romans 12:4–8 Paul argues that each member of the church and each spiritual gift is as important as the other, just as each part of the body works together for the good of the whole: "For as the body is one, and hath many members, and all the members of that one body, being many, are one body: so also is Christ. For by one Spirit are we all baptized into one body, whether we be Jews or Gentiles, whether *we be* bond or free; and have been all made to drink into one Spirit" (1 Cor. 12:12–13). Milton makes numerous references to the body in his prose, but in *Areopagitica* it is often linked to reading and to the church in general.[35] Books are compared to the fertility of dragon's teeth in the Greek myth of Cadmus, the "life-blood of a master spirit," the "entralls of many an old good Author," and the "issue of the womb" (*CPW* 2:492, 497, 505).

When Milton does turn to the myth of Osiris to describe the progressive search for truth, the constellation of metaphors linking the body to reading and both to the ongoing literary activity of the church is powerfully suggestive. It is through reading and writing in the pursuit of Christ's scattered truth that the church becomes the body of Christ. In fact, the parallel between Typhon and his "wicked race of deceivers" and Satan's influence on the church since the apostolic period could have led Milton's readers to a more specific conclusion. English divines share in the corruption of the true church when they fail to embrace the unity of the Spirit, welcome diverse gifts within the church, and recognize that reading and writing in Christian liberty are the church's lifeblood. This suggestion is more literal later in the same paragraph when Milton turns the tables on the Presbyterians who insist on prepublication censorship, accusing them of disunity and schism for trying to prevent others from uniting "those dissever'd pieces which are yet wanting to the body of Truth." This time the image of the church is both corporeal and geometrical. "The best harmony of the Church" is achieved when "the golden rule in Theology as well as in Arithmetick" is followed: members should "search[ing] what [they] know not, by what [they] know," adding truth to truth, "for all her body is homogeneal, and proportional" (*CPW* 2:550–51).

The process of temple building presupposes progressive rev-elation, which calls for the continuous exercise of Christian liberty, especially in reading and writing devoted to the Word, by all members of the church. The sermon is not the only, and perhaps not even the best way to proclaim the Word of God (*CPW* 2:548). If the goal of preaching is to change the will of the listener, and if this is best accomplished by combining delight with instruction, classical forms can also be useful in expressing the Word. By depriving believers of the opportunity to assess books themselves, those defending the Licensing Order are preventing believers from writing and reading them-selves into Christ's body. Truth's many shapes throughout history prove that the church's particular manifestations are less important than the Christian charity and liberty recom-mended by Saint Paul and Milton's appropriation of him (*CPW* 2:563). Moreover, God "dispense[s] and deal[s] out by degrees his beam, so as our earthly eyes may best sustain it" (*CPW* 2:566); consequently, reformation of the church must be an ongoing process of discourse made possible by the freedom of the inner Word promised in the New Testament.

The two principles of Milton's literary ecclesiology — the authority of the Word of God and the unity of the church as a textual community — remain consistent throughout his career, especially from 1644 onward. From the logical implications of Christian liberty and the metaphors of Pauline ecclesiology, Milton develops his vision of the church as a textual body con-tinuously transforming itself through encounters with the Word. Implied in this view of the church, although not fully explicated until much later, is his understanding of God's self-revelation to believers through the internal and external Word, since everyone has access to revelation through the guidance of the Holy Spirit. The church, as the textual community of believers, consists of individuals united by the Word and Spirit rather than the objective efficacy of the sacraments, the laws of church tradition, or the professional clergy. Due to the

Author's eternal presence and the limited forms of revelation, no one can claim infallible authority in matters of interpretation, opening the church to a staggering variety of doctrines and disciplines, as well as a dynamic process of Christian liberty based on the authority of the inner Word.

Milton's ecclesiology is literary, then, not only because each individual is saved by the Word, or because the Word is the central rite of a continually reforming church; it is also literary because concepts and practices derived from poetics and rhetoric modify traditional ecclesiological ideas in his work. Milton transforms the orthodox formulation of the Trinity, in which God the Father, the Son, and the Holy Spirit exist in the same essence, by an analogy of humanist, intentional textuality. For Milton, God is primarily an author/creator whose decrees/intentions are embodied in forms of the Word, the proper reading of which is guaranteed by the Holy Spirit. The Son, however, must always be temporally and essentially subordinate to the Father. In addition, Milton transforms the sacerdotal priesthood, in which priests are mediators of God's will and custodians of the sacraments, into a priesthood of believers, in which the office of the inspired prophet is open to anyone who has the appropriate literary gifts to administer words to the church. Milton redefines the orthodox Protestant doctrine of discipline as well: the purity of the community of faith maintained by spiritual law becomes self-discipline, in which each Christian, but especially the author, is edified and educated to become "a true Poem." Milton also reinterprets the liturgy, in which common prayers, sermons, homilies, and readings from the lectionary prepare the congregation for the Eucharist, and creates his own liturgy of the Word, in which inspired prayers, classical and Christian genres, and biblical expositions prepare the reader for the Word. Finally, the kingdom of God, or the church, is a textual relationship between readers, the Word of God, and other Christian authors rather than a gathering of the elect at a sacred time or in a sacred place.

Milton's ecclesiology is shaped profoundly by the assumptions about literary activity that he shared with many of his contemporaries.

Milton's decision to continue imagining what the church could be in *Paradise Regained* is the logical extension of the ecclesiology developed earlier in his career, for it was to church reformation that he devoted much of his life and it was to poetry that he believed he was called to perform his prophetic office. Each ensuing chapter outlines how one feature of Milton's literary ecclesiology is represented in *Paradise Regained*. Chapter 2 shows that the theology of the Word and church authority underlying his ecclesiology parallel the interplay of silence and the Word in the poem. Chapter 3 argues that Jesus represents just the kind of ideal priesthood of believers that Milton advocates in his prose. In his hermeneutic struggle with Satan, Jesus models self-discipline and the vigorous exercise of reason, both cornerstones of Milton's view of church discipline and both important features of humanist ethics. The liturgy of the Word emphasized in *De Doctrina Christiana* can be seen in the liturgical details, parallels, and forms of *Paradise Regained* as they are outlined in chapter 4. In the final chapter, the militancy and visibility of the church are engaged in the apocalyptic and astrological details of the poem, indicating that Milton continued to develop his radical, literary ecclesiology long after the Restoration. By overcoming Satan in hermeneutic combat, Jesus demonstrates how the will of God will be done on earth in the heart of each believer and reveals Milton's commitment to a holy community constituted by individuals who freely choose God's service through the Word and Spirit.

TWO

Silence and the Word

Like many Protestant reformers before him, Milton claimed that the Word of God alone was the clear and sufficient source of salvation. For Luther, Calvin, and Zwingli, Scripture was the only external authority capable of replacing the medieval church, but it was also much more. God is accommodated to human understanding in the incarnate Word and in the clarity and certainty of the scriptural text; as a result, everyone can be saved by hearing God's voice in the Word: "just as in men speech is called the expression of thought, so . . . He expresses Himself to us through His Speech or Word."[1] The reformers adapted principles of humanist scholarship — the study of original languages, the preference for rhetoric rather than logic, the use of historical contexts, and the location of interpretive authority in the author's intentions embodied in the authoritative texts — to a theology of God's sovereignty in all areas of life. By inward illumination, however, Protestants could return *ad fontes* in a way not foreseen in humanist methodology. The authority of classical texts is established by restoring the author's intentions, but the authority of Scripture was placed on the most certain foundation possible: the internal witness of the writer of Scripture, the Holy Spirit.

Even within the Protestant tradition, however, the meaning of "the Word of God" was challenged in a variety of ways throughout the seventeenth century in England, especially from 1643 to 1660 as Presbyterians and then Independents tried to formulate religious policy for the nation. John Goodwin, defending himself against the charge that he denied the divine authority of Scripture, argued that textual corruptions, different translations, and varieties of interpretations often obscure "the sense of the originals"; as a result, the Word of God, to be available to each reader and not just readers of Hebrew and Greek, must refer to what is contained in the letters of the Bible, rather than the letters themselves. The "glorious Truth" of the translated Scriptures "asserts their royal Parentage," but the Word itself "is not inke and paper, not any book, or books." Even if "a writing, or book, [is] a part, yea the most material part" of meaning, the material text holds the Word as a cup holds wine.[2] In this way, Goodwin resolves the conflict between the corruption of the biblical text, the immediate inspiration of the biblical authors, and the Protestant claim that the Word of God is sufficient in all matters of salvation for all members of the church. Even though the biblical authors and subsequent translations may have erred in some details, the Word of God is still authoritative because it survives intact.

John Owen, the most prominent Independent clergyman of the Commonwealth period, argued differently. Unlike Goodwin, Owen insisted upon the divine authority of the written word. The prophets and apostles "invented not words themselves . . . but only expressed the words that they received."[3] He defends the literal infallibility of Scripture in two ways. On the one hand, in *Of the Integrity and Purity of the Hebrew and Greek Text of the Scripture* (1659), Owen defends his view that the Word of God "is preserved unto us entire in the original languages . . . as also in all translations" against the suggestions of Goodwin, and especially Brian Walton.[4] According to Owen, by publishing parallel texts of Scripture in his *Biblia Sacra*

Polyglotta (1655–57), especially in the appendix of volume 6 where numerous textual variants from 15 authoritative texts are collected, Walton implies that "the same fate attended the Scripture in its transcription as hath done other bookes." Walton unwittingly supports "the Papists" claims Owen, since the multiplication of textual corruptions encourages the dependence of individuals upon the infallibility of the church rather than the Bible.[5] On the other hand, in *Pro Sacris Scripturis Exer-citationes Adversus Fanaticos* (1658), Owen attacks the Quakers — the other critics of the authority of the Word — who claim that "the word of God" should not be applied to Scripture since Scripture is neither Christ himself nor the light from Christ. Owen argues that both are called the Word because Scripture derives from Christ, reveals his will, and records his words.[6] Samuel Fisher answered Owen by suggesting that what Owen meant by "the word of God" was vague. Does he refer to the manuscripts of Moses, the prophets, and the apostles, or the spoken word preceding the writing? Does he refer to the first copies of the Scriptures or later transcriptions of them and, if so, does he also refer to translations of the transcriptions? The Quakers, according to Fisher, are at least consistent. The outward text is subordinate to "the Light of Christ in the conscience . . . the only firm Foundation of the Churches Faith."[7] For Fisher this view of authority leads to a belief in universal salvation, the corollary doctrine of the Atonement, for if each individual has Christ within, each individual is saved who acknowledges this presence. This doctrine is easily transformed into a justification of the rule of the saints, as the Ranter, William Erbery testifies. The mystery of the Gospel is that Christ's death liberated the Spirit, making God present in the flesh of his saints.[8]

The response of the magisterial reformers and English Puritans, with the exception of the Quakers, Ranters, and other radical spiritualists, to these and other challenges to the doctrine of scriptural authority was uniform, though different

in degree. In each case, inconsistencies led to a more authoritative professional ministry rather than a stronger lay presence in the church. When heretical doctrines were expressed,
banishment, excommunication, or imprisonment were rec-
ommended by ecclesiastical discipline; when obscurities in
the Scriptures were acknowledged, clarification was provided
by the clergy; in some cases, when arguments about "things
indifferent" arose, civil power was used to enforce the church's
authority. Milton rejected each of these compromises, maintaining from at least 1644 onward that the Word, when opened
by the Holy Spirit, was the only indispensable source of authority and unity in the church. God gave a "divine rule or autori-
tie from without us" in the holy Scriptures, and "no other within
us but the illumination of the Holy Spirit so interpreting that
Scripture," but because no one can be certain of the Holy
Spirit's presence at all times, "no man or body of men in these
times can be the infallible judges or determiners in matters of
religion to any other mens consciences but thir own" (*Treatise
of Civil Power*, CPW 7:242–43). For Milton, the unity of the
Spirit rather than external conformity, and the ministry of
believers rather than professional theologians, were the goals
of a thoroughly biblical reformation.

In his reform of the reformers, Milton consistently follows
the doctrine of the clarity and sufficiency of God's *sermo* for
salvation, a doctrine that becomes the cornerstone of his literary ecclesiology. Like the reformers, Milton argued that the
Word was a vehicle of grace, but unlike them, he believed its
authority rested in the conscience of each believer rather than
church tradition. Like the Anglicans, Milton argued that the
inner law of reason helped believers interpret God's revelation,
but unlike them, he believed tradition was not a significant
factor in interpretation. Like the Presbyterians, Milton asserted
that the Word was sufficient in matters of discipline as well
as doctrine, but unlike them, he believed the Word granted
individuals the freedom to worship as they chose. Like the

Independents, Milton assumed that the Word was the central liturgical activity of the church, but unlike them, he argued that the clergy should be independent of state sponsorship. Like the Quakers, Milton viewed the Spirit as the final authority in religious matters, but for him the Spirit enlightened a rational process of interpreting the Word rather than an ecstatic moment. This unique synthesis was made possible by Milton's rational exegesis of the biblical image of God's self-revelation in speech through the preexistent, incarnate, scriptural, and indwelling Word.

Milton follows to its radical conclusion the biblical and rhetorical image of God's *sermo* to believers, for if God's Word is revealed to each reader, the church consists of individuals gathered as a textual community over time and space to unfold and hear the Word. Derived from Milton's rhetorical and humanist understanding of representation, the features of textuality that underlie the Word as God's self-revelation in all of its manifestations are threefold: the indivisible, ineffable Author holds ideas that precede and shape the preexistent Word without being identical with it; the incarnate Word embodies the Author's intentions in words and flesh, but is accommodated to the understanding of the reader and limited by the words that become Scripture; the reader receives the scriptural Word, especially about matters necessary for salvation, by clarifying linguistic and historical contexts and by following the guidance of the Holy Spirit, but because the reader is fallen, the truth about many theological doctrines and things indifferent can never be fully recovered, authorizing multiple, though not unlimited, interpretations until the Second Coming.

In each case, absence and presence, silence and speech coexist as the Word is revealed. This rhetorical theology of revelation, grounded in Milton's rational exegesis of the biblical image of God speaking in and through the Word, leads to heterodoxy in each case. Since the Author's intentions or decrees precede their vocalization in the Word of Creation and Incarnation, the preexistent and incarnate Word cannot be equal to the Father. The real presence of the Son is with the Father after the Ascension, so he should not be confused with his representation in sacramental signs or material words; as a result, the scriptural and inner Word supersede the sacraments and the material words of the Scriptures as the preeminent modes of Jesus' presence in the church. Since the Holy Spirit is never fully present to any human being, revelation is progressive, resulting in a church that tolerates all doctrines and disciplines based on the Word of Scripture. A lay ministry and liturgy of the Word, which includes orations and poems in its canon as much as sermons and scriptural exegeses, and a discipline of the Word, which emphasizes self-government and edification rather than external compulsion, become signs of a true church. Milton's theology of the Word implies a rationale for Christian literary production, and reveals a literary ecclesiology grounded in reading.

The authority of the church in Milton's ecclesiology and the rhetorical theology of revelation and representation that it presupposes is reflected in *Paradise Regained* in two ways: in his depiction of the scriptural Word as the source of the church's authority and in his depiction of Jesus as the incarnate Word. Most obviously, in his hermeneutic contest with Satan, Jesus demonstrates the authority of the church dwelling in each reader of Scripture. The poem is based upon a scriptural narrative and both Jesus and Satan use Scripture to discover and understand their courses of action. The metaphor of the Word as spiritual food, important in *Areopagitica*, is repeated here (*PR* 1.347–51), and Jesus' hermeneutic method is exemplary. He corrects Satan's misreadings by clarifying intention and historical context (1.424–29), reads the text figuratively and typologically when it is appropriate (4.146–53; 1.351–54), and refuses to speculate about what hasn't been revealed (3.182–87). At the same time, Milton goes out of his way to emphasize that not Scripture alone but the nonverbal scripture — the silent, inner scripture of the Spirit written on the heart — is the final authority for Christians. This might be because he is depicting the New Testament in the process of being formed by oral tradition, but he is also showing how the Spirit and Word inform each other as mutually dependent forms of revelation and sources of authority for the church.

The contrast between the self-willed desire and aspiration of a young man whose "Spirit aspir'd" to "victorious deeds" (1.215) and the older, more experienced Jesus who surrenders his will, follows the Spirit to the wilderness, and reads the Spirit "in likeness of a Dove" (1.30) highlights the proper operation and meaning of the Spirit. The working of the Spirit upon memory and imagination as Jesus and Mary contemplate Scripture is also shown to be crucial. Confused and seemingly unready for the task ahead of him, whatever it might be, Jesus contrasts what he hears from others with impressions of his own and begins a process of remembering and imagining that eventually leads to a state of patient waiting upon God and the movement of the Spirit. He remembers his dedication to "the Law of God," his discovery that "persuasion" is better than "brute violence," and his mother's account of her experience. He confirms her account by returning to Scripture and finding that he is the Messiah, and reads the baptism experience as evidence of his spiritual authority, before concluding that waiting for further guidance about the purpose of his wilderness journey is the best course of action (PR 1.196–293). In this passage more than any other, Milton depicts how the Spirit works internally, shaping memory, imagination, and experience toward the interpretation that confirms Scripture.[9] More important than Jesus' dependence on both silence and the Word, the internal and external scriptures, however, is the nature of Jesus himself as the incarnate Word, the ultimate reference of the scriptural Word.

Despite Milton's emphasis on the scriptural and verbal battle between Christ and Satan in *Paradise Regained*, silence is a recurrent theme in the poem. The poet is "mute" without inspiration; Jesus is led by an inward "motion"; Mary and her son engage in silent meditation; Satan is confounded by the mystery of the Word and the angels praise the Son in songs unheard. Typological associations also draw attention to this thematic undercurrent. On three occasions (*PR* 1.353; 2.16–19, 2.266–78), Milton associates Jesus with Elijah who, after fasting for 40 days, heard God's "small voice of silence" (1 Kings 19:12). John Diodati, the Reformed theologian visited by Milton in Geneva in 1639, identifies silence and the Word in his commentary on Elijah's theophany: "the revelation and word of God, were specially joyned to the milde and quiet signe, to signifie unto us, that Gods saving revelation of himself is in the Gospell onely . . . and not in his terrible law. . . ."[10] In *De Doctrina Christiana,* Milton also refers to Elijah's experience in the wilderness as an example of "divine glory, in so far as mortals can comprehend it," which is consistent with the poet's view that "God is inaudible" (*CPW* 6:151–52, 239; *CE* 14:60, 239).

Silence is most eloquent, however, in the pinnacle scene of *Paradise Regained.* Faced with casting himself down and presuming God's protection or attempting to stand and falling to his death, Jesus recites the Word and stands by faith. The simplicity and finality of "he said and stood" (4.561) resonate in the silence which ensues, as the poem reaches its climax in the Son's fulfillment of the Father's decree. When Satan falls, silence emerges, between Christ's final words and the silent song of the angels, as the sign of divine presence and the mystery of Jesus' nature.[11] Having proven by his perfect obedience and hermeneutic victory that he is both divine and human, embodying both transcendent silence and human words, the Son can begin to redeem mankind and language through his prophetic ministry of preaching the kingdom of heaven. At the same time, Milton shows that Jesus derives all from the Father who "is far beyond man's imagination, let alone his understanding" (*Christian Doctrine, CPW* 6:133; *CE* 14:31) and who must be represented by negative attributes like silence, in addition to accommodated expressions like the voice at Jesus' baptism.[12] Thus, the silence on the pinnacle is two-sided: on the one hand, it authorizes and redeems language for the proclamation of the Word by the Word; on the other hand, as a minimal image of the Father's ineffable glory, it is also a reminder that such glory is never fully present in words or the Word. The interplay of silence and speech, especially in the pinnacle scene, represents the difficulty of representing the Incarnation — the irreducible mystery of Jesus' identity.

Critics have emphasized the opposition rather than the interplay of language and silence in *Paradise Regained*.[13] Steven Goldsmith, objecting to Stanley Fish's claim that in the pinnacle scene "speech finds its apex in silence,"[14] suggests that silence is "an emblem of nonexistence."[15] In my view, both Fish and Goldsmith are only partially correct. Fish is right to emphasize the culmination of the temptations in silence, but concludes that language is cancelled in silent "union with God."[16] Jesus' silence indicates his unity with the Father's will rather than his essence, and as Protestant traditions of commentary would have suggested to Milton, the temptations prepare Jesus for his preaching ministry, a process through which language is redeemed rather than denied.[17] Goldsmith, on the other hand, rightly stresses this redemption of language for the ministry of the Word in Christ's silencing of Satan in *Paradise Regained*, but neglects other details of the poem, other works by Milton, and Christian traditions of commentary which suggest that silence and the Word are not antithetical. The silencing of Satan and the silence of Jesus on the pinnacle are two completely different events: the first reveals the emptiness of words not linked to the Word; the second reveals the saving power of the Word as well as the inability of words to represent God's presence. By citing Scripture, Jesus demonstrates the renewal of language; by standing, he fulfills God's decree through perfect faith; by standing silently, he discloses the presence of divinity in both his words and deeds. In Jesus' silence and speech, Milton invites the reader to contemplate the Incarnation and the nature of divine representation. Christ is charged to represent the unrepresentable and is himself unrepresentable since his identity as both divine and human is a mystery of faith.

The problem of representing the Incarnation in *Paradise Regained* has been discussed by James M. Pearce and Ashraf H. A. Rushdy, neither of whom acknowledges Milton's integration of the "meta-argument" of divine representation and the "identity motive" in the pinnacle scene.[18] In fact, the coexistence of silence and the Word in theological traditions and throughout Milton's works generally forms a context in which Jesus' identity and the mystery of its representation are revealed at the same time, creating the formal as well as theological climax of the poem. For Pearce, God's speech in book 1.130–67 and the angelic hymn in book 4.596–635 "form the brackets within which the poem's meta-argument is deployed."[19] Although he does explain how Milton addresses the problem of representing the Incarnation by describing Jesus from shifting divine perspectives, Pearce reduces the dramatic impact of Jesus' recognition scene on the pinnacle, the poem's climactic event. Rushdy, on the other hand, explains the identity motive and maintains the pinnacle scene as a formal climax, but denies that the mystery of the Incarnation is a central issue. For Rushdy, Jesus "represents something like 'recta ratio' on the pinnacle by virtue of his insistent theocentricity," but the paradox of Jesus' theocentric self-representation is not a fulfillment of his nature — this can only occur in the future when God is fully present, and there is no need for mediation. Neither does the pinnacle scene represent the mystery of the Son's identity — this is revealed to Satan in the angelic hymn that follows.[20] The silence on the pinnacle refers to Satan's "amazement," his "absence of reason" while Jesus' standing on the pinnacle is not a miracle revealing Christ's divinity, but a simple, natural act since it is possible, though dangerous, for ordinary human beings to stand there.[21] Rushdy is right to dispel the miracle of Christ's standing, but this is not the only symbol of the mystery of the Incarnation. Nor does Milton's depiction of Jesus as divine and human reveal the essence of the Incarnation; rather, Milton reinforces the mystery of the Incarnation as the paradoxical coexistence of transcendent silence and human words in Christ. This confounds Satan even though silence and the Word have been associated with Jesus' identity from the opening lines of the poem. The mystery of the Son's identity as incarnate Word amazes Satan, an identity clarified through Jesus' refusal to limit his self-representation to Satanic or even verbal expression and through Jesus' resolute dependence on both parts of his identity throughout the poem.

The pinnacle scene, then, reveals the incarnate Word as a union of divinity and humanity, of unsayable presence and the words of the Word. Throughout *Paradise Regained*, but particularly in this temptation, Milton balances Christ's renewal of fallen language for his ministry with the silence which is both the origin and purpose of discourse, uniting Jesus' dual nature with his prophetic office of preaching the "Gospel of the kingdome of God" begun immediately following the temptations in the synoptic Gospels.[22] Just as divinity and humanity are joined in the Son, so ineffable presence and human words are joined in his preaching: he has shown, by the end of the poem, that he is worthy of speaking, as well as being, God's Word and can proceed to "Publish his Godlike office now mature" (1.188).[23] The emergence of silence on the pinnacle through Jesus' faithful use of Scripture and Satan's attempted appropriation of it is no coincidence. Nor is it accidental that Milton chooses Luke's order of temptations but adopts Matthew's "It is written" over Luke's "It is said." "It is written" reinscribes the authority of the Father's silent voice even as Jesus speaks and Milton recreates that speech. Glossing over the difference between the authoritative, originary text and the speaking subject by having Jesus *say* "it is written," Milton reiterates the difference in essence between the Father and Son while still maintaining the Son's status as God-man. All of these details underline the coexistence of silence and the Word in the Son's nature and prophetic office.

Patterns of silence and language in other poems by Milton and in Christian theology also show the implicit power of the saving Word and the limitations of language in the evocation of silence on the pinnacle in *Paradise Regained*. Before turning to *Paradise Regained,* then, it is necessary to discuss the theological traditions within which Milton worked, since these traditions provide reading strategies that help to explain the mystery of Jesus' identity, a mystery reiterated in the union of divinity and humanity, silence, and the Word on the pinnacle.

I

Writers of religious texts struggled with the problem of representing the unrepresentable long before the seventeenth century. Erich Auerbach has commented on the "heavy silence" that characterizes the biblical narrative of Abraham and Isaac.[24] According to Pseudo-Dionysius, the Areopagite of the late fifth century, attempts to say the unsayable in the Christian tradition led to a double tradition of Christian theology in which "what is not said is interwoven with what is said."[25] Dionysius's comment implies an especially incarnational view of textuality. Both transcendent silence and the written, incarnate Word are woven together, are textual. The discourse of positive theology is philosophical and persuasive, clarifying what can be said about God in prayer and argument. This kind of "God talk" is possible when God is immanent in the hierarchies of nature and the church, the Sacraments, the Incarnation, and the Scriptures.

In a passage foreshadowing Milton's doctrine of accommodation in *De Doctrina Christiana,* Dionysius suggests that as
much as can be known about God is revealed in the sacred texts:
"generally, then, one must neither dare to say nor conceive anything about the hidden, transcendent essence of divinity except
what has been divinely expressed in the sacred scriptures."[26]
As the reference to hidden divinity indicates, the tradition of
negative theology is mystical and nonverbal since "one must
ascribe non-logos to that beyond logos."[27] Even though God is
given many names in the Scriptures, the essence of divinity
is "not known, not spoken, not named"; in fact, because God
transcends speech, it is best to say what God is not, remembering that even this is saying too much:

> God is
> all in all
> nothing in none,
> known to all in reference to all,
> known to no one in reference to nothing.[28]

Whereas positive theology emphasizes God's volubility, accommodated and dispersed in human speech, negative theology
emphasizes silence. The closer believers get to God, the more
"language becomes restricted," resulting in being "wholly
united to the unspeakable."[29] As antithetical as they seem, both
traditions complement each other. According to his own principles, Dionysius never *declares* that positive theology is false.
More importantly, the two approaches respond to the paradox
of God's immanence and transcendence: dogmatic theology
affirms that God speaks in nature, the church, and Scripture,
while mystical theology denies all affirmations in order to
attain silent union with God.[30] To repeat, "what is not said is
interwoven with what is said."

In practice, however, Dionysius privileges "what is not
said" and, in the process, diminishes the importance of the
Incarnation as God's revelation in his Son, the Word made flesh.

Other early Christian writers were not as eager to endorse negative theology. Several early fathers of the church, although responding to christological and trinitarian disputes in vastly different contexts, insisted that God's Word was spoken in the Creation and the Incarnation.[31] Ignatius of Antioch, for example, whose works Milton read in Vedelius's 1623 edition, recognized the presence of silence in the Word when he explained that God is revealed in his Son "who is his Word which proceeded from silence."[32] Over 200 years later, but still before Dionysius, St. Augustine clearly outlined the dialectic between silence and language in *De Doctrina Christiana:* "And a contradiction in terms is created, since if that is ineffable which cannot be spoken, then that is not ineffable which can be called ineffable. This contradiction is to be passed over in silence rather than resolved verbally. For God, although nothing worthy may be spoken of Him, has accepted the tribute of the human voice and wished us to take joy in praising Him with our words."[33] Three features of Augustine's theology of silence reappear in *Paradise Regained*. First of all, silence represents an epistemological limit and identifies the distance between human understanding and the essence of God. Conversely, silence is the condition of speech and authorizes the use of words in God's service in spite of the limitations of language. Finally, silence is devotional and points to the humility and reverence with which believers should approach their Creator. In *Paradise Regained*, Christ's faithful reticence is a model of reverent deference to the Father, in whose service he finds perfect freedom. Moreover, God's ineffability is adumbrated in his decree, which is fulfilled in the inaction/action and silence/speech of the pinnacle scene. Christ's identity as the Word made flesh also underwrites the Word that he must proclaim and the words devoted to the Word written by the Christian poet. In each case, Milton demonstrates that silence and the Word are not mutually exclusive, but mutually dependent aspects of representation.

Not coincidentally, the seventeenth century Nonconformist community most familiar to Milton when he was writing his epics also emphasized God's silent transcendence of representation. For many Quakers, silence was the purest form of worship. According to Robert Barclay, "there can be nothing more opposit to the natural will and wisdom of man than this silent waiting upon God. . . ."[34] Alexander Parker urges the Friends to "sit down in pure stillness and silence of all flesh," while Isaac Penington the younger, probably known to Milton through Thomas Ellwood while he was at Chalfont St. Giles, asserts that "the ministry of the spirit and life is more close and immediate when without words." Finally, in a passage that could serve as a gloss on the pinnacle scene of *Paradise Regained*, Charles Marshall describes a liturgy of silence: "When a motion is felt, and openings are in the heart, and the power of the Lord is prevailing, then sink down in that in which no vain thought can be hid and stand single and passive . . . and then, in the power which warmeth thy heart, and moveth on thy spirit, enter into thy service."[35] A "motion" of the Holy Spirit led Jesus to the wilderness in the first place, while stillness, silence, and passivity are all associated with him in the pinnacle scene, as Milton explores the poetic and liturgical interplay of silence and the Word within his narrative of identity, Incarnation, and ministry.[36]

It is misleading to emphasize silence too much, however, because as Ignatius's comment reveals, God has broken silence by speaking the Word at the Creation and Incarnation through the Son and in Jesus, both in his body and speech. Barbara K. Lewalski has observed that Milton's Christology, following from his antitrinitarianism, "cannot be exactly classified in terms of any of the common christological positions."[37] Although Milton would rather leave the question of how the two natures coexist in one person as a mystery of the faith, since the Scriptures clearly attest to the mystery of the Incarnation (*Christian Doctrine, CPW* 6:420; *CE* 15:263), he does suggest

that the divine and human are unified in Christ's perfect manhood. The unity of the two natures derives from the way he
fulfills the Father's will and speaks his words.[38] In his human
preaching he is God's divine Word; in the sacrifice of the cross
he is God's incarnate Word, who fulfills the words of the law
in his body, in one act of atonement. Thus, Milton maintains
the biblical testimony of Christ's dual nature while diminishing
Jesus' divinity: the Son is the divine Word but not of the same
essence of God. At the same time, he elevates Jesus' humanity by emphasizing his mediatorial office as the incarnation
of the divine Word in words. Milton's heterodoxy arises not
from his attempt to negotiate between various received positions in the history of theology, despite his use of traditional
diction, but from his rational explication of the biblical image
of God's speech. His emphasis on Christ as a mediator, who
faithfully delivers God's Word in human words, ensures that
the Scriptures are a means of grace available to every believer
and a clear and sufficient statement of God's intentions on all
matters necessary for salvation.

Within the context of his view of revelation, in which the
words of Jesus convey the Father's Word to the church, Milton's
Christology is consistent, though no less unorthodox for being
so. In addition, not only the copresence of Christ's two natures,
but the unity of those natures in the person of Jesus is essential if Scripture is to be regarded as a means of grace and an
authority for believers. Those who tear apart the unity of
Christ "rob Christ's speeches and replies of all their sincerity,"
but uncertainties that arise from not knowing which of Christ's
natures is speaking at any given time disappear when readers
are assured that he speaks as God and man at once (*CPW*
6:228; *CE* 14:229); that is, Jesus' words are authoritative because
of their source in the Word that is spoken by God. The Word
of God is plain and sufficient for the church, then, because God
really speaks there, especially in the words and body of Jesus.
It is in this sense that the identity of the Son is revealed in

Paradise Regained. His silence on the pinnacle signals his dependence on the Father for his divinity, while his use of Scripture underscores the importance of his human ministry of the Word. The interplay of silence and speech in the pinnacle scene reveals the mystery of Jesus' identity as both God and man but also the extent to which Milton transformed the theological "topos" of divine representation into a powerful poetic symbol.

II

The coexistence of silence and the Word is a persistent theme in Milton's poetry before *Paradise Regained*, surfacing in different ways in *A Mask* (540–64), "Upon the Circumcision" (1–5), "Il Penseroso" (55–56), *Lycidas* (176), the Nativity Ode (116), and especially *Paradise Lost*. The first four lines of book 8, added by Milton in the 1674 edition of the poem, present a variation on the interplay of silence and speech found in Christian tradition and the early poems. In book 7.565–640, Raphael's account of creation culminates in liturgical sabbath hymns sung by the angels complete with echoes of Psalm 24:9 (7.566), Psalm 92:5 and Psalm 145:3–4 (7.602).[39] Like Dionysius and the Quakers, the angels assert that God is beyond thought and speech; on the other hand, like Augustine they do not rest in "silence holy" but proceed to praise and worship "Jehovah," the "great Creator." At the beginning of book 8, Adam stands transfixed as Raphael's voice, and presumably the angelic hymns, linger silently:

> The Angel ended, and in *Adam's* Ear
> So Charming left his voice, that he a while
> Thought him still speaking, still stood fixt to hear.
>
> (8.1–3)

This conjunction of silence and voice, where "endings" linger and continue to speak or sing in silence, is even more explicit earlier in *Paradise Lost* when Milton describes the onset of evening in book 4. Here "Silence accompanied" evening as birds and animals prepared for rest, but silence also accompanied them in a musical sense; it played with and offered accompaniment to the song of the nightingale and "Silence was pleas'd" (4.600, 604). The repetition of the word "still" in these references and elsewhere in Milton's work further emphasizes that the interplay of silence and speech is an intricately developed pattern in Milton's poetry before he uses it as a symbol of the Incarnation and Jesus' identity in *Paradise Regained*.[40]

The extent to which Milton continued to develop patterns of silence and speech, present in his earlier works, in *Paradise Regained* is evident from even a brief consideration of the poem's opening lines. In line 12 the narrator admits he would be "mute" without the inspiration of the Holy Spirit, the same Spirit who led Jesus into the wilderness, thereby linking his poem with the scriptural and incarnate Word. Just as Jesus will raise Eden in "the waste Wilderness" through his obedience, so too the poet will erect his poetic monument out of silence. His subject has remained "secret," "unrecorded," and "unsung" until now (1.15–17). The "Hymns" and "Celestial measures" of the angels circling the throne following the Father's decree (1.168–81) parallel Milton's representation of "sacred Song" in *Paradise Lost* (3.344–410), while the silence of the angels who "Admiring stood a space" before the song (*PR* 1.169) recalls the silence of the angels before the Son emerges to save humankind (*PL* 3.217–18).[41] The song after the pinnacle scene also alludes to the "marriage supper of the Lamb" (Rev. 19:9) and the "unexpressive nuptial Song" of *Lycidas* (176), both of which celebrate the kingdom of glory that will be established when Christ silences Satan with "the terror of his voice" (*PR* 4.627). Finally, Milton's representation of the Father as a voice at Jesus' baptism and during his "solemn message" or decree concerning the Son (1.130–67) illustrates not only the doctrine of accommodation, since "God is inaudible just as he is invisible" (*Christian Doctrine*, *CPW* 6:239; *CE* 14:252), but also the nature of the Son's divinity: as a silent idea precedes its vocalization or inscription, so the Father's silent foreknowledge precedes its revelation in the Word. As a result of Milton's use of the metaphor of speech to describe the Father, Jesus, although divine in his embodiment and enactment of the Word, is temporally and essentially subordinate to the Father's divinity.

Common as it is in Milton's works, the representation of Jesus' relationship to the Father as an immediate conversation is more pivotal in *Paradise Regained* than in his other poems because Jesus must demonstrate not only that he is the Son but also that he has acquired "the rudiments / Of his great warfare" (*PR* 1.157–58), or preaching ministry, uniting his nature as the incarnate Word with his office as the preached Word. Much has already been written on Christ's nature in *Paradise Regained*,[42] and it is beyond my purpose either to review or engage it; instead, I will outline three conclusions reached by Milton in *De Doctrina Christiana* that influence the interplay of language and silence in the poem: first, the unity of divinity and humanity in Christ is a genuine mystery (*CPW* 6:420; *CE* 15:262–63); second, Christ's divinity is not equal to the Father's (*CPW* 6:215; *CE* 14:198–99); and third, both natures are always present (*CPW* 6:228; *CE* 14:228–29), although the Son's divinity/humanity is not proven until he fulfills God's decree through the exercise of free choice. The identity motive is important, but only to Satan: he knows who the Son is (*PR* 1.356), but he is unable to fathom the unity of divinity and humanity in Christ's nature because it is a mystery of faith. Following Milton's advice to "let mysteries alone and not tamper with them" (*Christian Doctrine*, *CPW* 6:421; *CE* 15:264–65), Jesus is silent in response to Satan's questions about his nature in the debate leading up to the pinnacle scene (*PR* 4.500–01, 510–21, 522–30, 538–40). This reveals Satan's devotion to "monstrous controversies" and the Son's reverence toward the Father. Satan's real purpose in attempting to learn the Son's identity is much more selfish than his words suggest. He is afraid of the "fatal wound" from the "Seed of *Eve*" that will drive him from his kingdom (1.53, 54). To retain his kingdom, Satan attempts to separate words from the Word but is reduced to empty silence, while Jesus demonstrates that he *is* the Word and allows the silence of the Father to speak through him.

Milton likely expected his readers to know that the temptations were meant to prepare Jesus for the proclamation of the kingdom of heaven. John the Baptist's ministry immediately precedes the temptations and Christ's Sermon on the Mount immediately follows them, at least in the Gospel of Matthew. The temptations are linked to Christ's kingly vocation in *De Doctrina Christiana* as well. The temptations and the crucifixion are two forms of humiliation suffered by Christ to satisfy divine justice and to create his kingdom (*CPW* 6:438–39; *CE* 16:358–59), also known as the kingdom of grace and heaven. Although the "reign of grace . . . began with his first advent, when it was proclaimed by John the Baptist," it continues through the spiritual warfare of the church and will lead to the "kingdom of glory" at Christ's Second Coming (*CPW* 6:624, 436–37; *CE* 16:358–59, 15:300–01). The action of *Paradise Regained*, itself illustrating how the kingdom of Christ is attained by hearing the Father's voice, is framed by the "Kingdom nigh at hand" (1.20) proclaimed by the Baptist, the kingdom of Christ revealed after the temptations in Jesus' preaching ministry, and still further in the future, the kingdom of glory, which follows the final defeat of Satan foreshadowed in his fall from the pinnacle.

Commentators from a broad range of worshipping traditions were even more specific about the interpretation of the temptations. At his baptism, Jesus was named by God and anointed by the Spirit "to preach the Gospel to the poore" (Luke 4:18), while the temptations were a series of verbal and hermeneutic tests to prepare him for this ministry. The baptism, temptation, and vocation of Christ were seen as a coherent narrative sequence in the Son's early ministry. For Erasmus, Christ sets an example for God's ministers as he battles Satan through prayer, sobriety of life, and the holy Scriptures before accepting the sacred task of preaching the Gospel.[43] Lancelot Andrewes argues that Christ began his calling from his baptism and proved himself "too cunning for him [Satan] in disputing" by showing that *"Scriptum est"* is the best defence against the distrust, presumption, and idolatry of the devil, the "publisher of infamous reports."[44] William Perkins reminds the clergy that Christ, as the "sole Doctor and Prophet of Gods Church," must be "tempted before he go[es] to preach" just as ministers of the Word must "prepare themselves against Satans temptations."[45]

Milton also emphasizes the exegetical nature of the temptations, especially in the pinnacle scene. Not only is the last temptation the only one in which both characters quote Scripture, but Satan's attempt to have Jesus presume God's protection hides a more insidious sin: the distortion of the text and its meaning. As James H. Sims has clearly shown, Satan abuses Scripture throughout the poem, but his debasement of the text in the pinnacle scene differs from his previous abuses of the Bible in two ways: first, it occurs at a climactic moment in the poem and, therefore, is not one misinterpretation among many; secondly, while Satan's other misreadings are for secondary purposes — to gain sympathy for himself or to flatter Jesus, for example — his corruption of the Word on the pinnacle is meant to undermine the silent assent of the Spirit and Word, the source of Jesus' power in all of the previous temptations.[46] Whereas Satan wrests the meaning of the Word to serve his own purpose, Christ shows he *is* the Word by demonstrating that the "Scriptures of God are sufficient in themselves, truly to interpret and expound themselves."[47]

The commentaries of John Calvin and the annotations of scores of other exegetes all mention Satan's "craftie purpose" and Christ's hermeneutic victory on the spire of the temple.[48]

The interpretation of the Puritan divines responsible for the widely read *Annotations Upon the Books of the New and Old Testament* is representative:

> The devil now seeks to foil Christ with his own weapons, and cites Scripture. . . . There is no charge, or temptation of Satan more pernicious and dangerous, then that which is coloured with misseapplied Scripture, and shew of sanctity. . . . Here appeareth the venom of the old dragon, when he pretendeth the sacred authority of Gods H. word, to lead men to sin, and disobedience to God.[49]

By omitting "all thy wayes" from his reference to Psalm 91:11, Satan makes the text appear to say that God's people can do anything and expect divine protection. Most commentators, however, argue that the text does not apply to dangers in which people voluntarily throw themselves because "all thy wayes" refers to all the ways of faith set forth by God.[50] Thus, when Jesus cites Deuteronomy 6:16, he answers Satan's method as well as his intent. He shows that Satan's interpretation must be wrong, otherwise the commandment would be contradicted, and that Satan's intent is to undermine his faith by tempting him to ask God for a sign of his presence. Christ's text refers implicitly to Exodus 17:1–7, where the Israelites tempt God by demanding signs of his favour, saying "Is the Lord among us, or not?" In *Paradise Regained*, the question is answered by the voice of silence, which emerges after Christ's faithful use of language and Scripture on the pinnacle.

What Jesus must learn throughout *Paradise Regained*, then, is not his own identity or the nature of his kingdom. In his first, silent meditation he reveals the nature of his divine parentage and of his spiritual, eternal kingdom. What he must learn is

> How best the mighty work he might begin
> Of Savior to mankind, and which way first
> Publish his Godlike office now mature.
>
> (1.186–88)

Like Milton himself in sonnets 7 and 19, Jesus must "stand and wait" for the proper time to begin God's work and in this he must depend on his Father's call since his time "is not yet come" (*PR* 3.397). That God's work will begin with Jesus' preaching ministry is underlined throughout *Paradise Regained* by the interplay of language and silence as Jesus uses the word of God to "stand against the wiles of the devill" (Eph. 6:11).

The centrality of language in the conflict between Christ and Satan is emphasized even before the temptations. Prior to meeting Satan, Jesus learns his identity from Scripture (*PR* 1.259–63), adopts "winning words" for his "duel, not of arms" (1.222, 174), receives the witness of John the Baptist and the Holy Spirit (1.25–31), and "audibly" hears his Father's voice pronounce him the "beloved Son" (1.284, 285). Satan interprets the events of Jesus' baptism in a "carnal" and literal way that reveals his lack of faith and, therefore, his inadequate view of language. He fails to associate God's "Son belov'd" with his "first-begot" (1.85, 89), stands "Thunderstruck," silenced by the "voice divine" (1.36, 35), assumes that Christ's kingdom will be political (1.98–99), and sees the physical dove, "whate'er it meant," but not the Holy Spirit (1.83). The terms of the conflict are set from the beginning of the poem. By joining his will to his Father's voice, a voice essentially silent but accommodated to human limitations, Jesus correctly interprets the testimony of heaven and gains the "winning words" necessary for his preaching ministry; by denying the authority of the Father's voice, Satan misinterprets God's texts and falls in "shameful silence" (4.22), his "train of words" (3.266) vanishing like "froth or bubbles" (4.20).

In the first temptation, Satan tries to separate the Son of God's office from his nature by asking him to distrust God's providence in the performance of a miracle. Reading the trial typologically, Jesus links his prophetic office with Moses and Elijah and his nature with the manna from heaven given to the Israelites in Exodus 16:11–15. Jesus also shows that he fulfills both types since he *is* the "Word / Proceeding from the mouth of God" who has perfect trust in the Father, unlike the Israelites (*PR* 1.349–50). Jesus' refusal to separate his nature and ministry or to use words apart from the Father's plan sets the stage for the struggle between the Word and Satan in the following temptations.[51] Not only has the "inward Oracle" silenced the pagan idols, but Christ will reduce Satan to muteness as he withstands the temptation to use his words apart from the spiritual kingdom he has come to proclaim. Having rejected wealth and luxury, Jesus renders Satan speechless:

> So spake the Son of God, and Satan stood
> A while as mute confounded what to say.
>
> (3.1–2)

When he does begin to speak, Satan comes as close as he can to knowing Jesus as the Word, but fails to understand the significance of Christ's kingdom:

> Should Kings and Nations from thy mouth consult,
> Thy Counsel would be as the Oracle
> *Urim* and *Thummim*, those oraculous gems
> On *Aaron's* breast, or tongue of Seers old
> Infallible.
>
> (3.12–16)

Jesus reduces Satan to murmuring when he denounces glory and later fully reveals the absence of God, which is the source of Satan's empty words:

> Satan had not to answer, but stood struck
> With guilt of his own sin.
>
> (3.146–47)

At the beginning of book 4, Satan is silent once again; he realizes that Jesus will not separate his words from God's Word in order to establish his kingdom prematurely through force. When Jesus rejects the "smooth conceits" of Greece for the eloquence of the Word, his steady progress toward the proclamation of his own kingdom reaches a new level. By insisting upon the connection between eloquence and character and the source of both in God's revelation in his Word and the "Light from above" (4.289), Jesus lays down the first principle of language in his spiritual kingdom. Christ's redemption of language, however, reaches its symbolic height in the final temptation.

In this scene, Milton varies the pattern of temptation, Word, and silence in order to emphasize the source of Jesus' authoritative and authentic language in the presence/silence of the Father. Beginning with the Word in an attempt to appropriate the Son's authority, Satan omits phrases and deliberately distorts the text. Psalm 91:11–15 refers to the angels sustaining the faithful, not catching them if they fall. He cleverly omits verse 13, which refers to the dragon and adder being trampled under foot, an allusion to Genesis 3:15, a text Satan has been trying to understand since his opening speech (1.64–66). When Jesus paraphrases Luke 4:12, which itself paraphrases Deuteronomy 6:16, the force of truth linked with the performative Word and his faith that God will reveal his ministry in due time not only confound Satan, they also open the text to the silence from which the Word has proceeded. Present from the beginning in his decree but speaking only through Jesus' actions, the Father is revealed as the silent source of the inexhaustible, disseminative power of the Word (John 21:25).

Thus, whereas Satan's use of language reveals the silent void of faithlessness, the creative presence, which is silent in itself, speaks as language is redeemed for the ministry of the Word. Suspended momentarily between heaven and earth, Jesus fulfills the Father's decree and unites his office with the mystery of his nature as the incarnate Word. The song of the angels reinforces the presence of silence as well. The angels celebrate Christ's present victory and look ahead to the Apocalypse, when Satan's kingdom will be destroyed, but they do so with words only heard by Christ. The song itself, then, represents the apex of Milton's redemption of language since it is only through poetic and fictional recreation that he can move his fallen readers closer to the "Heavenly Anthems" that otherwise would have been silent.

Our knowledge of Jesus' ministry to preach the kingdom of God as well as of Milton's view of God's silent transcendence both play important roles in a balanced assessment of the pinnacle scene. If we emphasize only the former, we ignore Milton's effort to come to terms with the limitations of language; if we emphasize only the latter, we deny Milton's belief in the saving power of the Word. Milton would have readily agreed with Thomas Wilson's claim that eloquence was "first given by God, after lost by man, and last repaired by God again."[52] In *Paradise Regained*, this redemption of language is demonstrated in Christ's silencing of Satan and, most emphatically, in his faithful waiting as the divine Word upon God's silence in the pinnacle scene. It is necessary for Jesus' preaching ministry of the kingdom, for the writing of religious poetry, and for the unity and authority of the church. Just as Jesus' preaching ministry is sanctioned by God's presence in silence and in the Holy Spirit, and the poet receives his authority from the inward Oracle, so the church receives its authority as a textual community from the scriptural, incarnate, and indwelling Word. In keeping with the coexistence of absence and presence, silence and speech in God's *sermo*, the coexistence of silence and the Word in *Paradise Regained* clarifies the source of the church's authority: the scriptural Word illuminated by the Spirit, and the divine Word revealed in the Incarnation. By receiving such authority, the church can maintain itself in the hearts of believers during times of persecution as Jesus does in the wilderness and as Nonconformists did in the 1660s and 1670s. Silenced by ejection and muzzled by censorship in the first decade of the Restoration, Dissenters are shown the source of a more lasting silence. Although we may not be able to hear strains of the divine music in *Paradise Regained*, as perhaps we can in *Paradise Lost*, the reverent silence adopted by Jesus before he begins preaching the Word shows Milton's readers how best to compose themselves. This process of self-composition is an essential component of ministry and discipline in Milton's ecclesiology.

THREE

The Priesthood of Believers and the Vocation of Writing

For Milton, the Word is analogous to a sacrament. For in the practice of reading guided by the Holy Spirit — a practice Milton often compared to eating in his own works and in the works of his contemporaries — believers approach God's presence through the textual body of the Word, transforming the external temple into the temple of the heart. In his depiction of Jesus' rejection of Satan's first temptation in *Paradise Regained*, Milton connects the Word of God and the manna fed to the Israelites in the wilderness, a type of Jesus himself and of his body in the Lord's Supper (John 6:32, 35; Luke 22:19). He shows what is indispensable for the church's nourishment during all times but especially during the Restoration: feeding on the Scriptures. This does not mean that "the church is utterly invisible," as Malcolm Ross claims, or that "the old lines of communication between the visible and invisible are discarded," but rather that numerous "lines of communication"

are reduced to essentials: the Word and the community gathered to receive and recreate it.[1] Not only baptism, but also the Lord's Supper can be administered by the laity as well as the clergy given that the covenant of grace is received in the words of the New Testament before it is represented in the seals of the covenant. Clear and accessible to all, the external Word reveals God as the author wanted to be known.

Milton, however, did not confuse the signified with the sign, the Word with words. The true textual presence of Christ is disclosed only by the Holy Spirit and the internal Word written on the heart of each believer, the ritual of reading made efficacious by interpretation with the Spirit's guidance. Jeremiah foretold the coming of the internal Word (Jer. 31:31–4), which was fully revealed on the day of Pentecost (Acts 2), but no one since the apostles has received the direct and complete revelation of the Spirit. As a result, Milton emphasizes the authority of each individual's conscience rather than the authority of apostolic succession in his literary ecclesiology. No one but Jesus fully possesses the Spirit, so no one but Jesus is a mediator of God's truth. Accordingly, each individual conscience constitutes the final ecclesiastical authority, and the church is created when individuals voluntarily gather to worship according to their shared understanding of God's call in the Scriptures. Revealing truths within the sphere of the natural light of reason granted to all people in every dispensation, the texts of the classical canon can provide useful guidance on matters not prescribed in Scripture. Finally, since the individuals who make up the church are fallible and since revelation is progressive, the church is always in a process of building and edification until the Second Coming.

Milton's view of scriptural authority has important implications for his view of the ministry. Not only are bishops and "doctors" of theology eradicated, but distinctions between the laity and clergy virtually disappear. The ministry is a priesthood of believers, and England "a holy nation" in which

"all the Lords people are become Prophets" (Exod. 19:6;
Areopagitica, CPW 2:556; cf. Num. 11:29; Joel 2:28). For
Milton, the ministry of the Word is the responsibility of the
whole church and not a specialized, professional clergy. Of the
three traditional offices of Christian ministry — preaching
the Word, administering sacraments, and maintaining pastoral discipline — the prophetic ministry of the Word is preeminent for Milton because the prophetic office includes
exegesis and teaching, the principal methods of disseminating
the Word to the Christian community. Moreover, any believer
can be an ordinary minister or prophet, as long as the appropriate gifts are evident, especially "exceptional piety and wisdom for the purpose of teaching" (*Christian Doctrine, CPW*
6:572). Ordination and the laying on of hands can follow the
election of the ordinary minister by the congregation but only
as a ceremonial recognition of a previous call by God, the sign
of which is the gift of teaching. The office is neither occupied
permanently by one person of the congregation, nor is it authoritative in any way. Any member can preach and call the minister into question according to the Spirit of God within (*CPW*
6:595, 608). Only the gifts of the Spirit appropriate for the
ministry distinguish one believer from another, but this is a
difference of talent rather than office; the hierarchy of the
ministry in Milton's ecclesiology is based on merit rather than
apostolic succession.

Prophecy is preeminent among the three offices of the ministry, but the extraordinary ministry is the highest function
of the prophetic office because it requires not only natural gifts
but divine inspiration. The extraordinary ministry includes
those "sent and inspired by God to set up or to reform the
church both by preaching and by writing" (*CPW* 6:570). These
"prophets, apostles, evangelists and others" have special authority due to divine inspiration, but this also led to conflicts
with the authority of the particular, visible church. Most
importantly, Milton's conviction of his own extraordinary

ministry is reiterated throughout his prose and refashioned in *Paradise Regained*. Milton's theology of ministry helped to determine the shape of the visible church in his ecclesiology and to define his opposition to the Restoration church, its ministry dependent on political force and custom rather than scriptural authority and inspiration.

Convinced from an early age of his sacred poetic calling, Milton changed the form, not the office of his ministry when he turned to controversial prose in the 1640s. Persuaded by divine inspiration that he had special authority, Milton often found himself at odds with religious orthodoxies, "church-outed by the prelates," Presbyterians and Independents. Instead, he writes as a prophet sent to teach and exhort the nation and the church to reform. He addresses not only Restoration readers in his late poems but also a vast audience made possible by the printed book, an audience similar to the one he imagines in *The Second Defence of the English People* (1654): "Surrounded by congregated multitudes, [he] now imagine[s] that, from the columns of Hercules to the Indian Ocean, [he] behold[s] the nations of the earth recovering that liberty which they so long had lost."[2] For Milton, the visible church is embodied in a community of believers united, not by physical proximity, but by the progressive revelation of truth in reading, writing, hearing, and speaking the Word in all parts of the world at any given time.

Ministers, however, must not only interpret the Word but also live it, providing an example for the church widely dispersed in time and space. For Milton, the authority of the Word and the priesthood of believers are collective activities instituted by God to sustain divine presence in history and to satisfy the devotional needs of the church. Individuals must also gather for worship, and this requires laws that govern the congregation and its acts of worship as well as its relationships to other churches and the civil state. Order and harmony are needed in such organizations of people if they are to work toward understanding and living God's ways, but even when Milton defends most vociferously the need for an external form of church government and discipline in the antiepiscopal tracts, the key to the order of the church is self-discipline. The discipline of the church consists in the Christian life of its members, the process of self-government and edification undertaken by believers as they respond to the voice of God heard in the Word of Scripture with the guidance of the Holy Spirit. This is a process modeled by the minister's patience and temperance, especially during times of trial. Milton develops this view of church discipline as collective self-discipline in the antiepiscopal tracts of 1641–42 and reiterates it throughout his career, culminating in the portrait of Jesus in *Paradise Regained.*

Reformers such as Luther and Calvin both challenged the medieval priesthood, by emphasizing the prophetic rather than sacerdotal function of the clergy, and supported the medieval priesthood, by emphasizing the divine authority of the church. The divine inspiration claimed by poets as well as the direct illumination claimed by radical spiritualists were both secondary to the professional ministry's interpretation of the Spirit. Whereas Calvin was able to balance the authority of the individual and community, the inward witness of the Spirit and external witness of the Word, his spiritual heirs during the Civil War, Commonwealth, and Protectorate periods in England did not, resulting in the progressive fragmentation of the church's authority to the point where radical Quakers claimed the direct revelation of the Spirit without the Scriptures or ministry.

Milton clearly writes within this free church ecclesiological tradition but with four important differences. Unlike the Quakers, he never claims that the direct revelation of the Spirit is possible, but argues that truths revealed by divinely inspired, post-apostolic prophets are partial and incomplete. Moreover, the Spirit, the inner scripture that authorizes each Christian to be a minister of the Word, is manifested in a gradual, rational process rather than a sudden, mystical enlightenment, a process involving "the progressive restoration of the intuitive perception of the law of nature which was obscured but not obliterated by the Fall."[3] In addition, Milton's views of ministry and inspiration are as literary as they are theological and result in emphasizing the Word as much as the Spirit. The discipline that develops from the ministry of the Word is rooted in classical and humanist ethics as well as Scripture, leading to his emphasis on self-discipline rather than external order and on the universal rather than particular congregation. Further, Milton's literary rather than theological view of his divine inspiration and extraordinary prophetic ministry shapes the ecclesiology of the universal, visible church for which he writes. *Paradise Regained* is an act of discipline and ministry as part of Milton's prophetic and vocational office, but it also reconstructs true and false ministry and discipline in the conflict between Jesus and Satan, engaging in a critique of Restoration ecclesiastical politics in the process. The dependence of each office of the church on literary considerations indicates how unified Milton's ecclesiology truly is.

I

As Kerrigan has shown, in postapostolic Christianity, the prophetic ministry of the apostles was subsumed under the church's authority to interpret Scripture.[4] Christ and his apostles concluded the era of prophecy and inerrant inspiration, but, since the church extended Christ's presence on earth after his Resurrection and glorification, the Word was inseparable from how the ministry interpreted it. The decline of the prophetic office of the ministry in the Western church was the target of a strenuous critique by some humanists of the Renaissance and, later, by the leaders of the Reformation, which eventually led to the restoration of the prophetic ministry as a mediation of God's revelation. Erasmus condemned scholasticism because philosophical method could not move listeners to embrace Christ as well as rhetoric based on the Word.[5] The clergy should study rhetoric and literature to acquire eloquence so that they might accomplish the purpose of the preaching office — the conversion of souls. For humanists like Erasmus, the restoration of the preaching ministry did not contradict the church's authority; however, it was weakened when the early reformers, influenced by biblical humanism, undermined the sacerdotal priesthood, emphasizing the person rather than the office of the priest, and the personal experience of the Spirit and Word rather than the collective wisdom of councils and traditions. Calvin and Luther both separated the work of the Holy Spirit from the doctrine of the medieval church. They claimed a parallel inspiration with the prophets of Scripture, identifying their authority with the Protestant ministry after the "libertines" of the radical Reformation, as Calvin referred to various Anabaptist sects, denounced the Lutheran and Calvinist churches based on the inspiration of the Spirit, either in their own revelations or in their interpretation of Scripture.[6] Once the inward authority of the Holy Spirit was acknowledged, the individualism of the radical Reformation had begun, even if both Luther and Calvin actively fought against such conclusions.

A similar crisis underlies the theology of ministry as it developed throughout the seventeenth century in England. The Anglican priesthood, especially under Archbishop Laud, asserted the continuity and hierarchy of its offices from the time of the apostles until the present day, placing emphasis on the sacerdotal function of the priest and the sacraments of the church. In the Anglican view, the Spirit is synonymous with the church's interpretations guided by Scripture, tradition, and reason. Puritan confessions, whether separatist, semi-separatist, Presbyterian, or Independent also take for granted the need for a professional ministry of doctors, pastors, elders, and deacons.[7] Nevertheless, because they emphasize the authority of the Holy Spirit in the interpretation of Scripture, Independents were more likely to emphasize that any member of the congregation with the appropriate gifts could preach the Word of God.[8] As John Goodwin maintains, although no one has been filled with the Holy Spirit, and although the spirit of prophecy ceased with the Scriptures, sincere believers will be open to "quicknings, incitements, [and] impulses" in which the Spirit will "put forth himself, or his power abundantly" in many forms, including "prayers and songs to the Lord."[9] Based on similar assumptions, John Owen rejects both formal liturgies and direct revelations of the Spirit, but defends the preacher's inspired, prophetic office since the minister is the "mouth of God" blessed with the gifts of the Spirit for spontaneous prayer and evangelical preaching.[10] The authority of the Spirit, however, led radical spiritualists such as William Erbery to claim the direct revelation of the Spirit without the Word or the ministry. The authority of the indwelling Word in each Christian removed distinctions between clergy and laity.[11] The dispensation of the Spirit succeeded that of the Word, according to Erbery, making not only the ministry of the Word and sacraments redundant, but the visible church as well.

To add to the complexity of the prophetic ministry, Christian poets from Caedmon to Milton claimed to be divinely inspired. In the process of defending the study of Greek and Roman poetry and rhetoric against the aspersions of scholastic theologians, Erasmus and many Italian humanists before him, including Petrarch, Salutati and Boccacio, argued not only that ancient poets were the first divinely inspired theologians, but that much of the Old Testament was written in poetry. The first theologians were poets, including the legendary Orpheus, the supposed author of the Orphic mysteries, and Hesiod, the author of the *Theogony*. Virgil must have been divinely inspired when he wrote the "Fourth Eclogue," believed to prophesy the birth of Christ. More importantly, Moses and David wrote in verse in the Scriptures, while the prophets, and Jesus himself, used poetic figures of speech.[12] The prophets, and Moses in particular, used poetic language to convey the glory of God's creation.[13] Milton cites these and similar arguments in defending the dignity of his poetic office in *The Reason of Church Government* and cites them again in *Paradise Regained* (4.331–34, 353–60), this time to assert the superiority of Scripture as a model for poetry and prophecy. Although the argument that poetry should be studied because the Bible itself was poetic continued to be made in sixteenth and seventeenth century England, the more troublesome issue was left unresolved — if the poet, like the prophet, is divinely inspired, what is the status of a classical or Christian poet's authority in relation to the apostles, the Scriptures and, more importantly, the church?[14]

Despite the common origins of the sacred offices of poetry and preaching in the prophetic ministry of revealing God's Word by divine inspiration, poets rarely suggested that their authority contradicted the authority of the church. In the context of Renaissance critical theory, Weinberg has shown that Plato's theory of poetic, divine inspiration was contrasted with Aristotle's theory of art and imitation, but was never viewed as an alternative to the authority of the church.[15] From Castelvetro to Sidney and Jonson, critics maintain that true poetry begins with inspiration but is tempered by imitation and exercise; moreover, inspiration is often synonymous with the natural gift of verse rather than the immediate revelation of God's Word, which is generally reserved for the prophets and apostles, and occasionally, as I have suggested, the new prophets and apostles of the Reformation.[16] Sir Philip Sidney, for example, acknowledges the divine origins of poetry but only to contrast the dignity of poetry in the past with its degeneration in the present. The divine inspiration of classical poets was a "superstition"; in fact, Plato claims that poetry is "a very inspiring of a divine force, far above man's wit," which is more than Sidney himself asserts.[17] For Sidney, the divine purpose for poetry has no connection with the inspiration of the Holy Spirit or of a "divine force" in pre-Christian eras; rather, the "divine gift" or "genius" for putting words in "delightful proportion" and imitating ideal patterns of behavior helps people "know that goodness where unto they are moved."[18] In this sense, poetry "deserveth not to be scourged out of the Church of God."[19] Sidney thus denies the potentially heretical claims of poetic authority by associating inspiration with a gift and by denying the revelatory force of poetic inspiration altogether. A gift is from God but should not be confused with special insight or revelation; the latter was reserved, Sidney implies, for the writers of Scripture who were inspired by the Holy Spirit, but that special activity has ceased. Nevertheless, the poets should not be hounded out of the church as Stephen Gosson, Sidney's opponent, suggested in *The Schoole of Abuse* (1579). Poetry is a skill that can be used to lead people to a good life.[20] The Holy Spirit is the author of Scripture through the apostles and the prophets; on the other hand, the authors of poetry, even divine poems, were blessed with gifts from God to teach what had already been revealed to the church in Scripture.

Christian poets continued to petition God for the aid of the Holy Spirit in the early seventeenth century, as in the sixteenth, without any sense that they were contradicting the church. Donne and Herrick both acknowledge the inspiration of the Spirit, and use the "stylus Dei" figure to describe the relationship between God and the human author, but any association with direct revelation is avoided because they invoke the Spirit's aid for the gift of writing rather than the authority of revelation.[21] Even though the tone of Sylvester's translation of Du Bartas's *The Divine Weekes* is more personal and less conventional than previous invocations, reflecting a Calvinist's awareness of the inward witness of the Spirit, he too asks the "glorious Guide" to lift up his soul and refine his spirits rather than to inspire him with revealed truth.[22] Since the gift appropriate for writing and prophesying is cited as an ordinary grace bestowed by the Holy Spirit in 1 Corinthians 12:8–10, there is no conflict between poetic and theological appeals to the Holy Spirit. Literary references to divine inspiration begin to change, however, during the Commonwealth.

As far as he goes, Baker is right when he asserts that "in the connection between the literary and theological doctrines of inspiration . . . no problems of dogmatic theology are involved."[23] In the early stages of the English Reformation there were no problems because poetic inspiration in the composition and invention of fables was considered a gift of the Holy Spirit rather than part of a prophetic ministry. Later in the seventeenth century, however, when the authority of the Holy Spirit in each individual became such an important principle of the radical Reformation in England, and when Milton identified this authority in his own prophetic and poetic vocation, the results were no longer "within the limits of orthodox religious belief." Baker is on questionable ground when he concludes that Milton merely repeats "a centuries old literary and religious tradition" in which the appeal to the Holy Spirit is of "accessory value" only.[24]

Reacting to radical Independents and sectaries who claimed the direct revelation of the Spirit in fulfillment of the prophecy in Joel 2:28–32 and the Pentecostal dispensation of the Spirit in Acts 2, Royalist critics such as Thomas Hobbes, William D'Avenant, and Samuel Butler associate theories of inspiration with self-interest, heresy, political subversion, and enthusiasm, severing the traditional relationship between poetic and religious inspiration.[25] In his preface to *Gondibert* (1651), D'Avenant contrasts "Government and order" with inspiration, "a dangerous word which many have of late successfully us'd," referring to the inspired prophets both in and out of the pulpits of Commonwealth England.[26] For D'Avenant, "government and order" is needed as much in composition as in the state. He then goes on to discredit theories of inspiration by associating them with a corrupt and frenzied priesthood that has nothing but its own interests at heart:

> *inspiration* is a spiritual Fitt, deriv'd from the antient Ethnick Poets, who then, as they were Priests, were Statesmen too, and probably lov'd dominion; and as their well dissembling of *inspiration* begot them reverence then, equal to that which was paid to Laws; so these who now profess the same fury, may perhaps by such authentick example pretend authority over the people; It being not unreasonable to imagine they rather imitate the Greek Poets then the Hebrew Prophets, since the latter were inspired for the use of others; and these, like the former, prophesie for themselves.[27]

Divine inspiration is a political, religious, and poetic issue that D'Avenant associates with subversion, irrationality, and Nonconformity. Religious figures who "are Statesmen and Priests, but have not the luck to be Poets should not assume such fancy familiarity with a true God."[28]

Hobbes continues the same argument in his answer to D'Avenant's preface. He recognizes that ancient, "heathen" prophets were poets who claimed to speak "the word of God, and not of man," but goes on to condemn contemporary divines by associating them with this ancient superstition. There is no reason, argues Hobbes, now that we can "speak wisely from the principles of nature," for poets or divines to claim "to speak by inspiration, like a bagpipe."[29] The choice of the bagpipe image is a witty reminder of the political and religious associations of appeals to divine inspiration. Abraham Cowley, in a note explaining his invocation to Christ in *Davideis*, disclaims divine inspiration; the invocation is just a "custom" and he hopes "this kind of boast . . . will not seem immodest." On the other hand, the poet can "reasonably hope to be filled with a *Divine Spirit*, when it [the poem] begins with a *Prayer* to be so."[30] His careful use of the indefinite article removes him from the association of inspiration with sectarianism, but it is equally obvious that, as a poet, he wishes to claim divine

inspiration at the same time. Thus, even though only a limited number of preachers were claiming direct inspiration of
the Spirit, this was enough to force D'Avenant and others to
dissociate theories of inspiration from their theories of poetic
invention and from their views of the ministry of the Word in
general.

The inspiration and gifts of the Holy Spirit claimed by Independents are rejected more bluntly by Butler through his satire
of the "gifts" and "new-light" of Ralph, the empty-headed
squire in *Hudibras*.[31] His "new-light" is an *"ignis fatuus* that
bewitches;" it "inspires and plays upon / The nose of saint like
bagpipe drone" (1.482, 503, 515–16). Religious and poetic inspiration are then linked since the language of Ralph's inspiration is the same as that which

> Phoebus or some friendly Muse
> Into small poets song infuse
> Which they at second hand rehearse,
> Through reed or bagpipe, verse for verse.
>
> (1.521–24)

Reacting to Puritan claims about the revelation of the Spirit,
D'Avenant, Hobbes, and Butler dissociated religious and poetic
forms of divine inspiration by associating inspiration with
sectarianism, leaving sacred poets like Cowley, who wanted
to claim divine inspiration but resisted because of its sectarian associations, with nothing but a wish. When Milton invoked
the Spirit's aid in *Paradise Lost* and *Paradise Regained* he was
out of fashion, but he was also making a strong political statement of his own.

In both Reformation theology and Renaissance criticism,
potentially explosive claims to prophetic authority were
carefully contained and assimilated. In the theology of
Calvin, the personal and inward activity of the Holy Spirit
affirms thedivine origin of Scripture, speaks through the
prophets and apostles to each Christian, and enables every reader

to interpret the Scriptures. At the same time, only the preacher is the "mouth of God," only the church can confirm the internal witness of the Spirit, and only the doctors of the church can interpret Scripture with authority. Calvin was also unequivocal about the authority of poets, both ancient and modern — despite their harmful theology, ancient poets can teach morality, but prophetic and poetic vocations are distinct. Contemporary poets, therefore, must be guided by the church and have no authority comparable to the ancient prophets, prophecy having ceased with the apostles.[32] Similarly, in poetry and criticism, no sooner was the Platonic theory of divine inspiration rediscovered and poetry hailed as a gift "springing from God's bosom" than it was just as quickly subordinated to the Aristotelian discipline of imitation and *decorum*.[33] Nevertheless, the affinities between poetry and prophecy, particularly in their shared source of inspiration by the Holy Spirit, continued to be asserted, preparing the way for Milton's association of literary and theological doctrines of the Holy Spirit with his own extraordinary office of the ministry of the Word in poetry and prose throughout his career, but especially from 1640 onward.[34]

II

It was perhaps Milton's firmest inward conviction that he was called to perform an extraordinary ministry in poetry, and both his calling and the evidence that he received it are explored throughout his works. This vocation was interrupted when he was called to serve God and the nation in prose, but when he turned in the late poems to take up his former calling, the prophetic identity formed during the years of the Civil War and Commonwealth asserted itself in the Restoration epics with a new confidence and power despite his political and religious exile after 1660. Renaissance theories of poetic inspiration and radical theologies of lay ministry both helped to shape his prophetic, poetic identity.

The term *vocation,* or calling, had a variety of theological uses in the seventeenth century, but two were especially important for Milton: first, human beings are called to be reconciled to God through Jesus; and second, God calls every person to fulfill a specific function, one of which is the ministry. In theological accounts of vocation, every special calling has two parts: inner conviction, of which inspiration is the clearest sign, and external witness, consisting in the appropriate gifts and the acknowledgment of the community.[35] Milton, however, replaces the confirmation of the community with ethical discipline as an external witness of a person's worthiness for extraordinary ministry, demonstrating how classical ethics helps to shape his ecclesiology and how closely connected church discipline and ministry are in Milton's thought.

External evidence of an inward call to the ministry takes two forms in Milton's ecclesiology: "exceptional piety" and "spiritual gifts." In "Elegy VI," while he was still preparing to enter the ministry of the Church of England, Milton transfers the priestly regimen of Pythagoras to the moral character of the poet who "is sacred to the gods and is their priest" (52). Implied, of course, is the sacerdotal function of the priesthood: just as the priest must ensure a pure sacrifice, so the poet must have self-discipline in order to deliver God's Word. After Milton rejected the ministry of the Church of England, the same emphasis on the ethical discipline of the poet is continued but is transferred to the character of the prophet. Each member of the church is "call'd by the holy calling of God to be holy and pure; so is he by the same appointment ordain'd" (*Reason of Church Government, CPW* 1:843). Ministers, in particular, are called to teach by imitating Christ and the apostles (*Christian Doctrine, CPW* 6:595–96, 599), but all Christians, by virtue of their new dignity purchased by Christ's sacrifice, are holy enough to worship at the altar of God.

Milton's use of sacerdotal imagery in *The Reason of Church Government* implies that the character of the priest rather than the office of the priesthood is the essence of the ministry. He contrasts the sacerdotal priesthood's emphasis on the unworthiness of the laity, the ceremony of the altar, and the externality of the sacraments with the prophetic ministry's emphasis on the priesthood of believers and "the love of God," which is "a fire sent from Heaven to be ever kept alive upon the altar of our hearts" (*CPW* 1:841). He follows this conviction to its logical conclusion when he later states that "what chiefly constitutes the true worship of God is eagerness to do good works" (*Christian Doctrine, CPW* 6:637). Good works, however, like poetry and prayer, originate with the Holy Spirit rather than the human will. Good works conform not to "the written but with the unwritten law, that is, with the law of the Spirit which the Father has given us to lead us unto truth. For the works of the faithful are the works of the Holy Spirit itself. These never run contrary to the love of God and our neighbor, which is the sum of the law" (*CPW* 6:637). Thus, when Milton defends his character in *The Reason of Church Government* (*CPW* 1:801–23), *An Apology against a Pamphlet* (*CPW* 1:883–92), and *The Second Defence of the English People* (*CPW* 4:1.581–92, 611–29), he is providing testimonies of his "pure and honourable life" and, therefore, of his fitness for the ministry. Every human being, but especially a poet, "ought him selfe to bee a true Poem, that is, a composition, and patterne of the best and honourablest things" (*Apology, CPW* 1:890); otherwise, his gifts to God will be unworthy. Every believer can be a temple of God in which the Holy Spirit offers sacrifices on the altar of the heart and inspires true worship in the form of works of charity.

Milton's accounts of his learning also function as testimonies of the spiritual gifts he has received for his calling; however, "God even to a strictnesse requires the improvement of these his entrusted gifts" (*Reason of Church Government, CPW* 1:801). Milton's various claims for being unprepared, then, are inseparable from his calling to the ministry. In

"Sonnet VII" (1632) and the "Letter to a Friend," which accompanies it in the Trinity manuscript (*CPW* 1:318–21), Milton shows that he is troubled by his failure to use his talents as Jesus teaches in the parable of talents (Matt. 25:14–30). At the same time, because of the seriousness of his calling, he must devote himself to learning in order to honor God properly. In the letter, he defends himself against an unnamed friend's charge of "tardie moving" into the professional ministry. Milton replies by arguing that love of learning is not to blame for his delay in taking orders. For how, he asks rhetorically, could it surpass the desire for "immortal fame," "worldly gaine" and "house and family," which commonly occupy a young man's thoughts at this stage of life? On the contrary, he reasons, it is his "sacred reverence" for the Scriptures, and his awareness of the parable of talents, which urges each person to use the gifts that God has provided, that delay his entry into the ministry. It is better to be late for his ministry, he claims, than unfit to perform it. Curiously, though, he offers "Sonnet VII" as evidence of his awareness of this lack of "inward ripeness," and apologizes for preaching, which is precisely what he is being criticized for not doing, claiming that he would "deale worse with a whole congregation, and spoyle all the patience of a Parish" (*CPW* 1:320). These last comments are witty and ironic rather than direct; there is no evidence that Milton has chosen to abandon the ministry at this early stage, but he certainly seems to be hedging his bets. Even though the poem suggests that he has a sacred poetic calling that will employ his gifts for God's glory in a way unavailable in the traditional ministry, his desire for preparation does not exclude the ministry of the Church of England at this point.

Milton again appeals to his youth and unreadiness in *Lycidas* (1–5) and *The Reason of Church Government* (*CPW* 1:749, 806–07). In the latter, he also refers to the parable of talents, this time defending his decision to prepare for his ministry at his father's house instead of entering the priesthood. These are not just literary or theological *topoi*, however; they are public covenants announcing his calling and gift for the ministry. He proves that he has the gifts of language and literature, gifts suitable for the preacher as well as the poet, but also points out that he writes "out of mine own season" (*CPW* 1:807). "The full circle" of his "private studies" is incomplete, and his true vocation is sacred poetry rather than controversial prose; nevertheless, when God calls someone to an extraordinary ministry, the call must be answered. Education and preparation were needed to make the minister a fit vessel of the Holy Spirit, and also to provide evidence of inspiration and extraordinary ministry. Milton's humanism, his preoccupation with his unreadiness, his self-defences, and his references to the parable of talents can be seen, then, within the context of his preparation for the ministry, first in the Church of England, and then in the universal, visible church gathered to search the Word. Called by God to reform the church, Milton shifted the sacred calling of the ministry to prophetic poetry and prose.

More than external witness was needed in the acceptance of a calling, however; inner conviction was also crucial. Drawing on theories of literary inspiration and lay ministry, Milton demonstrated his inner conviction that he was called to an extraordinary ministry in the universal church. In his most explicit statement of personal calling to the extraordinary ministry, Milton links the songs of the prophets with the "inspired gift of God" which is given only to a few in each nation who "are of power beside the office of a pulpit" (*Reason of Church Government, CPW* 1:816). Although this identification of poetic and prophetic calling takes place after he has decided not to enter the professional ministry of the Church of England, a similar prophetic calling informed his poetic designs while he was still intending to enter the ministry. Believing himself called to serve the church and to write sacred poetry, when God called him to write controversial prose in 1640, Milton did not abandon his ministerial vocation; his ministry simply changed from an ordinary to an extraordinary, inspired ministry of the Word.[36] Prepared as a child for the ministry of the church and demonstrating gifts "for the study of literature," Milton assumed that the two offices were compatible until the late 1630s and early 1640s, when it became obvious that he could not enter the Laudian church (*CPW* 1:823; *Second Defence, CPW* 4:1.612).

Ministerial and poetic callings are both prophetic because they have teaching as their objective and literary gifts as their witness. Milton also links the inspiration of the prophet Isaiah to his poetic office in the Nativity Ode (27–28) and his prophetic office in *The Reason of Church Government* (*CPW* 1:820–21). In both cases he compares Isaiah's experience of purification and dedication to the Lord by means of a seraph's hot coal to his own illumination and purification by the Holy Spirit for the sacred office of writing. In *Il Penseroso* he identifies the poetic experience of inspiration with the "Prophetic strain" (176), while in *Lycidas* the poet, priest, and prophet are identified not only in the figure of Lycidas, but also in the speaker of the poem who ascends to prophecy when he proclaims that the corrupt clergy will be destroyed by "that two handed engine" (130).

Milton intended to enter the professional ministry and to write sacred poetry, but neither office was sacerdotal. In writing he claims his "right of lamenting the tribulations of the Church" (*Reason of Church Government, CPW* 1:823), while early statements of his poetic calling were sacerdotal only in his superficial use of the imagery of Greek mystery cults. He is self-conscious and hyperbolic in his appropriation of priestly imagery for the poet in his early poetry: "By song Apollo's priestesses and the trembling Sibyl, with blanched features, lay bare the mysteries of the far away future. Songs are composed by the sacrificing priest at the altar . . ." ("Ad Patrem," 24–26). Representative in the years before the civil war were the unqualified, though still conventional statements of divine inspiration in "At a Vacation Exercise" (29–52), "Elegy V" (11–12), and "Elegy VI." Here he claims that "the bard is sacred to the gods and is their priest"; the poet's "hidden heart and his lips alike breathe out Jove" (77–78). He then offers Charles Diodati a "gifte for the birthday of Christ" (87): the Nativity Ode.

With the possible exception of the Nativity Ode, "Sonnet VII," and a few lines in *Lycidas,* Milton's prophetic vision of his poetic calling before 1640 was conventional and defensive. The invocation of the frenzied, divinely inspired poet of Plato's *Phaedrus* in "Elegy V" (11–12), for example, is predictable in a poem that celebrates the *topos* of spring, for the rebirth of poetic powers corresponds to the regeneration of the earth. Side by side with this conventional belief in his divine inspiration as a poet, however, must have been a growing, more deeply felt sense of divine calling for the ministry, especially when his calling and inward prompting were manifested in the literary gifts granted by the Holy Spirit for use in the church.

In stark contrast to Milton's conventional, literary appeals to divine inspiration in his early poetry, Puritans within the Church of England in the 1630s, with whom Milton later sympathized, identified England with Israel and themselves with the prophets of the Old Testament who speak the Word of God. This tendency to identify the preacher with the inspired prophet grew as conflict with the Laudian church reached a crisis as a result of the martyrdom of Prynne, Bastwick and Burton; the Bishops' Wars (1639, 1640); the failure of the Short Parliament; and the imposition of the *Constitutions and Canons Ecclesiasticall* (1640). William Prynne, for example, wrote "of the breath of the mouth of God in his word breathed by one poore Minister," while Edmund Calamy — the "ec" of the acronym, Smectymnuus, whom Milton defended in *Animadversions* — assures the Long Parliament that "God hath sent me hither this day as his Angell."[37] The prophetic calling of the Puritan ministry, erupting in the late 1630s and early 1640s, may have helped Milton to clarify the relationship between his own vague poetic vocation and the ministerial vocation for which he had been training since he was a boy. When the opportunity arose to defend his country and lead the reformation of the church, Milton's callings converged in the prophetic office of an inspired writer of prose called by God to exhort the church to build Christ's kingdom in England.

The first indication that Milton's ministry is extraordinary and prophetic is that it depends on inward calling and inspiration rather than ordination or apostolic succession. In *The Reason of Church Government* he writes of the "supreme inlightning assistance" which makes up for his lack of experience and of the "inward prompting" that he "might perhaps leave something so written to aftertimes, as they should not willingly let it die" (*CPW* 1:749, 810). When these testimonies of inward calling are considered with his belief that poetry is an "inspired gift of God . . . of power beside the office of the pulpit," it is likely that Milton is providing his readers with a testimony of his extraordinary ministry. In the autobiographical section of *The Reason of Church Government,* Milton declares his divine calling and offers his talents and gifts as evidence of his fitness for his vocation. He makes his extraordinary office even more plain by identifying himself with the prophet Isaiah:

> Neither doe I think it shame to covnant with any knowing reader, that for some few yeers yet I may go on trust with him toward the payment of what I am now indebted, as being a work not to be rays'd from the heat of youth, or the vapours of wine, like that which flows at wast from the pen of some vulgar Amorist, or the trencher fury of a riming parasite, nor to be obtain'd by the invocation of Dame Memory and her Siren daughters, but by devout prayer to that eternall Spirit who can enrich with all utterance and knowledge, and sends out his Seraphim with the hallow'd fire of his Altar to touch and purify the lips of whom he pleases. (*CPW* 1: 820–21)

Louis Martz argues that in addition to identifying Milton with Isaiah, the appearance of this covenant with the reader in the middle of his discourse recalls the structure of a similar personal testimony in Jeremiah.[38] Milton's identification of the Holy Spirit as the source of vocation and inspiration, "of utterance and knowledge," the purpose of which is the teaching of God's Word, also links him to a specific extraordinary ministry.

He explicitly associates himself with the divine inspiration of the prophets by identifying himself with the burden of the Word reluctantly taken up by Jeremiah. Milton declares himself one of "Gods . . . selected heralds of peace," but such a task is a burden: "This is that which the sad Prophet *Jeremiah* laments, *Wo is me my mother, that thou hast born me a man of strife, and contention.* And although divine inspiration must certainly have been sweet to those ancient profets, yet the irksomnesse of that truth which they brought was so unpleasant to them, not every where they call it a burden" (*CPW* 1:802–03). Like the prophet, Milton has been divinely inspired and, despite the burden of truth, must deliver the message to the nation: "But when God commands to take the trumpet and blow a dolorous or a jarring blast, it lies not in mans will what he shall say, or what he shall conceal" (*CPW* 1:803). God's "*word was in my heart as a burning fire shut up in my bones,*" declares Jeremiah, and with him, Milton (*CPW* 1:803). Temporarily unable to perform his prophetic task in poetry, he will turn with his "left hand" in the "cool element of prose" to the reformation of the church, the denunciation of the clergy, and the exhortation of the nation. This ministry, as Milton reminds his readers in *An Apology Against a Pamphlet*, depends on God's will alone: "And against such kind of deceavers openly and earnestly to protest, lest any one should be inquisitive wherefore this or that man is forwarder then others, let him know that this office goes not by age, or youth, but to whomsoever God shall give apparently the will, the Spirit, and the utterance" (*CPW* 1:875).

The divine inspiration experienced by Milton as the internal testimony of his poetic and prophetic callings shows that the two offices were essentially the same — the ministry of the Word. The divine source of his calling, however, differs markedly from representations of the inspired poet in the early poetry. In the Latin elegies Milton invokes the conventional image of the frenzied poet possessed by the divine presence, while in the antiepiscopal tracts his inspiration is exegetical and prophetic. Even though his indignation and scorn reach an irrational pitch, he justifies it on rational grounds. His are "sharp, but saving words," which, like the prophet's, are "a terror, and a torment in him to keep back" (*CPW* 1:804). God has given him "ability the while to reason against that man that should be the author of so foul a deed" as the oppression of the church. Moreover, the "two most rationall faculties of humane intellect [are] anger and laughter"; consequently, he is fully justified in using harsh invective in God's defense (*Animadversions, CPW* 1:664).

His specific office, however, is to teach, and what better way to teach those who are "proud and obstinate" than to adopt methods used by God:

> For as in teaching, doubtlesse the Spirit of meeknesse is most powerfull, so are the meeke only fit persons to be taught: as for the proud, the obstinate, and false Doctors of mens devices, be taught they will not; but discover'd and laid open they must be. For how can they admit of teaching who have the condemnation of God already upon them for refusing divine instruction . . . therefore we may safely imitate the method that God uses; *with the froward to be froward, and to throw scorne upon the scorner,* whom if any thing, nothing else will heale. (*Apology, CPW* 1:874–75)

As Kerrigan has shown, this representation of the indignation of the prophet inspired to interpret God's Word correctly was appropriated by Christian exegetes in order to distinguish their reception of divine revelation from the "furor" of pagan poets and oracles. In this tradition, the reception of divine revelation results in ferocity but not frenzy.[39] Here Milton appropriates the tradition for his own ministry of prophetic, inspired teaching. He hopes to be "an interpreter & relater of the best and sagest things among mine own Citizens throughout this Iland in the mother dialect" (*Reason of Church Government, CPW* 1:811–12).

Milton also distinguishes the rational prophecy of the writer in "the cool element of prose" from the office of the poet "soaring in the high region of his fancies." Whereas the poet appeals to the imagination, the controversialist persuades by argument, but both are dedicated to inspired teaching of the Word of God. The inspiration that is the basis of both callings is not direct or complete as it was for the prophets, apostles, and evangelists; God now reveals truth progressively rather than instantaneously or inerrantly.[40] Although his prose work may only be "a plain ungarnish't present" and "thanke-offering" to God compared to the "elaborate Song to Generations" that he plans, he has been called and inspired by God to perform his task and cannot refuse what the Lord asks of him. The imagery of gifts and offerings is also used in the Nativity Ode, in which he gives testimony of his prophetic calling, and suggests that writing is an act of worship, for it is the Word given to him that he offers back to God in words, whether in prose or poetry.

In the antiepiscopal tracts, Milton accepts God's call to be an inspired teacher or prophet who will instruct the nation, but he does so with reluctance, not because that is the biblical convention, but because his gifts and education have prepared him for a poetic expression of his prophetic vocation.[41] As the "digression" in *The Reason of Church Government* and the outlines of compositions in the Trinity manuscript show, his new calling interrupted and delayed his calling to write a poem which, as he hints in *Of Reformation*, would celebrate God's favor of England and the nation's reformation of Christ's kingdom (*CPW* 1:616). This intermediate stage in Milton's prophetic vocation, characterized by his reluctance to leave poetry for prose, is left behind by the time he writes the tracts of 1643–1644.

In his works of "domestic liberty," Milton fully adopts the prophetic activity of rational exegesis in order to advise Parliament and the Westminster Assembly of the scriptural proof of divorce and freedom of the press. In fact, as Hill notes, as opposition to his views on divorce grew, Milton became more and more convinced of his prophetic role, standing with the people of England, "a Nation of Prophets," against "the whole noise of timorous and flocking birds" (*Areopagitica*, *CPW* 1:554, 558) gathered in the Westminster Assembly. [42] Later he will stand against the backsliding nation in *The Readie and Easie Way* (1660), but at this early stage he feels that the nation and the true church can still be transformed according to the Word. In *The Doctrine and Discipline of Divorce*, for example, he declares that "by the favour and appointment of God" the Parliament and Assembly have "a great and populous Nation to reform" and that he, a "Scribe instructed to the Kingdome of Heav'n" (Matt 13:52; *CPW* 2:223), has a special calling since he has been inspired by the Holy Spirit. This inspiration is not simply a gift of talents or a conventional trope but a claim to truth and insight through the Holy Spirit's guidance, a claim which is prophetic in its origin and authority. "[T]he way to get a sure undoubted knowledge of things," he explains, "is to hold that for truth, which accords most with charity. Whose unerring guidance and conduct having follow'd as a loadstarre with all diligence and fidelity in this question, I trust, through the help of that illuminating Spirit which hath favor'd me, to have done no every daies work" (*CPW* 2:340). When he discovers that Martin Bucer, the respected Strassburg reformer, confirms his views, he interprets it as a further sign of God's favor. Bucer was God's servant, so it can be no strange thing if in this age he [God] stirre up by whatsoever means whom it pleases him, to take in hand & maintain the same assertion. Certainly if it be in mans discerning to sever providence from chance, I could allege many instances, wherein there would appear cause to esteem of me no other then a passive instrument under some power and counsel higher and better then can be human, working to a general good in the whole course of this matter. For that I ow no light, or leading receav'd from any man in the discovery of this truth. . . . Yet at length it hath pleas'd God, who had already giv'n me Satisfaction in my self, to afford me now a means wherby I may be fully justify'd also in the eyes of men. . . . So as I may justly gratulat mine own mind, with due acknowledgement of assistance from above, which led me, not as a lerner, but as a collateral teacher, to a sympathy of judgement with no lesse a man than Martin Bucer. (*Judgement of Martin Bucer, CPW* 2:433, 435–36)

In part a defence of his own industry and authority apart from Bucer's, and in part a testimony of God's inspiration and guidance, Milton's letter to Parliament indicates that he has fully accepted the office of inspired teacher, the most important function of the extraordinary ministry.

When, in the same year, he declared in *Areopagitica* that the nation is like the prophet Samson, waking from its sleep, and like Israel, fulfilling Moses's wish that "all the Lords people are become prophets," Milton asserted his prophetic vocation in its most optimistic and visionary form. Not only he, but the whole nation will "walk in the Spirit," "musing, searching, revolving new notions . . . reading, trying all things, assenting to the force of reason and convincement" (*CPW* 2:558, 567, 554). More importantly, Milton clarifies the nature of the truths proclaimed by prophets inspired by the Spirit. The Truth, as a whole, will not be revealed until Christ's Second Coming. Until then the truth "may have more shapes then one," for "what else is all that rank of things indifferent, wherein

Truth may be on this side, or on the other, without being unlike her self" (*CPW* 2:563)? As Milton concludes in *De Doctrina Christiana*, truth is revealed "with the help of the Holy Spirit, promised to each believer. Hence the gift of prophecy, 1 Cor. xiv." If there is disagreement, people should "tolerate each other until God reveals the truth to all" (*CPW* 6:580, 584).

In *Areopagitica*, Milton expresses his most idealistic hopes for the extraordinary ministry of the Word in which the whole church and nation will work in the unity of the Spirit toward the building of the true reformed church, the kingdom of Christ. Like the prophet of Isaiah 40–55, he exhorts people to embrace a new world in which each member of the church can also be an active minister witnessing God's Word in reading, writing, speaking and listening. The prophet Haggai reveals that the Lord will "shake all nations" (Haggai 2:7) just as Milton declares that God now "shakes a Kingdome . . . to a general reforming" (*CPW* 2:566). The prophet Joel declares that the Lord "will pour out [his] spirit upon all flesh," (Joel 2:28), and Milton declares that all have the opportunity to become prophets.

Milton uses allusions to the prophets not only to persuade his audience, but also to convey his own authority as a prophet and extraordinary minister of the Word. From 1649 to 1660, however, Milton comes to realize that England has refused God's promise to make it "a holy nation," but this only intensifies his sense of prophetic identity and extraordinary ministry. He instructs, warns, condemns, and laments the nation as it turns from the possibility of freedom to the slavery of the Restoration. In *The Tenure of Kings and Magistrates* (1649), Milton curses false prophets who mislead the nation (Jer. 48:10; *CPW* 3:236), defends the prophets who have slain kings (Jer. 22:1–9; *CPW* 3:215–16), and reminds the nation of God's Word to Samuel: "they have not rejected thee, but they have rejected me, that I should not reign over them" (1 Sam. 8:7; *CPW* 3:202, 204).

In *Eikonoklastes* (1649), he condemns the idolatry of an "Image doting rabble" just as Jeremiah condemns the "stiffnecked" people of Israel who disobey God and worship idols (Jer. 7:22–26, 10.1–15; *CPW* 3:343, 601). In *The Second Defence of the English People,* he thanks God for defeating his enemy, praises the remnant of the faithful who lead the nation, and warns them of backsliding (*CPW* 4:1.549, 674, 680; Jer. 50:1–18; 50:20; 7:23–26). Finally, in *The Readie and Easie Way,* he once again warns the nation of "chusing them a captain back for *Egypt.*" He laments, in the anguished voice of Jeremiah, the perversity of "a misguided and abus'd multitude": "Thus much I should perhaps have said though I were sure I should have spoken only to trees and stones; and had none to cry to, but with the Prophet, *O earth, earth, earth!* to tell the very soil it self what her perverse inhabitants are deaf to" (Jer. 22:29; *CPW* 7:462–63). Although the explicit identification of Charles II with Coniah (Jer. 22:24–30), which Milton made in the first edition of *The Readie and Easie Way,* disappears in the second edition, the reference is still pointed enough. Milton, as Jeremiah, curses the king even if his emphasis is on the "perverse inhabitants" who reject the prophet and choose slavery. Adapting the words of another prophet, John the Baptist, he then offers hope for rebirth. There is a remnant "whom God may raise of these stones to become children of reviving libertie." On the eve of the Restoration, the solitary prophet rails against the nation and its lost opportunities, hoping that, even in this perverse time, when inner liberty is abandoned for the slavery of monarchy, a few righteous individuals will remain to congregate in God's name. Thus, like Jeremiah, Milton receives the call reluctantly, depends on divine inspiration, condemns idolatry and false prophets, laments the weakness of his people, and stands in solitary allegiance to God, linked to other prophets only by the Word.

The formal theology of *De Doctrina Christiana* codifies what Milton learned by hard experience and literary tradition.

In *De Doctrina Christiana,* Milton defines prophecy as a gift of teaching, the central form of which is interpreting the Word in the church. Since ordination was less important than a previous, more direct inspiration from God manifested in the gifts of prophecy and ethical fitness, any member of the church, provided they had these gifts, could perform this function. Given Milton's personal experience of inspiration as a poet, it is fitting that he would be attracted to theologies of ministry and the Spirit that would emphasize the personal, internal witness of the Spirit as the authority for a lay ministry. Preeminent within the ministry, however, are those extraordinary ministers such as the prophets, apostles, evangelists, and Protestant reformers, who have been divinely inspired to reform the church by writing or preaching. Milton identifies himself with this extraordinary ministry. He emphasizes his divine favours and inspiration, his self discipline, his teaching and exegetical office both in poetry and prose, and his fellowship with the prophets.

His views of progressive revelation and the partial illumination of the understanding by the Holy Spirit, however, differ from both the literary and the theological views of inspiration that were current during this time. Literary invocations of the early seventeenth century tend to petition the Holy Spirit for literary gifts, while Royalist critics dismiss the role of inspiration on political grounds. Milton, especially in the Nativity Ode and *The Reason of Church Government,* identifies his inspiration with the "hallow'd fire" of prophetic revelation by the Spirit. His is a claim to illumination and not just the ability to write. He also differed from conservative theologians, like John Owen, who maintained that prophetic revelation ceased with the apostles, and from sectarians, like William Erbery, who claimed to have received infallible, immediate revelation. For Milton, inspiration did not reveal the truth, since human comprehension is always incomplete, nor was prophetic

revelation immediate or ecstatic. For him, inspiration illuminated the mind in a rational process of teaching and debating
that defines the church and that would continue until the
Second Coming, when truth would be revealed in glory. Until
then, all offices of the ministry, including preaching, administering the sacraments, and maintaining discipline, were
accessible to all members of the church.

Like moderate humanists in the Church of England such as
Hooker and Taylor, Milton asserted that reason guided by the
Holy Spirit is the best authority when scriptural commands
are absent.[43] Unlike Hooker and Taylor, however, Milton
ignored the authority of church tradition, leaving the individual
conscience and the exercise of reason guided by the Holy Spirit
in the interpretation of Scripture the final authorities in religion. Like sectaries such as Erbery, Milton granted final authority to the Spirit, but for Milton the truth of the Holy Spirit is
manifested progressively in rational activity and in other gifts
suitable for the ministry rather than in sudden and direct revelations apart from Scripture. In addition, like the sectaries,
Milton downplayed distinctions between the clergy and laity,
creating a ministry of believers, but unlike them, Milton
acknowledged ranks within the ministry, ranging from divinely
inspired, extraordinary ministers to gifted, ordinary ministers
and deacons.[44] Like the Presbyterians of the Westminster
Assembly, Milton defended the degrees of the ministry, but
unlike them, denied the ministry of doctors and the authority of synods, asserted the equality of clergy and people, and
recognized the authority of the Holy Spirit in each person.[45]
Finally, like the Independents, he denied the authority of
the councils, rejected set patterns of prayer, and recognized the
particular, visible church as a "self-contained and complete
church" because each congregation enjoyed "the scriptures and
promises, the presence of Christ and the guidance of the Spirit"
(*Christian Doctrine, CPW* 6:601). Unlike them, however,

Milton condemned the confusion of ecclesiastical and civil power in the collection of tithes and the ministry of university educated doctors.[46]

Milton's view of the ministry, therefore, cannot be identified with the ministry of any particular, visible church of his time. This does not mean that the visible church disappeared from his thought; it was still possible for those unable to join a "correctly instituted church" in "good conscience" to share in "the blessing which was bestowed on the churches" (*CPW* 6:568). In particular, although he was "Church-outed by the prelates," the Presbyterians, and the Independents, he continued his extraordinary ministry in the universal, visible church, defined as "the whole multitude of those who are called from any part of the world, and who openly worship God the Father in Christ either individually or in conjunction with others" (*CPW* 6:568). Milton's late poems, then, are central to his literary ecclesiology both in their relationship to his own ministerial calling and to the audience that the printed book allows him to reach.

III

Milton's conception of his own prophetic office of writing parallels the emphasis on the Word in the free church tradition. When the church is regarded in its universal rather than particular dimension and when the media of the Word are expanded to include books as well as sermons, we can begin to appreciate Milton's prophetic and poetic vocation in *Paradise Regained*, and what he meant when he said that those who have "the inspired gift of God . . . are of power beside the office of a pulpit, to inbreed and cherish in a great people the seeds of virtue and public civility" (*Reason of Church Government*, *CPW* 1:816). Poetry, in particular, can be as incarnational as Jesus's parables and metaphors. The parables of the kingdom are important not just for the doctrine they convey; they are paradigms of religious language and how religious truth is revealed.[47] They are incarnational in that they bear the reality to which they refer and invite the reader's participation in that reality. As Eberhard Jungel suggests, the kingdom cannot be separated from the parables that are used to proclaim it: "Jesus's parabolic language *is* the event of the Kingdom of God. . . . Jesus's parables are the real presence of the Kingdom."[48] Similarly, for Milton the church is constituted by the Word and its readers, but literature also has a special role since in the invention of scriptural narratives, parables, and metaphors, authors invite readers to participate in the creation of the kingdom in the act of making interpretive choices and forming metaphors and narratives themselves.

When Milton asks for the inspiration of the Holy Spirit at the beginning of *Paradise Regained* and depicts Jesus being led and inspired by the Spirit but still rational and measured in his reading of Scripture, he deliberately defies the poetics of Royalist *decorum* according to D'Avenant and Hobbes and the stereotypes of Nonconformists found in Restoration discourse, particularly Butler's *Hudibras*. Calm rather than frenzied, patient rather than impetuous, disciplined rather than disorderly, Jesus' response to the Spirit leading him to the wilderness and guiding his reading subverts the Royalist construction of delirious Nonconformists under the influence of the "new-light" of the Holy Spirit. The prophetic office of the Word is demonstrated in the hermeneutic battle with Satan in which Jesus acknowledges the transcendent silence of the Father. In this acknowledgment he finds the unity of his two natures and the power of the Word to embody the Father's wishes. In addition to embodying the church's authority, Jesus is also an exemplary minister, while Satan is a demonic parody of one: whereas Jesus opens the text through the Spirit, Satan abuses it by enslavement to the letter; whereas Jesus interprets figurative speech, Satan is confounded by it; whereas Jesus depends on the Word alone, Satan reaches for pagan philosophy; whereas

Jesus represents the ministry of the whole church, Satan represents a professional class separate from the laity; whereas Jesus
accepts God's mysteries, Satan insists upon debating them;
whereas Jesus patiently endures suffering, Satan anxiously
hopes to avoid it; whereas Jesus separates church and state, Satan
unites them.

These differences between Jesus and Satan in *Paradise
Regained* are similar to the differences between true and false
ministry defined in many of Milton's prose works. As I showed
in chapter 2, Jesus is a model of faithful exegesis in *Paradise
Regained,* and this is the primary function of the ministry, but
for Milton Jesus taught by example as well, providing the ministry with the only essential pattern of Christian life. Through
his actions he taught how to gain "wisdom by simplicity,
strength by suffering, [and] dignity by lowliness" (*Reason of
Church Government, CPW* 1:824). In particular, Christ's servanthood, accomplished through the act of *kenosis,* when he
emptied himself of pure Godhead in order to become the Word
made flesh, is inseparable from his teaching. According to
Milton, "the form of a servant was a mean, laborious, and vulgar life aptest to teach; which form Christ thought fittest,
that he might bring about his will according to his own principles choosing the meaner things of this world that he might
put under the high" (*CPW* 1:825–26).[49] "The Lordly life, the
wealth, [and] the haughty distance of Prelaty," then, contradict Jesus' servanthood and "that misterious work of Christ,
by lowlines to confound height, by simplicity of doctrin [to con-
found] the wisdom of the world" (*CPW* 1:824, 829–30). By
using force to ensure church unity, the prelates show contempt
for Jesus' doctrine of "strength by suffering." Through their accumulation and display of wealth, the prelates deny Jesus' doctrine of "dignity by lowliness." Emphasizing human traditions
of learning, the bishops ignore Jesus' doctrine of "wisdom by
simplicity." "Despising the mighty operation of the spirit by
the weak things of this world," the bishops act "contrary to

the whole end and mistery of Christ's coming in the flesh" (*CPW* 1:833, 835).

In *Paradise Regained* Satan unwittingly reinforces Jesus' ministerial calling. By mocking Jesus' low birth, he gives Jesus the opportunity to reinforce the "dignity of lowliness." Satan insists that political power is necessary for Jesus' kingdom, but Jesus counters with the strength of patience and suffering. Temporarily giving up on political power, Satan offers a kingdom of the mind instead. Jesus, on the other hand, insists on the "wisdom of simplicity" derived from the "Light from above" (4.289). Satan offers political power, the trappings of wealth, and worldly wisdom, three subjects that Milton returns to repeatedly in his critique of the bishops and the "hireling clergy."

Milton emphasizes Jesus' servanthood not only to condemn episcopacy but also to celebrate that "the privilege of teaching was anciently permitted to many worthy Laymen" (*Reason of Church Government, CPW* 1:839). True ministry occurs when members of the church, "in true imitation of Christ," and "enobl'd to a new friendship and filiall relation with God" (*CPW* 1:842), act with reverence toward each other. Since every lay Christian is "Gods living temple," which is "more sacred than any dedicated altar or element" (*CPW* 1:843, 844) by virtue of each member's "filiall relation," the church consists of a voluntary congregation of equal believers joined by the Spirit. When the laity is restored to its active place in church affairs, then the "congregation of the Lord [will] soone recover the true likenesse and visage of what she is indeed, a holy generation, a royal Priesthood, a saintly communion, the houshold and City of God" (*CPW* 1:844). In Jesus' rejections of Satan's temptations in *Paradise Regained,* Milton provides his readers with just such a model of "royal Priesthood," a ministry which includes each member of the church.

The true minister is not a "Carnall textman," (*Apology,* CPW 1:951) who "scan[s] the *Scriptures* by the Letter" (*Of*

Reformation, CPW 1:522) as Satan does in his futile attempts
to understand the figurative and typological meaning of Christ's
baptism at the beginning of the poem and the nature of Christ's
kingdom in the second temptation. True leaders of the church
are "Herald[s] of heavenly truth" (*Animadversions, CPW* 1:721)
who interpret by "the quickning power of the *Spirit*" (*Of
Reformation, CPW* 1:522). Jesus prefers "Sion's songs" which
are "from God inspired" (*PR* 4.347, 350), and his trust in the
Spirit enables him to unfold David's prophecies of his kingdom as well as the figurative meaning of the dove at his baptism. Jesus embodies a principle of the ministry proclaimed
in the antiepiscopal tracts but also taken up in *Considerations
Touching the Likeliest Means to Remove Hirelings Out of the
Church*. Because of "their spiritual priesthood," lay members
of the church have "equal[ly] access to any ministerial function whenever calld by their own abilities and the church" (*CPW*
7:320). Jesus shows in his dependence on the Father and Spirit,
and in his thoroughly human suffering, that the only thing separating the ministry and the laity is the vocation to teach, while
Satan, on the other hand, by elevating him on the pinnacle of
the temple, tempts Jesus with the sacerdotal ministry, separated from the laity.

In the temptations of the kingdoms, Satan also tempts Jesus
to violate the spiritual jurisdiction of the minister by using
wealth and political force to build his kingdom, but Jesus
maintains the spiritual nature of the church, just as Milton
does throughout *A Treatise of Civil Power in Ecclesiastical
Causes* and *Considerations touching the Likeliest Means to
Remove Hirelings out of the Church*, published within months
of each other in 1659. In *Hirelings* he argues that the ordained
clergy, when they insist on the necessity of tithes and a university education, are implicated in this corruption of the
church by civil power. This concern is continued in the first
temptation in *Paradise Regained* as well. Milton first presents Satan disguised in "rural weeds" following "a stray

Ewe" — a conventional figure of the minister, whose duties include pastoral care for the flock and the persuasion and discipline of lost sheep back into the fold of the church through "winning words."[50] The whole passage recalls Matthew 18:11–18, the proof text commonly cited in Protestant schemes of pastoral discipline (*PR* 1.314–34). The "Son of God" comes to save lost sheep, not false priests; he comes in preaching, not in miracles. If church members are led astray, it should be told "to the church" not to the "Town or Village" of the "heathen man and [a] publican." Finally, when the church binds or loosens on earth it does so to open or close the doors of the kingdom of heaven rather than to increase the fame of a member or to satisfy those who "curious are to hear" (*PR* 1.333). Satan's abuse of Scripture throughout the poem also marks him as a false teacher, one of the signs of the Second Coming of Christ mentioned in *Christian Doctrine* (*CPW* 6:616).

Not only is Satan a false priest, identifying himself with the lying spirit that inspired the false prophets of Ahab's court (*PR* 1.371–77; 1 Kings 22:13–23), but his advice to Jesus is clearly unsound as well. If Jesus is, as Satan suggests, a lost sheep "far from path or road of men," Satan should put him on the right path not toward "Town or Village" to gain fame (*PR* 1.322, 332). Jesus' answer confirms this. Instead of accepting the mediation of a false priest, he acknowledges "no other Guide" but the Spirit, and no other food but the "Word/Proceeding from the mouth of God" (1.336, 349–50). Satan's temptation of Jesus to distrust God's providence — to provide his own food by turning stones into bread, fearing that God has abandoned him to starve — is also a temptation to distrust God's spiritual kingdom founded on the Word alone and to submit to the temporal, carnal power offered by Satan.

Similar arguments were used by Milton against the state church in *Hirelings* 12 years earlier.[51] Milton claims that the clergy turn Christ's "heavenly kingdom into a kingdom of this world, a kingdom of force and rapin," transforming the church into "a beast of many heads and many horns." The clergy reveals its distrust of providence when it takes tithes and insists that a university education is necessary for every minister of the Gospel (*CPW* 7:313, 308). Tithes are "tempting baits" that lure unfit ministers into the church; instead, clergy should "trust in God and the promise of Christ for thir maintenance" (7:300, 303). The argument that tithes are necessary to support a university educated clergy is equally distrustful of God's providence, argues Milton, since "the providence of God and the guidance of the Holy Spirit" are sufficient to sustain the church just as they are sufficient to sustain Jesus in *Paradise Regained* (7:304; *PR* 1.335–36). Jesus depends on the "inward Oracle" and the "Light from above" just as whatever "makes a fit minister, the scripture can best informe us to be only from above" (*PR* 1.463, 289; *CPW* 7:316). By tempting Jesus to turn stones to bread, Satan is also tempting him to turn the church into a worldly kingdom. Milton, unlike the defenders of the Restoration Act of Uniformity, continues to insist that religious and civil jurisdictions should be separate.

In his rejection of Satan's temptation of learning, Jesus reflects Milton's view of the role of education and learning for the ministry outlined in *Hirelings* and, to a lesser extent, the antiepiscopal tracts. When education is part of an attempt to conflate spiritual and civil power, as it is when Satan offers the wisdom of Greece to Jesus apart from the revealed Word, and when the necessity of a university education is used as an argument for the maintenance of tithes, as Milton's opponents argued in the learned-ministry controversy, a humanist education must be rejected. In *Hirelings*, Milton does not condemn learning outright, but only if it is used as an argument in support of tithes and a state-supported clergy. Similarly, Jesus reveals his knowledge of the classics and praises such figures as Socrates, but rejects them when they are offered as substitutes for Scripture or as means to acquire a worldly kingdom. Just as in *Paradise Regained* Jesus returns to "his Mother's house private" (*PR* 4.639) in a humble condition to begin his ministry, so Milton argued that a minister could learn everything necessary for his calling in a "private house" (*Hirelings*, *CPW* 7:316). He urges the ministry to abandon the pomp and wealth of the world and to teach throughout the countryside like the apostles. The teaching ministry should depend on providence by accepting "the benevolence and free gratitude of such as receive them" or support themselves with "an honest trade" (*CPW* 7:309, 306). In his special prophetic ministry, Jesus represents both the ideal clergyman and the ideal layman since both are one in the priesthood of believers that Milton imagines for the church.

For Milton, "Christ . . . came downe amongst us to bee a teacher," and this prophetic ministry was perpetuated by the church in the ministry of the Word (*Animadversions*, *CPW* 1:722). Not only did Milton conceive his own vocation in these terms, seeking "to be an interpreter & relater of the best and sagest things" (*Reason of Church Government*, *CPW* 1:811), but as H. R. MacCallum has suggested, Jesus' pedagogy in *Paradise Regained* reflects the teaching methods attributed to him by Milton in his early prose.[52] The pedagogical context of the temptations is similar to the context in which Jesus meets the Pharisees throughout the New Testament, and in which Milton debates the clergy in his prose. Satan, like the Pharisees and the clergy, is proud and obstinate, refusing divine instruction; as a result, he cannot be taught but must be "discover'd and laid open" (*Apology*, *CPW* 1:874). In the Bible, Jesus "discovers" his unsympathetic listeners by being "froward with the froward," by giving them "a sharp vehement answer to a tempting question" (*Divorce*, *CPW* 2:282). In *Paradise Regained*, he "sternly" and "sharply" rebukes Satan and his temptations (*PR* 2.406, 468). Christ's terse and sometimes cryptic answers to Satan's questions are meant to "discover" the adversary. They reveal Satan for who he is since he is unable to interpret a text that a believer would understand with

ease. The pinnacle scene, then, is a discovery scene in a pedagogical as well as a dramatic sense.

Bent on trapping Jesus in a verbal conundrum motivated by
their literal interpretation of the law, the Pharisees are rebuffed
time and again by parables, hyperboles, and paradoxes.
Throughout his ministry, Milton argues, Jesus teaches by indirect speech in order to drive the interpreter from the letter to
the spirit, and to confound his enemies, the Pharisees. His intention was to "blind and puzzle them the more who could not
understand the Law" (*Tetrachordon, CPW* 2:678; *Divorce,
CPW* 2:301). Jesus uses "short, and vehement, and compact sentences," scattering the seeds of truth in order to confuse his
enemies and reward the "laborious gatherer" (*Divorce, CPW*
2:301, 282–83, 338). In *Paradise Regained,* Jesus' terse replies,
as well as his oblique references to his kingdom, ensure that
Satan, lacking the guidance of the spirit of truth and charity,
will continue in his ignorance, while Milton's readers will
grow in their understanding of the spiritual sense of Christ's
words. Jesus gives "a sharp and vehement answer to a tempting question" in book 1, when he rejects Satan's attempt to
gain his sympathy, and in book 4, when he quotes the Scriptures
on the pinnacle. Jesus also scatters epigrammatic truths like
pearls throughout his speeches (*PR* 1.335–36), answers questions with questions (1.422–26), and absolutely rejects Satan's
offers, only to adopt a modified and purified form of the same
temptation later. A good example of this occurs when Jesus
curtly rejects Satan's banquet only to accept the celestial banquet later on. This use of hyperbole, in which we "bow things
the contrary way, to make them come to thir naturall straitnes"
(*Divorce, CPW* 2:283), is also evident in the temptation of the
kingdoms. When Satan offers wealth, Jesus rejects it in favor
of its opposite — the spiritual kingdom — and Satan is left mute
as truth is revealed to him (*PR* 2.406–86).

In keeping with his tendency to answer Satan in ways that
will encourage him to reveal himself for what he is, Jesus uses
parables to heighten the mystery of the kingdom rather than

to reveal it. Although the image of David's throne as a tree "Spreading and overshadowing all the Earth" (4.148) will be interpreted metaphorically by Milton's readers, Satan is unable to unravel its meaning, manifesting the absence of the Spirit. Mary and the disciples are in a similar state of uncertainty about the meaning of the kingdom at the beginning of book 2, but instead of tempting Jesus to begin the kingdom immediately, they resolve to wait patiently until he opens their understanding, revealing their faith that truth will emerge in due time.

Although Jesus is the exemplary teacher and the Bible the true source of wisdom, Milton also includes classical texts and teachers as sources of inspiration and edification for the church. In *The Reason of Church Government*, Milton praises the "method of instruction" followed by Plato and Moses, who both introduce their lessons on the nature of law with a "well temper'd discourse" designed to "charme the multitude" before the harsher doctrines which follow are outlined (*CPW* 1:746). Even though Moses's authority is "better & more ancient . . . then any heathen writer," he shares with Plato a common method, consisting in the use of "true eloquence" to teach the people about "that which is really good as to imbrace it ever after, not of custom and awe . . . but of choice and purpose, with true and constant delight" (*CPW* 1:746–47). Milton praises Plato's belief that "persuasion certainly is a more winning, and more manlike way to keep men in obedience then feare" (CPW 1:746) just as in *Paradise Regained* Jesus realizes early in his life that "winning words" accomplish more than "the work of fear" (1.222, 223).

This recognition of the importance of classical learning seems to contradict Jesus' later rejection of learning in *Paradise Regained*, but the context of the learning temptation must be kept in mind. As exemplary teachers, Jesus and the church leaders who follow him need only the simplicity of heavenly doctrine, not abstruse philosophical doctrines pursued for their own sake. Satan offers classical learning as a means of attaining fame and worldly empire through contemplation. Jesus has already rejected the temptations of premature action, glory, and political kingdoms; learning must be rejected since in these terms it is an aimless pursuit. Learning, under these conditions, might "entertain / The irksome hours" of the rebel angels in *Paradise Lost* (2.526–27), and it will serve a similar aimlessness when it is "with Empire join'd" (*PR* 4.284) without saving faith. Learning is fine, Satan further implies, until Jesus matures enough to turn his attention to what is really important. As Jesus goes on to argue, and as Milton himself argued in the antiepiscopal tracts, eloquence and learning without truth is frivolous, the realm of "learned fools," and those who pursue it are like "Children gathering pebbles on the shore" (4.330). In this confrontational setting, Jesus must reject Satan by rejecting what he offers, and by offering biblical models of eloquence and poetry instead; to do otherwise would be to acknowledge Satan as a wise teacher. However, as Jesus' understanding of classical wisdom indicates and as his explicit defence of those authors in whom "moral virtue is express'd/By light of Nature" (4.351–52) acknowledges, classical learning, although perhaps not "God inspir'd," is still useful, if not absolutely necessary, for Jesus and the ministry. Both Job and Socrates serve as valuable exemplars of patience, temperance and suffering for truth's sake (3.91–98). "Quintius, Fabricius, Curius, [and] Regulus" (2.446) as well as Gideon, Jephtha, and David (2.439) are models of the "dignity of lowliness" and how men in "lowest poverty" can accomplish the "highest deeds" as long as they exercise "Virtue, Valour, [and] Wisdom" (2.439, 431). Learning from these examples, Jesus derives his wealth from virtue and discipline rather than riches, asking rhetorically,

> And what in me seems wanting, but that I
> May also in this poverty as soon
> Accomplish what they did, perhaps and more?
>
>   (2.450–52)

In his literary ecclesiology, Milton reiterates that reading the Word and responding to it in writing for those who have a special calling are the essential acts of ministry and authority in the church. For Milton, however, the inspiration of the Christian author/minister should lead not only to interpretation and invention but to action as well. The discipline of the Word is an integral part of Milton's literary ecclesiology, for if God speaks in Scripture, and the ministry disseminates this speech to the community, the purpose of the speech is to change individuals, to persuade them to live the Word more fully in their daily lives. To accomplish this purpose, the minister must be an exemplar of the Christian life and the poet "ought him selfe to bee a true Poem, that is, a composition, and patterne of the best and honourablest things" (*Apology Against a Pamphlet, CPW* 1:890).

Almost from the outset of the Reformation, church discipline was a subject of fierce debate within the Church of England.[53] Initially directed against the retention of Roman Catholic vestments in the church, such as the cope and surplice, Puritan criticisms of the tardy Reformation in England eventually included ceremonies, such as the sign of the cross during baptism; orders, such as the episcopacy; powers, such as the "power of the keys" held by priests to prescribe forms of penance; and jurisdictions, such as the supremacy of the king in the church. Even though in its ecclesiastical use church discipline referred specifically to the powers of spiritual censure held by the clergy, by the 1640s it was also applied to the expression and application of doctrine in ceremonies, vestments, orders, and ecclesiastical laws in general.

Milton uses church discipline in this general sense in the title of his first work of ecclesiastical prose, *Of Reformation Touching Church Discipline In England*. Underlying his vituperative and wide-ranging attack on the English church, however, is a specific and coherent view of church discipline — the discipline of the Word. For Milton, the discipline of the church consists of the Christian life of its members, the process of self-government and edification undertaken by believers as they respond to the voice of God heard in the Word of Scripture with the guidance of the Holy Spirit. Each individual *is* the church and a member of the church at the same time. Just as the body is the temple in which the Holy Spirit dwells in each individual, so the church is the body of believers united by the Holy Spirit through the Word. Any external order, whether Presbyterian, Anglican, or Independent, is idolatrous if it hinders the reformation of the church through the edification of its members by the Word and Spirit. Thus, only vestments, ceremonies, powers, and jurisdictions clearly outlined in the Word and used by the apostolic church are acceptable because any addition to God's Word amounts to the worship of idols forbidden in the second commandment. Moreover, the proliferation of visual symbols in the church hinders the edification of believers and their attempt to understand God as a spiritual presence approached through the Bible. Finally, searching the Word, which Milton identified with the church itself in *Areopagitica,* is also implied in the process of edification and self-government that constitutes the external order and discipline of the church in the antiepiscopal tracts. The ministry and discipline of the Word, then, are inseparable: not only is the ministry open to all members of the church, but interpreting and expressing the Word in words and actions, poetry and self-discipline are bound together as well.

Milton's publication of his views of church discipline in 1641–42 coincided with the ascendance of the Presbyterian party in the Long Parliament. Their attacks on episcopal jurisdiction, as well as the vestments, ceremonies, and powers of the English church under the leadership of Archbishop Laud, were relentless. More particularly, Milton's antiepiscopal tracts are clearly linked to the controversy between Bishop Joseph Hall and the five Presbyterian clergymen — one of whom was Thomas Young, Milton's former tutor — known as Smectymnuus.[54]

Critics as different in method as Arthur Barker and Stanley Fish have concluded that Milton's doctrine of church discipline in the antiepiscopal tracts is poorly developed but essentially Presbyterian.[55] The acceptance of this thesis by later readers has led to the view that the tracts are of rhetorical interest only; that they are empty but colorful outbursts expressing the "straight Presbyterian party line."[56] Without denying the importance of the rhetorical dimensions of Milton's early prose, when we consider the importance of self-discipline in Milton's thinking, his position on church discipline appears more coherent than has been previously argued. Milton's main purpose is to discredit the bishops, not to present a systematic proposal; as rhetorical occasions permit, alternatives to episcopacy are suggested, some of which support the Smectymnuans and many others which do not. This lack of agreement was not uncommon in the early 1640s since nothing resembling a unified Presbyterian party existed for those who sought more local autonomy for the church through government by lay elders elected by the congregation.[57] Moreover, the principle of interpretation upon which Milton's discipline is based clearly distinguishes him from the Presbyterians he is supposed to be defending. While the Smectymnuans argue that the church, led by the ordained ministry, is the final authority in matters of interpretation, Milton insists that each individual, guided by the Holy Spirit, needs only the Word for salvation. Each Christian, as "God's living temple" (*Reason of Church Government, CPW* 1:843) is free to act according to conscience. Church discipline, then, includes more than ecclesiastical censure, church government, liturgy, or applications of doctrine; for Milton, "discipline" refers to self-discipline or "likeness to God" (*Of Reformation, CPW* 1:571), the measure and proportion of action as the Word becomes incarnate in daily life.

At least since 1572, the year of the *Admonition to Parliament,* the reformation of church discipline and government according to an apostolic model was a goal of many English reformers, but even at this early stage of the debate, "discipline" could be used in a variety of ways.[58] In its ecclesiastical context, "discipline" could refer to church government and worship generally or, more specifically, to the rules used to maintain order in the church, especially as they related to the censure and excommunication of wayward members of the congregation.[59] "Discipline" was also used in an ethical context to refer to orderly conduct, moderation, and self-government. In practice, this sense of the word was never far below the surface of its ecclesiastical use because the purpose of discipline in most Puritan churches was to strengthen the church as a witness to Christ by excluding from communion those who did not have discipline in the ethical sense.[60] Thus, the possibility of conflating the ecclesiastical and ethical meanings was available even before Milton turned in this direction in 1641.

In *The Reason of Church Government*, Milton associates discipline with the circumscribed limit or measure that is inherent in each person and goes on to show how the attainment of self-discipline leads to the building of the church. God has "cast his line and level upon the soule of man which is his rationall temple, and by the divine square and compass thereof forme[s] and regenerate[s] in us the lovely shapes of vertues and graces, the sooner to edifie and accomplish that immortall stature of Christs body which is his Church, in all her glorious lineaments and proportions" (*CPW* 1:758). In an earlier passage, Milton turns to images of music rather than geometry to explain the relationship between the divine Word and human actions guided by self-control. Discipline is prescribed in Scripture, heard in the divine voice and imitated in virtuous action; "And certainly discipline is not only the removall of disorder, but if any visible shape can be given to divine things, the very visible shape and image of vertue, whereby she is not only seene in the regular gestures and motions of her heavenly paces as she walkes, but also makes

the harmony of her voice audible to mortall eares" (*CPW*
1:751–52). This music imagery emphasizes the convergence of
the divine and human in virtue, the highest expression of
divine discipline available in human life.[61] The ideal of discipline as the measure and proportion inherent in individuals
is also linked by Milton to the order of creation itself through
the imagery of planetary orbits. As a result of true discipline
"our happinesse may orbe it selfe into a thousand vagancies
of glory and delight, and with a kinde of eccentricall equation
be as it were an invariable Planet of joy and felicity . . ." (*CPW*
1:752). Far from encouraging the "repetition of that which is
prescribed," discipline allows the planets to have a variety of
orbits and still participate in a more inclusive order. In the same
way, Christians are free to live out their own discipline and
still participate in the church.

As Arnold Stein argues, the music imagery associated with
discipline in Milton's work also suggests that his notion of
self-discipline and temperance is Platonic in origin but Christian in application, indicating again how Milton's ecclesiology
is informed by classical and humanist sources.[62] Unlike the
Stoics' view of temperance as the eradication of emotions and
Aristotle's view of it as a prudent choice between extremes,
Plato's view emphasizes the harmony achieved in the soul
when action or will is directed by reason. Temperance and
self-discipline do not exclude emotion, but they imply "the
subordination of lower faculties to higher."[63] For Milton,
temperance and self-discipline consist in the exercise of right
reason in the service of God's will as it is revealed in Scripture.

Music imagery is often used to describe this state of freedom in which God's will and human action coincide. Music
and song at the end of *A Mask* symbolize the Lady's attainment of virtue through self-discipline and temperance, while
the angelic song at the end of *Paradise Regained* celebrates the
Son's enactment of Christian liberty and the incarnation of the
internal Word in heroic action. Jesus also hears the morning

"chant of tuneful Birds" twice (2.290; 4.437) and is the subject of three hymns (1.182, 242; 4.593–94). On the other hand,
sin is represented by the inability to hear the divine harmony
or to act in harmony with God's will. "At A Solemn Music"
refers to the "harsh din" of the Fall and the struggle to "keep
in tune with Heav'n" (20, 26), and Comus is associated with
harsh dissonance and noise. Satan, in *Paradise Regained*,
doesn't hear the heavenly "Odes and Vigils" (1.182) sung in
heaven or the "Anthems" (4.594) sung to the Son, while the
rebel angels are associated with "clamor" (2.148). In book 4,
Satan claims to have heard and understood the significance of
the "Angelic Song" accompanying the Nativity (4.505), referred
to as the "glorious Choir" by Mary (1.242), but in book 1, in
his address to the rebel angels, the opposite is true. He argues
that Jesus' birth is not a significant cause for fear, unlike his
growth into manhood (1.66–69). This indicates that he wasn't
listening to the angel and the choir cited in Luke 2:10–15, or
that he heard but didn't understand what he was listening to,
or that he is lying to or misleading his audience for his own
purposes. Satan's accounts clash, creating the impression that
the divine music has not created harmony and order in the self,
but fear and agitation instead. The purpose of discipline, on
the other hand, is to "set the affections in right tune" (*Reason
of Church Government, CPW* 1:817). According to Milton, "all
the movements and turnings of human occasions are moved
to and fro as upon the axle of discipline. . . . [S]he is that which
with her musical chords preserves and holds all the parts
thereof together" (1:751).

The discipline of the Word, so important in achieving church
discipline, is synonymous with the virtue of temperance dis-
played by Christ throughout *Paradise Regained*. Jesus' self-mas-
tery is the visible representation of that "true and substantial
liberty, which must be sought not without, but within, and
which is best achieved, not by the sword, but by a life rightly
undertaken and rightly conducted" (*Second Defence, CPW*

4:1.624). On the scale of virtues explored in *Paradise Regained,* wisdom is the highest, and it is manifested in the Son's obedience to the Father's will manifested in Scripture, but temperance and patience are the most important manifestations of this wisdom and, indeed, wisdom and self-discipline are virtually interchangeable. By linking temperance to wisdom understood as obedience, however, Milton again implies that the classical conception of virtue, however insightful, is dependent on the Christian view of revelation, for virtue, whatever form it takes, arises not from the self but from one's personal relationship to God.

In *De Doctrina Christiana,* temperance is the preeminent special virtue of the self concerned with the regulation of appetite and the discriminating use of material things (*CPW* 6:724–28), and Jesus is associated specifically with temperance twice in *Paradise Regained* (2.378, 408). The role of temperance in moderating appetite, however, also connects it to the general virtue of "righteousness towards ourselves," which refers to "right reason in self-government and self-control" and includes two main parts: "the control of one's own inner affections" and the "resistance to or endurance of evil" (*CPW* 6:720). The virtue of self-control and discipline is implied in many of the words, especially the negatives, used to describe Jesus' responses to the temptations: he is "unmov'd" (3.386; 4.109), "unshaken" (4.421), "untroubl'd" (4.401), "unapall'd" (4.425), "unalter'd" (1.493), and calm (3.43; 4.425) as he bears suffering without complaint.

To endure evil with "equanimity" (*aequo*), another word implying balance and discipline, and to acquiesce to "the promises of God, through a confident reliance on his divine providence" demonstrates patience (*Christian Doctrine, CPW* 6:738). Another of the heroic virtues exemplified by Jesus in *Paradise Regained,* patience is temperance and self-control as it relates to how we think or act in response to present suffering. Jesus' refusal to act prematurely, to turn stones to bread, or to speculate about the time of his kingdom's arrival all illustrate his patience and self-discipline. They also illustrate that the source of his wisdom is his "confident reliance on his [God's] divine providence," his complete reliance upon God to show him the way out of the wilderness. The numerous references to Job, the biblical archetype of patience (1.147–49, 369, 424–26; 3.64–67, 93–95), the association of Jesus and Mary with patience (2.102, 432; 4.420), and the attainment by Job and Jesus of glory for God through "wisdom eminent, / By patience, temperance" show again that self-discipline, the virtue that ties together patience, temperance, and "righteousness toward ourselves," is an important quality of Jesus' character and, by extension, of the ministry and the church as a whole.

The connection between personal discipline and the building of the church is made more explicit in the temptation of the kingdoms where Christ's kingdom, the church, is defined as an inner kingdom ruled by self-discipline.[64] Although this connection is explored in more detail in chapter 5, it is worth noting here that the true king is one who "reigns within" and "governs the inner man" (2.466, 477). The Romans and, by analogy, the English were once "temperate" but became "inward slaves" after being ruled by "lust, and rapine," luxury, greed, ambition, and vanity (4.134–41). When Jesus asks,

> What wise and valiant man would seek to free
> These thus degenerate, by themselves enslav'd,
> Or could of inward slaves make outward free?
>
> (4.143–45)

he echoes passages in *The Second Defence of the English People*. Milton describes Cromwell's "government of himself" through his control of "passions which infest the soul," depicts the Romans as "enervated by luxury" and enslaved by their inability to govern themselves, and asserts that "many" people are undeserving of freedom before concluding with this warning: "learn to obey right reason, to master yourselves" (*CPW* 4:1.671, 683–84). If individuals lack self-discipline, Milton argues, the state will degenerate into slavery and the church into idolatry.

In his ministry of the Word, Milton develops to a logical conclusion the implications of his doctrine of scriptural authority and provides a theological foundation for the literary activity that underlies his ecclesiology as a whole. A beneficiary of the rediscovery of classical rhetoric during the Renaissance and the renewed emphasis on the saving power of the preached and written Word during the Reformation, Milton emphasizes throughout his works the clarity, infallibility, and sufficiency of God's communication to humanity about the essentials of salvation. The external Word, when it is illuminated by the inner scripture written by the Holy Spirit on the heart, allows all Christians to participate in the unity of Christ's body, the church, and its progressive revelation of truth through reading, writing, hearing, and speaking the Word. The authority and ministry of the Word are complementary in this process of church building. On the one hand, the authority of the Word is concerned primarily with the reception of Scripture in reading and hearing; on the other, the ministry of the Word is concerned with the reproduction of the Word in writing, speaking, singing, and teaching, but also in the disciplined Christian life of the ministry, in its ordinary and extraordinary forms.

The authority and ministry of the Word, including works of religious poetry, are also interrelated because the Holy Spirit is the author of both Scripture and the gifts of the ministry shared by the poet and priest. Whereas the authors of Scripture were verbally inspired by the Spirit and were instruments of immediate revelation, the ordinary ministers of the Word receive the aid of the Spirit in composing tracts, sermons, and prayers, but do not receive immediate, inerrant truth as the prophets, evangelists, and apostles did. Extraordinary ministers of the Word, like Milton himself, are divinely inspired to reform the church through writing, but their inspiration and illumination are also limited, even though they possess greater authority than the ordinary minister. Each individual is fallible and receives the truth of the Holy Spirit only according to God's gift of illumination. Thus, even though by reading and hearing the Word each individual is saved, and even though by writing, preaching, and prayer each individual contributes to building the church, the ordinary ministry is reserved for those who manifest the gifts of the Spirit, while the extraordinary ministry is reserved for those who have a special calling to reform the church in addition to those gifts.

More than anything, however, Milton's literary ecclesiology is a relationship between the authors of the Bible, Christian writers, exemplary non-Christian writers, and the whole spectrum of readers and writers since the death of Christ. The authors of Scripture were inspired immediately and infallibly by the Holy Spirit, but since subsequent readers were not inspired to the same degree, Christian authorship was needed to clarify the Word and to disseminate it, a process Milton identifies with the church itself, and more particularly, with ministry and discipline. The congregation in Milton's ecclesiology is essentially a readership, a textual community united over time and space by the author and minister's repetition of the Word. Even if each repetition is incomplete, the continuing inspiration of the Holy Spirit, both in the act of composition and in the act of interpretation, ensures that God's original acts of speech in Creation, the Incarnation, and Scripture will continue to be heard and remembered in the prayers, sermons, and written works of Christian authors. Thus, Milton's literary ecclesiology is a fully developed and coherent Christian literary pragmatic, a set of interrelated assumptions about textual production and reception that allows communication to occur between God and the church and between individuals in the church, regardless of the separation of space and the passage of time. In the church without walls imagined by Milton, the church's ongoing engagement with the Word is the only necessary rite, and this ritual of reading is the subject of chapter 4.

FOUR

The Renovation
of Worship

The ministry of the Word, in its prophetic, vocational, and ethical dimensions, is central to the literary ecclesiology of *Paradise Regained*. Under normal conditions, the Lord's Supper and baptism — the sacraments, or external seals of the covenant of grace — were marks of a true, visible church and, like the Word, could be administered by anyone who had the community's authority. Throughout his work, however, Milton implies that the Word in all of its forms is the only necessary sacrament of the church, taking over the ritual activity and semiotic structure of the sacraments in the liturgy. Further, because poetry rather than preaching or exegesis is the pre-eminent form of expressing the Word, it performs a ritual function in Milton's literary ecclesiology. In this sense, *Paradise Regained* is an act of worship.

Throughout his career, Milton participated in a "revolution in ritual theory" that profoundly changed public forms of worship both inside and outside the Protestant church.[1] One of the underlying causes of this revolution was a "semiotic crisis" that would redefine the relationship between the sacred and the material world in the early modern period.[2] Beginning with the objections of figures such as Wycliff and Erasmus to clerical and lay abuses of sacramental rites and continuing in the detailed sacramental theologies of Luther, Zwingli, and Calvin, this crisis paved the way for the emergence of the biblicism of various sixteenth and seventeenth century English Puritan communities. However important ritual signs and actions were in constituting the identities of medieval men and women and informing their magic and medicine as well as their religion, by the seventeenth century the assumption that signs conveyed presence — that by enacting a rite the thing signified by the sign was brought into being — could no longer be accepted by most Protestants as an explanation of the nature of rituals. Instead, a "hermeneutic conception of ritual" was developed by both reformers and humanists in which rituals consisted not of communal experiences that "created presences and enacted being" but of signs that communicated meanings existing independently of the signs that conveyed them.[3] The relationship between the sacred and the material world was constructed on a communicative model, restricting the appearance of the sacred to the Word and the forms of worship found in Scripture.[4]

A paradigm of this change in perspective can be found in the sacramental theology of Zwingli, a sign theory that clearly resembles Milton's. Rather than identifying the bread and wine of the Eucharist with the body and blood of Jesus, the "is" of the words of institution simply means "signifies" or "stands for." Thus, "this is my body" means "this bread stands for my body," by metonymy encouraging participants to remember and live by Christ's sacrifice, an event already presented in Scripture (*Christian Doctrine, CPW* 6:555–56). This shift from presence to representation, flesh and blood to signs, from ritual to reading made it necessary for English Puritans and Nonconformists to examine all details of worship and ritual,

from gestures to music and ornaments, for their biblical meaning and significance. Far from being "adiaphora" or indifferent to salvation and, therefore, subject to the authority of the
church, as they were for defenders of the English church, rituals were symbolic means by which God communicated with
believers and believers communicated with God.

Archbishop Laud's preoccupation with sacramental devotion
in the 1630s, and the attempt to return the church to this condition in the 1660s, should be seen against this background of
ritual theory and practice. According to Laud, the Puritans were
"depravers of the Book of Common Prayer" who contented
themselves "with the hearing of Sermons onely." In doing
so, they broke the unity of the contemporary church and the
practice of the primitive church. Laud's attempt to regulate
sacramental devotion, however, was doomed; his desperate
enforcement of conformity in outward worship indicates the
extent to which the "revolution in ritual" had already occurred.
The Puritans, however, did not reject forms of outward worship entirely; they modified their forms of service to suit their
emphasis on the Word and Spirit and their changing cultural
conditions.

The hermeneutic approach to ritual led to a broad spectrum
of ritual practices in the Puritan tradition, from the liturgical
conservatism of Richard Baxter's "Savoy Liturgy" (1660) and
the "Westminster Directory" (1645) to silent waiting for the
Spirit in Quaker worship. In each case, however, the rich tex-
ture of symbols and symbolic actions that had embroidered
church and society 100 years earlier was extremely threadbare
by the time Charles II was restored and Milton completed his
great poems. Not only did the Bible become the sole criterion
for public worship, but the ante-communion service, or liturgy
of the Word, with its emphasis on readings and the sermon,
became the normative order of service in those Nonconformist
churches that still maintained an interest in liturgical forms.
In the "fractured religious culture of Restoration England," indi-

viduals could also read Scripture, pray and, increasingly, receive the sacraments in small, family gatherings or simply avoid the sacraments completely.[5]

The legacy of Puritan iconoclasm and the reduction of ritual in controversies involving the sign of the cross in baptism, the symbol of the ring in marriage, the posture of communicants during the Lord's Supper, and other ritual acts have been well documented in studies of Milton's prose and, more generally, in histories of theology and worship in seventeenth century England.[6] What scholars are now beginning to discover, however, is the extent to which "the method of reform was often to substitute one ritual for another."[7] Above and beyond the liturgical diversity that developed in England between 1645 and 1662, when Presbyterians failed to replace the *Book of Common Prayer* with the "Westminster Directory" as a source of common worship, iconoclasm is itself now understood as a purification ritual. The Word, both read and heard, became "virtually a third sacrament alongside Baptism and the Lord's Supper," conveying grace in a ritual of verbal presence both in the sacred space of the church and in the sacred space of the reader or listener's heart, the real *"house and church of the living God,"* according to Milton (*Christian Doctrine, CPW* 6:589).[8]

The decline in the force of traditional ritual theory encouraged innovations in liturgy and opened a "space for ritual invention" in literature as well as the church, especially literature that was religious but not specifically liturgical. According to Thomas Greene, texts by Dante, Boccaccio, Petrarch, Erasmus, Rabelais, and Shakespeare "suggest that the questioning of ceremony during the Renaissance left open a space for creative play with ceremonial symbols."[9] A. B. Chambers has provided a more thorough taxonomy of "transfigured rites" in seventeenth century English verse, from liturgical parodies and formal parallels to evocations of a "sacramental view of the world" and uses of the Christian calendar. Chambers brilliantly analyzes the contrast between chronological time and *kairos,* time fulfilled and made meaningful by divine events, in *Paradise Regained,* but downplays "the heterodoxy of Milton's personal views" during the period when the poem was written.[10] It is true that the contrast between time schemes is "entirely traditional," but Milton's association of *kairos* with a hero whose activities consist of debate, silent waiting, and free choice based on Scripture suggests a view of worship that is anything but traditional.

Throughout the poem, Jesus models true worship, the universal form of which is good works, those actions performed "when the Spirit of God works within us through true faith, to God's glory, the certain hope of our salvation, and the instruction of our neighbor" (*Christian Doctrine, CPW* 6:638). Absent, of course, is the church and set forms of prayer, but this does not mean that Milton ignores ritual in *Paradise Regained;* rather, throughout the poem authentic worship is grounded in the ritual of presence associated with the encounter with Scripture and acts of "substantial liberty" consecrated to God. Prayer, like inspired writing, has its origin in the Holy Spirit and, therefore, should not be forced into predetermined forms. This does not mean that forms of prayer should be abandoned, any more than literary genres or meters should be; rather, the forms are given in Scripture to be freely modified according to the will of the worshipper under the guidance of the Holy Spirit. In *Paradise Regained* Milton models a "spontaneous liturgy" of the kind P. G. Stanwood finds in the hymns of *Paradise Lost,* in which "the poet does not deliberately set out to write in a liturgical environment or in obedience to any liturgical form, yet in avoiding the form comes inevitably to have it."[11] I would only add that Milton sets out to foreground worship in *Paradise Regained,* and in the process of demonstrating true worship without liturgy offers an act of worship to his God that also alludes to and transforms various rituals in his Restoration context.

Milton's *Paradise Regained* illustrates a creative response
to the revolution in ritual theory and the semiotic crisis that
underlies many ritual experiments in the seventeenth century.
Milton's is a rigorously plain, restrained form of worship, the
result of a thorough critique of the sacramental signs and rituals that bound both "popular" and "official" religion before
the Reformation. In the process of showing what is essential
for worship, however, Milton goes where no clergyman would
follow, even while he alludes to traditional ceremonies; for him,
true worship does not depend on a visible church in the conventional sense, but on reading and writing with the Holy Spirit.
Thus, allusions to sacraments, liturgical forms, and frames of
time engaged in worship do not legitimize a specific church;
instead, by appropriating them, Milton demonstrates how
forms of true worship can be enacted and defended during the
Restoration, including his own "minimal mysticism."[12] Milton
attempts to unify readers in a ritual of presence through his
recreation of ritual time. The spatial order of the particular,
visible church is replaced by the verbal space of discourse, in
which inspired Christian authors perform the liturgy of the
Word, uniting readers in an imaginative order of time characterized by the creative repetition of scriptural events. Ritual
time, according to Mircea Eliade, exists when chronological
time is redeemed by the repetition of singular events in a god's
life, uniting participants in the god's presence.[13] Although a real
presence is impossible for Milton, the imaginative and visionary apprehension in literature of divine presence in a frame of
time beyond the chronological is the next best thing.

I

Called by Parliament to reform the doctrine and discipline
of the Church of England, the Westminster Assembly first
met in July 1643. By October, Parliament had passed an ordinance giving the Assembly the authority to create a liturgy to

replace the *Book of Common Prayer*. The Assembly failed to produce a liturgy of set forms, however, because two Independent members on the subcommittee empowered to produce the liturgy — Thomas Goodwin and Philip Nye — refused to impose a form of prayer on the ministry. As the "dissenting Brethren" explained in their *Apologetical Narration,* "public Prayers in our Assemblies should be Framed by the meditation and study of our own Ministers, out of their own gifts, (the fruits of Christ's Ascension) as well as their Sermons use to be."[14] In the Independent church, according to John Cotton, prayers were offered to God "not in any prescribed forme of prayer, or *Studied Liturgie,* but in such a manner, as the Spirit of grace and prayer (who teacheth all the people of God, what and how to pray, Rom. viii, 26, 27) helpeth our infirmities."[15] As Cotton's order of service for the Boston church and Goodwin's support of Baxter's "Savoy Liturgy" indicate, although Independents were against prescribed prayers they were not against an ordered service in the church. Paradoxically, however, Cotton's suggestion that the Spirit teaches all people how to pray contains the beginning of the ministry's end since the authority of the Spirit could supplant the authority of a human ministry. The logical outcome of the Independent emphasis on the Spirit in prayer is a ministry of believers; any believer with the gifts of the Spirit, whether he or she has been ordained, can pray and preach in public. This is exactly what many Quakers and Ranters did in the 1650s. William Erbery, just to take one example, claimed that "if the Saints could stay a while, and wait for the Spirit . . . if men could be content with God alone, live in God onely, behold God dwelling in them and they in God: [then] they had not run so fast into the *Church* nor the *Churches* hastened to send forth their Ministers to baptize: these being not Gospel Order, nor Ordinance among them."[16] Initially sympathetic with the Independents but eventually alienated by the intolerance of their "hireling clergy," Milton became an independent Independent in his liturgical views. In the years leading up to the Restoration, he emphasized, like Erbery, the importance of the Spirit in worship, but avoided the irrationality that often characterized the English radical Reformation in the 1650s. The seeds of Milton's radical position on liturgy and prayer, however, had been planted earlier in the antiepiscopal tracts and in *Eikonoklastes*.

The preeminence of the Holy Spirit in prayer is especially evident when Milton attacks the liturgy of the Church of England in *Animadversions* (*CPW* 1:677–92), *An Apology against a Pamphlet* (*CPW* 1:935–43), and *Eikonoklastes* (*CPW* 3:503–08). The liturgy is idolatrous, since believers are forced to say words that have no relationship to their inward convictions or to God's stated will, and to impose the liturgy "is a supercilious tyranny impropriating the Spirit of God" to the fallen nature of human understanding (*Animadversions*, *CPW* 1:682). Moreover, in *An Apology against a Pamphlet*, Milton clearly links the ministry and liturgy of the Word: "they whom God hath set apart to his ministery, are by him endu'd with an ability of prayer. . . . And if prayer be the guift of the Spirit, why do they admit those to the Ministery, who want a main guift of their function, and prescribe guifted men to use that which is the remedy of another mans want; setting them their tasks to read, whom the Spirit of God stands ready to assist in his ordinance with the guift of free conceptions" (*CPW* 1:936). If the purpose of the ministry is to declare the Word in prayer, this purpose cannot be achieved if the source of prayer — the Holy Spirit — is denied in favour of prescribed forms.

The author of *Eikon Basilike*, the "icon" that Milton hoped to shatter in *Eikonoklastes*, is a particular example of one who prays without the Holy Spirit and exemplifies the idolatry encouraged by the liturgy.[17] Lacking "true righteousness in the person," the writer's petitions are "clapt together," the "lip-work of every Prelatical Liturgist" (*CPW* 3:360). He mindlessly repeats the words of others so often that "imitation seem'd to vie with the Original" (*CPW* 3:361). The most blatant form of false prayer, however, is plagiarism, the clearest example of which occurs when the author uses Pamela's prayer from *Arcadia* without acknowledging Sidney's authorship (*CPW* 3:362). Such rote repetition is to be expected from one who is devoted to the liturgy, for the liturgy forces ministers "to seek affections fit and proportionable to a certain doss of prepar'd words" rather than to gather "words from thir affections"; it "imprison[s] and confine[s] by force, into a Pinfold of sett words, those two most unimprisonable things, our Prayers <and> that Divine Spirit of utterance that moves them . . ." (*CPW* 3:505). Thus, Milton's conception of his prophetic ministry inspired by God also shapes his liturgy of the Word. The Spirit inspires the minister and provides the gifts that ensure that prayers are not simply imitations of others but original creations arising from the Spirit's own activity in the minister's process of composition.

The literary nature of the liturgy of the Word is emphasized because both poetry and prose have the Holy Spirit as their author. Whereas in *extempore* prayer and in inspired composition of any kind, "wholesom words will follow of themselves" from "good desires rightly conceav'd in the heart," in the prayers of *Eikon Basilike*, the writer "had it not in him to make a prayer of his own" (*CPW* 3:504, 367). Without the Holy Spirit, the true source of the minister's authority and literary gifts, ministers are reduced to puppets who blithely repeat other people's words rather than create their own compositions in response to the Holy Spirit. Following Renaissance rhetorical theory, Milton distinguishes between mindless repetition and creative repetition — the essence of both inspired composition and prayer. "It is not hard for any man, who hath a Bible in his hands," explains Milton, "to borrow good words and holy sayings in abundance; but to make them his own, is a work of grace onely from above" (*CPW* 3:553).[18] Rather than simply repeat the classical or biblical models of the past, the minister, like the poet, must alter them to suit the conditions of the present if the prayer or the poem is going to have any hope of moving listeners to greater love of God. The work of application and creative repetition, of making the words of the past "one's own," is the work of the Holy Spirit.

As a result of the minister's dependence on the inspiration of the Holy Spirit for composing prayers, Milton's critique of the liturgy, and of those who defended it, is often literary in nature. Resulting not from his distrust of images or of his distrust of his audience, the plain style of *Eikonoklastes* is deliberately constructed to oppose the "smooth style, and pathetical composure" of the King's Book.[19] The former style is the medium of true prayer while the latter is representative of the false prayer of the Church of England. Moreover, he frequently refers to the author's vain repetitions, which convey no spiritual teaching (*CPW* 3:551, 507, 505, 432), a form of prayer he later condemns in *De Doctrina Christiana*.

In *An Apology against a Pamphlet,* Milton associates poor style with the absence of the Spirit in the prayers of the established church. He mocks the "coy flirting style" of *A Modest Confutation of a Slanderous and Scurrilous Libell, Entitled, Animadversions Upon the Remonstrants Defense Against Smectymnuus* (1642), a tract written by "one who makes sentences by the Statute" (*CPW* 1:873). Poor style reveals not only the bad taste of the writer, but also his alienation from the only source of true prayer and composition — the inspiration of the Holy Spirit. In *Eikonoklastes* Milton derides the style of *Eikon Basilike,* its "curtal Aphorisms" hiding the desperate emptiness of an author who relies on imitation and tradition rather than the zeal of the creative spirit and the "solid proofs of Scripture" in prayer (*CPW* 3:496). The author's "petty glosses and conceits" are "weake and shallowe, and so like the quibbl's of a Court Sermon" that they were likely "fetcht" from the "Cymbal Doctors" of the Church of England (*CPW* 3:430). His prayers consist of "empty sentences, that have the sound of gravity, but the significance of nothing pertinent" (*CPW*

3:431). The words of liturgical prayer are "stale and empty" because they have no relationship to the spiritual state of the minister uttering them.

In contrast, just as God "left our affections to be guided by his sanctifying spirit, so did he likewise our words to be put into us without our premeditation; not only those cautious words to be us'd before Gentiles and Tyrants, but much more those filial words, of which we have so frequent use in our access with freedom of speech to the Throne of Grace" (*CPW* 3:506). These are "filial words" because every human being has the potential of becoming a son or daughter of God by virtue of Christ's sacrifice and the presence of the Holy Spirit, the new covenant written on the heart and the basis of Christian liberty. The possibility of receiving words sanctified and inspired by God is part of a Christian writer's inheritance. True prayer and liturgy, composed of "filial words," arise from the regenerate heart moved by the Spirit not from "outward dictates of men" which stifle God's "gift, who is the Spirit." Set forms of prayer ensure that God's messengers will not "procreate a number of faithfull men, making a kind of creation like to Gods, by infusing his spirit and likenesse into them," but will set up, in the pulpit or in books, empty idols in the form of words dislodged from active faith and true creation (*Animadversions, CPW* 1:721). Without truth, or a portion of it, a minister cannot hope to have the appropriate style necessary to move the audience; this style is accessible only to those who allow the Spirit to operate freely to offer words to God's glory.

Milton's defence of his own style in *Animadversions* and *An Apology against a Pamphlet* anticipates his theology of prayer in *De Doctrina Christiana* and *Eikonoklastes*. In *De Doctrina Christiana*, Milton cites zeal in the sanctification of God's name as an admirable feature of prayer while in *Animadversions* he refers to Solomon, "Christ and all his followers in all Ages" as authorities for his harsh invective. All of them "have wrought up their zealous souls into such vehe-mencies, as nothing could be more killingly spoken" (*CPW* 1:663). More importantly, Jesus not only authorizes the use of "tart rhetorick in the Churches cause" (*Apology, CPW* 1:901), but contains within himself the styles of classical rhetoric nec-essary for eloquence on any given occasion. The Word, in fact, *is* eloquence:

> Our Saviour who had all gifts in him was Lord to expresse his indoctrinating power in what sort him best seem'd; sometimes by a milde and familiar converse, sometimes with plaine and impartiall home-speaking regardlesse of those whom the audi-tors might think he should have had in more respect; otherwhiles with bitter and irefull rebukes if not teaching yet leaving excuse-lesse those his wilfull impugners. What was all in him, was divided among many other[s] . . . teachers of his Church. (*CPW* 1:899–900)

After the ascension of the Word, eloquence is divided, like truth in *Areopagitica,* among the teachers of the church, only to be reunited when he comes again.

Milton links his denunciations of the prelates with the prophets as well. There is not a "more proper object of indig-nation and scorne together than a false Prophet" such as his opponent, Joseph Hall, bishop of Exeter and author of *A Defence of the Humble Remonstrance* (1641) (*Animadversions, CPW* 1:664). When Hall mocks Milton's "canting" language and his "holy fire of zeal," Milton again defends his combative stance by citing Scripture and the freedom of the prophet to denounce God's enemies: "thus did the true Prophets of old combat with the false; thus Christ himselfe the fountaine of meeknesse found acrimony anough to be still galling and vexing the Prelaticall Pharisees" (*Apology, CPW* 1.700–01).[20] The prophets themselves with their "sanctifi'd bitternesse against the enemies of truth" (*CPW* 1:901) are models for the prayers and curses of the antiepiscopal tracts. For Milton, ministers of the Word are called upon to curse God's enemies in public; his harsh denunciations reveal his conviction that in writing against the prelates he is performing a sacred, prophetic office.

Milton's liturgy of the Word, then, is linked to literary activity by the common operation of the Spirit in both activities. The literary style of the liturgy and of the defenders of the *Book of Common Prayer* is evidence of the absence of the Spirit and is based on a false view of literary invention as a mere repetition of human tradition. The zealous style of *extempore* prayer and its defenders, such as Milton, reveals the presence of the Spirit and a view of composition as a gift of God's grace. In this tradition of prayer, repetition is a creative process of appropriation, of making the past "one's own" in the present, a process guided by the Holy Spirit in prayer and reading. The Spirit inspires words and brings them forward, offering them on the altar of the writer's heart to God's glory.

In addition to the emphasis on the Spirit in prayer and on zeal in the defense of the true church, many other characteristics of public prayer mentioned in *De Doctrina Christiana* appear in Milton's prose long before he turns to *Paradise Regained*. Milton prepared metrical psalms prior to the Restoration, probably for a new psalter to replace the old version attached to the *Book of Common Prayer*, and also referred to both *Paradise Lost* and *Paradise Regained* as songs, suggesting that the poems themselves can be seen as liturgical performances. Throughout his prose works, he emphasizes that his offerings are derived from the Word alone, either the Word of Scripture or the Word written on the heart, the inner scripture of the Spirit. In *Of Reformation*, he petitions God to save England from "the Sorceries of the *great Whore*," promises to thank God in the form of a poem which will celebrate his deliverance of England, and curses God's enemies with vehemence and indignation (*CPW* 1:613–16). In the prayer of *Animadversions* (*CPW* 1:703–07), he begins by cursing those who hinder reformation, cites England's past as evidence of God's favor, petitions God to come again to complete reformation, and promises to sing "an elaborate Song" of praise before once again petitioning Christ to return. Curses and petitions are both genres of prayer identified by Milton in *De Doctrina Christiana*.[21]

In both prayers Milton uses repetition, but it is repetitiveness arising from "vehement disturbance of the mind" (*Christian Doctrine, CPW* 6:673) rather than prescribed forms: "Come therefore O thou that hast the seven starres in thy right hand, appoint thy chosen *Priests* according to their Orders, and courses of old, to minister before thee, and duely to dresse and poure out the consecrated oyle into thy holy and ever-burning lamps; thou hast sent out the spirit of prayer upon thy servants over all the Land to this effect, and stirred up their vowes as the sound of many waters about thy Throne" (*Animadversions, CPW* 1:706). This particular prayer is remarkable because it echoes the *Veni Creator Spiritus* and the *Veni Sancte Spiritus* used in the Anglican rite of ordination, but what follows this prayer is a vow to write a "Song to Generations" in praise of God, a vow he repeats when he "covnant[s] with any knowing reader" in *The Reason of Church Government* to make payment "for what he is now indebted" (*CPW* 1:820). Although he is indebted to God for not using his talents for poetry, he will pay the debt by writing the poem in the future with the help of "prayer to that eternall Spirit who can enrich with all utterance and knowledge" (*CPW* 1:821). Vows, of course, are also cited in *De Doctrina Christiana* as forms of prayer authorized by Scripture. Finally, Milton's oath in *The Second Defence of the English People* indicates the extent to which all of his literary activity is consecrated to God's glory: he invokes God to witness that his doctrine is derived from Scripture alone, not ambition, party politics, or the works of others (*CPW* 4:1.586–87). Convinced by the Spirit that he is revealing God's truth, not his own prejudices, Milton offers his

prose as "a plain ungarnish'd present" and "thank-offering" for
the purpose of glorifying God. By offering prayers of praise and
thanksgiving, which are truly God's to begin with, Milton
performs the liturgy of the Word, not because he uses set
forms of prayer in his offerings, but because offering words to
God is the highest form of sacramental action in Milton's
church.

Milton's view of worship as it is expressed in *De Doctrina
Christiana* and later woven into the narrative of *Paradise
Regained* is best described as "liturgical congregationalism"
in the free church tradition. Written liturgies were not used
in free churches because "if God's word is clear to everyone
who reads, each community can discern what is God's will by
itself and must be free to act accordingly." This did not result
in "liturgical chaos; indeed, the degree of predictability is usu-
ally almost as high as in other traditions of worship."[22] Instead,
the free churches became preoccupied with the origins of true
expression in the Spirit and the Word of Scripture, and with
the church as a voluntary gathering of individuals united by
the Spirit and Word rather than by unscriptural traditions or
prescribed prayers in which "imitation seem'd to vie with the
Original" (*Eikonoklastes, CPW* 6:361). Repetition and ritual
did exist in this tradition, but only in a ritual of presence and
a repetition of the original Spirit in the words, prayers, songs
and gestures of worship. Milton's vivid, sometimes brutal
attack on "the repetition of that which is prescribed" (*Reason
of Church Government, CPW* 1:752) in the Anglican liturgy
is well known and does not need to be reiterated though its
theological basis deserves mention.[23] The liturgy, whether
Anglican, Presbyterian, or Independent stifles the gifts of the
Spirit in prayer and makes idolatrous additions to the supreme
liturgical handbook: the Word of God. Although Milton may
have worshipped only with his family during the Restoration,
he was not a "church of one" in worship or ecclesiology. His
reliance on the Word and Spirit and the ritual of presence in
reading and prayer clearly place him in a varied and innovative

free church tradition whether he would have acknowledged it or not.

The suggestion that Milton has anything to do with the church or with ritual, even of the reduced kind that was typical in the free church tradition, is bound to be met with skepticism by Milton critics. The failure to acknowledge the imperative of worship in Milton's writing emerges most clearly in Samuel Johnson's claim that Milton "grew old without any visible worship . . . [and] omitting public prayers, he omitted all."[24] As with most of Johnson's Milton criticism, there is some truth in this, but not enough. Writing over 100 years after the poet's death, Johnson could have been repeating a commonplace created by John Toland who, in 1698, attached his biography to the first collected edition of Milton's prose. According to Toland, "in the latter part of his Life, he [Milton] was not a profest Member of any particular Sect among Christians, he frequented none of their Assemblies, nor made use of their Rites in his Family."[25] Toland offers these speculations in spite of the importance of the church in Milton's youth, his passionate commitment to church reform up to and including 1659, and evidence that not only his third wife, Elizabeth Minshul, but also his daughters attended church. Toland does not comment on why Milton failed to worship in a particular, visible church, and also fails to explain what the church means to Milton. These omissions cast doubt on his account, for if he knew what he claimed to know about Milton's devotional life, he likely would have had an explanation for Milton's avoidance of public worship. In addition, despite following the previous four biographies of Milton closely in most other respects, Toland clearly adds this detail on his own. Neither the anonymous biographer nor Edward Phillips, the poet's nephew, in their independent biographies mention anything about patterns of worship, a curious omission if there were anything irregular or unusual about Milton's worship, or lack of it. More than likely, Toland found in Milton a kindred spirit and amplified into fact what was at best unverifiable, for

Toland's portrait of Milton is more like Toland than Milton. The deist author of *Christianity not Mysterious* illustrates his own thesis that a disinterested and rational Christianity is possible without the church by carefully selecting and embroidering details from Milton's life, but especially by emphasizing his disinterested search for Truth and his avoidance of all sects and parties. Thus, although we cannot conclude from the evidence of the early biographies that Milton worshipped in a particular church or followed a particular rite, neither can we conclude that Milton "grew old without any visible worship."

More serious evidence of Milton's rejection of visible church worship comes from his own works, but this testimony must also be treated carefully. In *De Doctrina Christiana* he claims to "follow no . . . heresy or sect," but this refers to his reliance on Scripture alone rather than his abandonment of the visible church (*CPW* 6:123). Milton also argues that people who cannot join a properly constituted church "conveniently, or with good conscience" are not destitute of the blessings bestowed upon the churches (*CPW* 6:568), but this is a common argument advanced by orthodox theologians such as William Ames, who also admits that silent prayer is sufficient for God and that it is a sin to participate in worship against one's conscience.[26] God does command believers to abstain from idolatrous worship, and although there are precedents for attending idol worship under the auspices of a civil duty, Milton advises that it is safer to avoid these duties altogether, but these situations likely reflect Milton's relationship with the Anglican church rather than all churches (*CPW* 6:694). Finally, Milton's belief that the church exists wherever there is charity and that inward worship is sufficient for God (*CPW* 6:565, 668) has led some critics to conclude that, for Milton, all earthly churches pervert the true church of the Spirit.[27] Even in book 12 of *Paradise Lost*, however, where Milton describes the progressive degeneration of the church, he also celebrates the eventual triumph of those who persevere in the worship "Of Spirit and Truth" (12.532–33), which is consistent with the free church tradition. In his "religion of the Spirit," then, Milton does not exclude public worship or the church, but neither does he adopt traditional forms of worship or ecclesiology without adapting them to suit what he finds in Scripture. Although Milton likely did not worship in a particular church in the conventional sense after the Restoration, this does not mean that he rejected public worship altogether or that forms of worship did not influence his poetry. Solitary, family, and Nonconformist worship of various kinds were viable alternatives to the Presbyterian, Independent, or Anglican worship that might have offended his conscience.

Despite the importance of reading and writing, listening and speaking, praying and singing according to the Word and Spirit, true worship consists of good works, and good works "are those which we do when the Spirit of God works within us" (*CPW* 6:638). Milton's whole discussion of worship in *De Doctrina Christiana* hinges on this notion that the origin of true worship, and the universal form of good action, is the Holy Spirit, "the secret agent" of *Paradise Regained*, according to Georgia Christopher.[28] Virtues or "good habits" are the immediate causes of good works, and the special virtues related to God are internal and external worship, which "are never separated except by the viciousness of sinners" (*CPW* 6:666). Internal worship consists of several virtues, including love, humility, patience, obedience, and confidence in God, a virtue that is contrasted with distrust, presumption, "trust in the flesh" and idolatry (*CPW* 6:658). All of these virtues lead to good works, and all are prompted by the Holy Spirit. Ethics and right action, then, are forms of ritual and worship, for believers glorify and praise God when they act to obey the divine will, returning again and again to Scripture and waiting patiently to discern what the Spirit illuminates there.

Even though internal worship is sufficient for God, external worship is not; it must be accompanied by true sincerity and faith. In keeping with his emphasis on the Word and Spirit, Milton divests the ordained clergy of all authority in interpretation, prophecy, and administration. Any man — women seem to be excluded from Milton's account — who has the gift of the Spirit may lead the community in prayer, preaching, and prophecy, or teaching; in addition, he can also administer the sacraments since they are only signs of the grace promised in Scripture. Milton's hermeneutic approach to the sacraments is seen in his discussion of baptism. Because external signs, like baptism in a moving stream, refer to biblical precedents, recipients of baptism must be adults, for "how can infants, who do not understand a word be purified by the word?" (*CPW* 6:544–45). He also makes a clear distinction between "the symbol and the thing symbolized," eliminating any potential confusion between the symbols of the bread and wine and the real presence of Christ's body and blood (*CPW* 6:555).

The time, place, and posture of worship are also dependent upon the Spirit since the Spirit acts in a voluntary manner, not only on Sundays in the church. In fact, to worship God "only one day in seven, is to disparage the Christian religion"; any time is appropriate for prayer, but "morning, midday, and evening are particularly suitable," presumably so that prayer can bring worshippers closer to God by being part of the natural cycle God created (*CPW* 6:714, 704, 674). Prayer can be solitary or collective, silent or audible, and can be offered on behalf of those praying or for others. It can be delivered kneeling or standing in any chosen space not only because these practices are found in Scripture, but also because the internal disposition of the believer guided by the Holy Spirit determines where the church is, not the quasi-sacramental nature of the church building itself. For the same reason, "tautological repetitiveness" such as occurs in litanies should be avoided, although repetitiveness arising from holy zeal and a "vehement disturbance of the mind is not to be counted in vain" (*CPW* 6:673).

There are two kinds of prayer prescribed in Scripture — invocations and the sanctification of God's name — and four kinds of invocations: petitions, thanksgivings, oaths, and casting lots. Because prayer occurs by "the instigation of the Holy Spirit" and by "divine helpers, not human" ones, there is "no need of a liturgy"; even the Lord's Prayer is a model "rather than a formula to be repeated" (*CPW* 6:670). Petitions take two forms — the petition for good and the petition to take away evil — while prayers of thanksgiving in which we give "thanks with a joyful heart for divine benefits" often take the form of songs and hymns (*CPW* 6:683). Making vows, taking oaths, cursing God's enemies, and fasting also have scriptural warrant and, therefore, can be used when circumstances demand them.

The sanctification of God's name is the second genre of prayer discussed by Milton and is often associated with zeal in defending and promoting God and professing the faith, even in the face of death. God's name should be sanctified by deeds as well as words "in every circumstance of our life" and in "consecrating anything we use to his glory" (*CPW* 6:700). This form of worship takes us back to good works as the essential form of worship since both occur throughout life rather than within a specific sacred space. A life in which the image and Spirit of God are manifested in freely choosing to obey God's ways revealed in Scripture by the Spirit is the best way to sanctify objects and to worship God.

Milton's engagement in the revolution in ritual throughout the early modern period is consistent and thorough. Like Zwingli he empties the sacraments of real presence by revealing the flawed sign theory on which they are based and by appealing to the hermeneutic basis of God's communication with believers — the Word of God. This reduces worship to writing, speaking, reading, and hearing the Word, receiving baptism and the Lord's Supper as scriptural seals, and praying and singing in biblical forms. Unlike Zwingli, however, Milton recognizes the authority of the Holy Spirit as the possession of each individual. As a result, prescribed liturgies, ordained ministers, and sacred times and places of worship are unnecessary. Instead, a believer enacts the ritual of the Holy Spirit's presence in good works generally, but especially in encounters with the Word, including religious poetry. This encounter is paradigmatic of "a whole new kind of anti-liturgical ritual that emphasized the spiritual significance of mundane materiality within a religious worldview that had supposedly disenchanted material objects."[29] Milton's theology of worship in *Paradise Regained* is embodied in Jesus, where the ritual of presence is manifested in patience, obedience, restraint, and, above all, in searching the Scriptures and acting by the Spirit. As Georgia Christopher points out, "in this tradition the word becomes the sacramental reality when and only when the Holy Spirit moves the mind to understand and embrace the scriptural word."[30] Milton's opening prayer to the Holy Spirit indicates that the rituals of presence are enacted as well as represented in *Paradise Regained*, the prophetic poet recreating a sense of ritual time for the reader through the narrative repetition of events in his hero's life.

II

The importance of worship and ritual in *Paradise Regained* is evident in both the details and structure of the opening sequence depicting Jesus' baptism. The Holy Spirit, the source of good works and true worship, is especially prominent: the Spirit is called upon by the poet in the opening invocation, the Spirit is received in fullness by Jesus at his baptism, the Spirit is unacknowledged by Satan who sees only a dove, "whate'er it meant," and the Spirit leads Jesus into the wilderness to begin "his great warfare." Jesus refers to "my Spirit" in his recollection of his youthful preparations, but the Spirit conferred now is much different. Whereas Jesus' youthful Spirit is admirable but limited by his political conception of his destiny, the Spirit conferred at his baptism is complete, for the baptism "conferred the gifts of the Spirit straight away" (*Christian Doctrine, CPW* 6:551). As the narrator suggests, it is the Spirit, silent and present, who "brought'st him Hence/By proof th'undoubted Son of God" (*PR* 1.10–11) not his own will. Underlying the ritual of reading in the poem, then, is Jesus' guidance by the Spirit.[31]

The poem as a whole depicts a rite of passage of the kind described by Victor Turner, but what is most noteworthy is how carefully Milton has appropriated the structure of the rite into his narrative, shaping the biblical materials to emphasize Christ's trial.[32] Jesus is briefly called and separated from the world, crosses a threshold into an extended liminal stage where everyday standards are suspended in spiritual combat, and then is briefly incorporated into the community again, renewed and strengthened in his identity at the end of the poem. That Milton should use this structure in his poem is no surprise since baptism itself is a specifically Christian rite of passage. As a naming ceremony it confirms the participant's identity and symbolically enacts a process of regeneration and rebirth through the Spirit, a passage from death to life. It also announces the inclusion of the believer into the church and reenacts the death and Resurrection of Christ. In the baptismal rite described by Milton in *De Doctrina Christiana*, the believer is called out of the world and takes a vow or pledge of faith before being immersed in a flowing stream and welcomed into the church. In the poem, a similar structure is apparent, but Milton, following Scripture, alters the order of events to highlight Jesus' "hermeneutic combat" with Satan, to suggest that the temptation narrative is typologically equivalent to Christ's Crucifixion and Resurrection, and to emphasize Jesus' identity. Jesus, like all others who have come to the Jordan, is fully immersed in the flowing or "laving" stream; only *then* is he separated from the world through his naming by the Father, his reception of the Holy Spirit, and his journey to the wilderness. Milton thus implies that the ritual trial by temptation is Jesus' initiation into his incarnate identity before he emerges fully prepared to enter and transform the human community when he leaves the wilderness. The falling and rising movement of baptism and Crucifixion/Resurrection is also replicated in the way Jesus moves downward and inward before he moves upward to the spire of the temple and outward to his Galilean ministry. He communes with "deep thoughts" (*PR* 1.190) and "descends" into himself (2.111), suggesting that this is a spiritual, visionary trial, but also that he has been purified by plunging into himself.

Milton's critique of sacramental efficacy in *De Doctrina Christiana* is also explored in the contrast between how Jesus and Satan interpret the baptism. Satan claims sarcastically that the "Consecrated stream" (*PR* 1.72–73) washes away sin simply in the action of baptism, but this is precisely the confusion of the symbol with the thing symbolized that Milton identifies with Roman Catholic doctrines of efficacy. Nor has the consecration of the water any scriptural basis. Jesus, on the other hand, recalls the Spirit, and especially the Father's voice, before immediately jumping into action, interpreting the signs as pledges of the Father's word rather than as signs conveying purity in and of themselves. For Satan, the dove is literal and, lacking the Spirit, he is unable to understand its real meaning; for Jesus, the literal is the spiritual, for the Spirit descended "like a Dove" not in it. Jesus' response to and fulfillment of the Father's word through reflection on Scripture, personal recollection, and silent meditation are typical of how Jesus worships the Father through his acts throughout the poem.

Milton extends the semiological critique of sacramental efficacy to his representations of the Lord's Supper in *Paradise Regained* as well. As I have discussed, in the free church tradition the central role of the sacraments in the liturgy was taken over by the Word itself; not only was the ante-communion service, or liturgy of the Word more prevalent, but the Word revealed Christ's presence more directly than the "visible words" of the sacraments, turning the Bible and the sermon into the spiritual food that sustains the church until Christ comes again in the flesh.[33] In *Paradise Regained*, Satan attempts to undermine the Son's prophetic office as the Word in the first temptation, where he is urged to abandon "each Word/ Proceeding from the mouth of God" (1.349–50) for bread. The food/Word imagery continues throughout *Paradise Regained*, showing that Christ not only *is* the Word but *speaks* the Word in human terms, providing the means for his celebration.[34] Satan, on the other hand, is associated with the *ex opere operato* theory of sacramental grace, in which the sacrament is efficacious regardless of the priest's spiritual state. God lets impure ministers handle "holy things"; therefore, Satan argues, God should allow him access to the Son (1.486–90).

The culmination of sacramental imagery, however, occurs in the banquet scenes. The first is a demonic feast served on a table "richly spread, in regal mode" (2.340) like the communion tables of the Church of England. The second is a celestial banquet, "A table of Celestial Food, Divine" (4.588), which prefigures the communion of saints after the Apocalypse (Rev. 19:7–9; Mat. 8:11, 22:1–10, 26:29). This is particularly important because in the liturgies of the free church tradition, the memory of Christ's death and resurrection and the hope of future union with Christ signified in the banquet are often emphasized rather than his real presence.[35] Between these two banquets and implied throughout the poem, however, is the figure of Christ, the word of God, the spiritual food of the church.

Forms of worship figure in *Paradise Regained* in structural features that the poem shares with other Nonconformist liturgies and in the poem's evocation of ritual time. For example, the overall structure of the ante-communion service is analogous to some features in *Paradise Regained*. As the liturgies of Zwingli, Calvin, Bucer, Knox, the Middleburg Puritans, the Westminster Assembly, and Baxter show, the liturgy of the Word in the Puritan tradition consists of four parts in the following order: the confession, the *extempore* prayer for illumination, the sermon, and the blessing before dismissal, in addition to readings and psalms that are sung at intervals throughout.[36]

There are, of course, variations in form and content in each service, but this general structure is observable in each of the liturgies. There is no analogue of the confession at the beginning of *Paradise Regained*, an omission that might indicate that Milton did not share the penitential tone of orthodox Puritan devotion, but the opening invocation of *Paradise Regained* does parallel the *extempore* prayer for the illumination of the Holy Spirit which precedes the sermon in Puritan and Reformed liturgies. Milton asks for the inspiration of the Holy Spirit just as Calvin does, despite the contrast in genre and purpose: "let us beseech Him, in whom is all fullness of wisdom and light to vouchsafe to guide us by His Holy Spirit into the true understanding of His holy doctrine."[37]

Moreover, just as the sermon based on a scriptural text follows the prayer for illumination, so the narrator's exposition of the temptations follows his prayer. His exposition, however, takes the form of a poetic "harmony of the gospels" rather than a word by word exegesis or a sermon following the doctrine, reason, use pattern.[38] Like the "friends of Truth" in *Areopagitica*, the narrator laboriously gathers, at the beginning of book 2 (2.5–7, 18–24, 30–57), scriptural texts that do not appear in Matthew or Luke's accounts of the temptations. References to the incarnate Word, the disciples, and John's baptismal ministry from the Gospel of John (1:14, 35–40, 3:23) and details from Acts (1:6) and Mark (16:11–14) evoking the disciples' post-Crucifixion anxiety and doubt, are woven together with invented material and classical motifs into a unified dramatic structure. The narrator thereby demonstrates how to read by the Spirit, moving his audience and drawing them closer to the same Spirit that inspires authentic interpretation.

The songs that occur at significant intervals in the worship service, such as before the prayer for illumination, after the sermon, and before the final blessing, also occur in *Paradise Regained* as the angels break into "Hymns" following the Father's decree and "Heavenly Anthems" after Jesus' victory over Satan. We should include, too, the morning songs of the birds, which refresh the Son after troubled nights of dreams, remembering that Milton approved of songs in worship and felt that even though no time is prescribed for prayer, morning, noon and evening were most suitable (*PR* 2.279–81, 290; 4.432–38). Once again, however, it is not the content of the liturgy that is used by Milton but its structure and feeling, as an event is solemnized by ritual song and poetry. Finally, the tone and structure of the blessing and dismissal are also incorporated by Milton into *Paradise Regained*. The closing angelic hymn, the return of Jesus to where he began in "his Mother's house private" (*PR* 4.639), and the final four lines of the poem, written in perfectly melodic iambic pentameter, capture the peace and serenity offered by the closing prayer of the liturgy of the Word. Thus, although Milton condemned formal ritual and its rote repetition, he nevertheless adopted enough of its structures and strategies to enable "prompt eloquence" to emerge within a recognizable and repeated form.

Milton also uses repetition at the textual and narrative levels to create an imaginative ritual through which the reader participates in ritual time, an order of time in which chronological time is suspended in the imaginative re-living and re-membering of Christ's life. This is not a detached perspective in which "we watch, as we always watch in ritual acts, with God" as Jackson Cope suggests because Jesus' temptations are Milton's readers' temptations too; as a result, readers participate in the rhythm of repetition and return throughout the poem.[39] Ashraf Rushdy, developing the insights of Mircea Eliade, captures the richness of Milton's treatment of time. Sacred time, inhabited by Jesus and inaccessible to Satan, is the "primordial mythical time made present." As Rushdy suggests, "in Milton's poem that moment is part of the strategy of representing the renovation . . . of a culture."[40] Sacred time is present in Christian ritual, where the original moment of salvation is recreated. By creating this unique temporal perspective for his readers, Milton recreates the temporal conditions of ritual and allows readers to participate in an imaginative ritual in the fullest sense.

The formal characteristics of Christian ritual have been described most concisely by Mircea Eliade. Eliade sees underlying most rites a desire for union with divine presence through the creation of a sacred order of time symbolized by the cyclical, yearly, and daily repetition of events in the life of a god. From the Christian point of view, this redemption of time occurs in the repetition of the Christian calendar throughout the sacred year and in the repetition of the eucharistic rite, not a temporal occasion at all, but an eternal present in which Christ's sacrifice not only makes chronological time meaningful, but suspends time by making Jesus present and incorporating the believer into God's body.[41] Eliade highlights the difference between sacred and profane time by adopting Nietzsche's phrase "the eternal return" to characterize the relationship between the redemptive repetition of the Eucharist, which incarnates Christ's body and blood, and the compulsive repetitions of modernity, desperately hoping to reclaim lost moments through fruitless repetitive acts.

Milton, of course, rejected any sense of real presence just as he rejected liturgical repetition when it was associated with the mindless reiteration of ritual acts that have no connection with commitment and faith. The Word, however, and to a lesser extent, texts written in response to it, is a kind of sacrament, especially when the hermeneutical view of ritual shared by Milton and many reformers is considered. Like the Eucharist, the Word with the help of the Holy Spirit, is a vehicle of grace and unites believers in a ritual of presence by returning readers to Christ in imagination. Above chronological time but below the real presence of sacred time, the ritual time of literature promises metaphors of presence.

The repetition of the Word as part of a ritual of presence can be seen in some of the smallest details of *Paradise Regained*.

The identification of Jesus as the Son of God by both John the Baptist and the Father is turned into a ritual of naming when Milton has Jesus use schemes of repetition to describe the baptism. The anaphoric repetition of "Mee him" in lines 276–77 of book 1 and the epizeuxis in lines 284–85, where "me his" is repeated without intervening words, both transform the event into verbal ritual. Here the repetition is more of an accretion, a repetition with a difference. In the first "me his" the metrical emphasis falls on "his", that is, on the Father, while in the second the emphasis is on Jesus, illustrating the divine but also mediatorial role of the incarnate Word, and reminding us of the subordinate position of the Son in Milton's doctrine of the Trinity.

The narrator's description of the disciples at the beginning of book 2 is a further example of Milton's use of repetition to recreate the conditions of ritual in the return of the same events in Christ's life and in the words in which he chooses to deliver the Word. In this speech, the narrator recalls the circumstances of the disciples, conveys their doubt because of Christ's absence, and emphasizes their hope for the future when they will see their "joy return." The interrelationship between the past and future in ritual time is reflected in the disciples' attempt, in their present, to resolve the scriptural past with the promise of the Son's return in the future. This is analogous to the Lord's Supper itself, as the physically absent Son is present imaginatively in the ritual, inspiring hope for his return in the future. The transition words convey this convergence of time: "meanwhile" suggests ongoing, present time; "yet," "lately," and the past tense throughout the speech until line 54 convey the disciples' unrest as they search the past in order to make sense of the present; the future tense in lines 54–57 indicates their faithful resolution, but also the convergence of the past and future in the present. The speech is also highly patterned. The use of parallel phrases (2.6), anadiplosis in conjunction with antithetical parallel phrases (2.9–10), polyptoton (2.11), and epizeuxsis (2.12) all verbally recreate the repetition of ritual. Milton's rhetorical and verbal repetition reinforces his repetition of larger units of discourse to the point where we soon realize that repetition and its relationship to time are recurring concerns in the poem.

A. B. Chambers has outlined the "double time scheme" in *Paradise Regained* and has linked it to liturgical time. In Christian ritual, *kairos*, consisting of unique events in which God has intervened in history, converges with sacred time, consisting of the repetition of those unique events in the liturgical life of the church. Through participation in such rituals worshippers are redeemed from *chronos*, the succession of events and moments that slip into the past and culminate in death.[42] Chambers's attempt to link the repetitions of the poem to Lent, however, is unconvincing. Instead, Milton's own sense of ritual — the spontaneous, rather than prescribed, use of verbal repetition to redeem the present with reference to the past and future — should be considered.

We should first notice that Jesus, Satan, and the disciples each stand in a different relationship to time and repetition. Satan, afraid of the future due to lack of faith, views time as a meaningless, chronological succession of events, each following the other into oblivion, unless they can be used to maintain his power by destroying Jesus. The only source of the redemption of time is Satan's will to power, but this proves futile since it is grounded in despair and dread. The result of this view of time is self-destructive compulsion in which he is doomed to repeat the same actions over and over again without hope of completion or redemption.[43] The "circling hours" slip over his head like a noose; his "dreaded time" has "compast" or encircled him (*PR* 1.57). Satan experiences time not as a "datelesse and irrevoluble Circle of Eternity [which] shall clasp inseparable Hands with joy, and blisse" (*Of Reformation, CPW* 6:616), but as a meaningless, cyclical repetition of actions motivated by dread and desperation. Just as

surging waves against a solid rock,
Though all to shivers dash't, th' assault renew,
Vain batt'ry, and in froth or bubbles end;
So Satan, whom repulse upon repulse
Met ever, and to shameful silence brought,
Yet gives not o'er though desperate of success,
And his vain importunity pursues.

(PR 4.18–24)

Because time is a succession of moments culminating in his downfall, Satan is doomed to compulsive repetition in a desperate attempt to reclaim the passage of time. Jesus, on the other hand, is a rock of patience since his faith allows him to await the "due season," or *kairos* which God has appointed for him, and to realize that he not only repeats but fulfills the experience of previous prophets such as Job and Elijah. In fact, Jesus *is* the "fullness of time" since all events, for a believer like Milton, begin and end in him. The passage of time in the present does not concern Jesus as much as it does Satan because of Christ's unshakeable faith that God will reveal his purpose in the future. Repetition is meaningful since he is the Truth who fulfills previous incarnations of his presence.

The experience of unredeemed chronological time by Satan and the experience of redeemed chronological time by Christ are balanced by the experience of ritual time by the narrator, in which chronology and *kairos* converge in the creative repetition of events in Christ's life. Repeated references to Job, Elijah, and other figures and events from the scriptural past show how the narrator creatively recreates the past in the present, creating meaning where it otherwise would have been absent, and providing for future creative acts. The baptism is repeated three times, once each by the narrator (1.18–32), Satan (1.70–85), and Christ (1.273–86), while Jesus' ritual appearance in the temple and the nativity are interpreted three times as well, once each by Christ (1.211; 1.242–54), Mary (2.96–99, 66–75), and Satan (4.216–17; 1.64–66). Speculation about the nature of Christ's kingdom is also repeated by the disciples (2.30–48), Satan (3.152–53; 4.389–90), Mary (1.234–41) and Jesus (1.265; 2.467–86; 4.146–53). Through these repetitions of the same event Milton reveals not only his hermeneutics but also his attitude toward worship. In the process of responding to the scriptural past creatively, each interpreter redeems the present by imaginatively reliving the past and providing hope for the future. Except for Satan, who fails to respond creatively to the present because he has no faith in the future, each character succeeds in creatively repeating the past, not as a prescribed form of ritual, but as a voluntary act of love and faith. The ritual of presence, then, includes repetition but only as it is performed by each individual creatively responding to God's revelation in the past in order to live the fullness of time in the present and future. Similarly, the temptations themselves enact ritual time: as the repetition of events in Christ's life, we know what is going to happen, and when the expectation is fulfilled three times in essentially the same way — by the quotation and application of Scripture — the Word is disclosed as the still centre of the turning world controlled by Satan.[44]

Milton's view of worship as good works inspired by the Holy Spirit and revealed in free choice guided by Scripture and reason is especially forceful in his characterization of Jesus throughout the poem. In his struggle with Satan, Jesus is tempted to abandon the ritual of presence that constitutes true worship. *De Doctrina Christiana* cites confidence or trust in God, patience, and obedience, three virtues manifested by Jesus in *Paradise Regained*, as "devout affections" related to internal worship (*CPW* 6:656). More importantly, Milton seems to read the temptation narrative as a specific example of Satan's attempt to undermine Jesus' trust in God. Distrust, idolatry, "carnal reliance," and presumption are all cited in *De Doctrina Christiana* as the opposites of confidence "which is placed entirely in God, as an effect of love and a constituent of internal worship" (*CPW* 6:657). These opposites of trust in God

underlie the temptations in *Paradise Regained:* the temptation to turn stones to bread is a temptation to distrust providence (*PR* 1.355); the temptation of the kingdom combines idol
worship and "carnal reliance," or a reliance on the things of
this world, associated by Milton with kingship and civil power
(4.162–67); the temptation of the temple is a temptation to presume God's protection (4.561).

The importance of the temptation of the kingdom to Milton
is reflected in the length of the temptation in the poem, and
this is paralleled by the extent to which idolatry is involved
in flawed internal worship in *De Doctrina Christiana*. It is the
antithesis of trust in God (*CPW* 6:657), gratitude toward God
(*CPW* 6:659), and true fear of God (*CPW* 6:660). It is also
implied in will worship, or the worship of superstitions and
non-Christian rites, hypocritical worship, or the worship of
external forms (*CPW* 6:666–67), and oaths sworn to objects other
than the true God (*CPW* 6:687). The adoration and invocation
of God — true forms of prayer in Milton's view — become
false and perilous when the divine name is identified with a
representation, whether the object is meant to represent the
true God or a false one (*CPW* 6:690–91). Milton's association
of carnal reliance with distrust of God and kingship, and all
three with idolatry and false worship, stands as a bold condemnation of the Restoration church, which used civil power
to enforce uniform worship, a worship that included features
of idolatry, hypocrisy, and will worship in Milton's view. Jesus'
choice to continue internal worship grounded in the Word
and Spirit emerges as the central rite in a church without
walls.

In *Paradise Regained*, through allusion, assimilated form,
and imagery, but especially in the figure of Jesus, Milton continues to explore his interest in the renewal of worship that
began in the 1640s. The need for liturgical reform that united
the Puritan party within the English church in 1640, however,
had divided it by 1660, when persecution by the established

church increased the isolation and fragmentation that Puritans had already brought on themselves in the decade before the Restoration. In this context of divided and defeated Nonconformity, Milton's representation and enactment of worship in *Paradise Regained* are both consolatory and visionary. The poem provides a model and theology of worship in the Spirit appropriate for persecuted and isolated Nonconformists, but also plants seeds for the future, portraying a source of unity for a renewed religious culture. Literature plays a central role in forming and sustaining this community of imagination, for it creates an order of time in which passing moments are temporarily suspended in the shared experience of reading. The condition of the true church in the wilderness of the world, a condition of militancy which includes the Restoration but also continues until the Second Coming when the church will become triumphant and visible, is the subject of the next chapter.

FIVE

Astrology, Apocalypse, and the Church Militant

The close relationship between the authority, ministry, and liturgy of the Word in *Paradise Regained* reflects the relationship between the invisible and visible church in Milton's literary ecclesiology. Following Augustine and Calvin, Milton defines the true church as the invisible, mystical body of the regenerate in union with each other and with the Father and Son.[1] The mystical church is not subject to space or time since it includes all of the regenerate from the beginning of the world; as a result, absolute knowledge of membership in the invisible church belongs only to God (*Christian Doctrine, CPW* 6:498–500). The visible church, on the other hand, is a "mixed society" of regenerate and unregenerate, elect and reprobate. However, unlike Augustine and Calvin, Milton views each member of the visible church, by virtue of the clarity of Scripture and the illumination of the Holy Spirit, as the supreme authority in religion; consequently, the visible church

consists of a textual community united by progressive revelation, a community of "skilfull and laborious gatherer[s]"
(*Divorce, CPW* 2:490) dedicated to the pursuit of Truth until
the revelation of the invisible church.

Through the ritual of reading, each member participates in
a particular, visible church and, more importantly, in the universal church, which includes all Christians professing biblical faith throughout the world. Membership in a national
church or an Independent congregation, therefore, is not a
necessary condition of membership in the universal church.
Thus, Milton does not conflate the invisible and visible
churches; this was, as Hooker also argues, the error of both
Congregationalist and Roman ecclesiologies.[2] On the one hand,
Independents use conversion as a criterion of visible church
membership in order to separate the elect from the reprobate
because the visible, gathered church is identified with the
mystical communion of saints as closely as possible. Conversely,
Augustine admits the coexistence of the elect and reprobate
in the visible church, but because there is only one true, visible church, whose authority was derived "from the time of
the [earthly] presence of Christ, through the dispensation of
the apostles and through a regular succession of bishops in their
seats . . . to our own day throughout the world," membership
in the invisible church depends upon membership in the
Roman church.[3] Calvin, like Augustine, also defends both the
mystery of election and the necessity of particular, visible
church membership, except that he rejects the authority of
everything but Scripture interpreted by the professional ministry.[4] For Milton, however, the mystery of election and the
doctrine of "sola scriptura" lead to voluntarism in his ecclesiology. He asserts that the mystery of invisible church membership gives authority in religious matters, not to the church
as an external body, but to each individual guided by the Holy
Spirit and united to the body of Christ and the church by the
textual body of the Word. Because election is mysterious,

glorification is incomplete, and assurance is conditional, the visible church cannot be identified with the invisible church until the Second Coming; as a result, the church militant finds itself in spiritual combat with Satan until the Apocalypse, while both the elect and reprobate are included in the visible church. The authority of the church rests with each member who voluntarily participates in the interpretation and performance of Scripture and, to a lesser extent, the reading of works compatible with "the Spirit of Christ" (*Divorce, CPW* 2:282), or "charitie, the interpreter and guide of our faith" (*CPW* 2:236).

Each area of Milton's ecclesiology is modified by its literary and textual context. The visible church is a textual community unified by the silence and Word of God. Church ministry and discipline can be derived from words as well as the Word, from education as well as edification, resulting in the progressive building of the church through the reading and writing of religious poetry and prose as well as sermons and treatises. Moreover, the divine calling of poets and prophets to lead the church, despite their lack of ordination, makes the ministry and liturgy of the Word profoundly literary. The inspired poet/prophet is "beside the office of the pulpit" in authority, while the "filial words" of poetry and prose can surpass the sermon in persuasive power and, therefore, in usefulness to the church. The central liturgical act of the church becomes the proclamation of the Word, but in a more exact way, the style of the work — its repetitions, allusions, and patterns — simultaneously uniting its readers with a past that is present, with a time that is timeless.

Milton's literary ecclesiology would have been incomplete, however, had he only outlined the nature of the church and the relationship between Christians and Christ within the visible or invisible body. The church is also called to perform its ministry in the world and maintain a relationship with civil society. Although Milton's view of the relationship between church and state changes throughout his career, it always changes to protect the individual's freedom to interpret Scripture according to conscience against the encroachment of both church and state. Only by defending Christian liberty could the kingdom of Christ be built and the church militant sustained until the Second Coming, when the veil between the invisible and visible church will be lifted and the church triumphant revealed. Such a defense was particularly important during the Restoration, when the kingdom of Christ, as Milton understood it, was under seige.

The kingdom of Christ imagined in *Paradise Regained* is Milton's most compelling representation of the church and the problems facing it at all times, but especially during the Restoration. The interplay of silence and the Word in Jesus' hermeneutic battle with Satan reconstructs Milton's emphasis on the Holy Spirit in interpreting Scripture and on Jesus' incarnate nature. Temperance and self-governance are important in Christ's ethical battle with Satan, reiterating Milton's emphasis on self-discipline in his discipline of the Word. The centrality of the Word in Christ's ministerial and liturgical battle with Satan illustrates the prophetic and priestly offices of Christ, which Milton refers to throughout his prose. Finally, the spiritual nature of the kingdom in Christ's battle with Satan develops further the separation of church and state in Milton's view of the kingdom of Christ in the antiepiscopal tracts but also in *A Treatise of Civil Power.*

In scriptural and astrological references to the Apocalypse in *Paradise Regained*, Milton continues his critique of the English Reformation and its failure to recognize Christ's spiritual rule of the church and, therefore, the separation of church and state.[5] Thus, in *Paradise Regained*, Milton not only advances a consistent view of Christ's kingdom, but he also participates in his literary ecclesiology in the process of formulating it. Christ's kingdom, the kingdom of the Word, is the invisible, spiritual fellowship made possible by the Word, and words devoted to the Word; it will be perfected when Christ comes again, but will depend until then only on the Word, and never on force, for its perpetuity. As Milton argued in *De Doctrina Christiana*, Antichrist arose within the church, thriving during Constantine's reign and persevering well into the Restoration. In Jesus' rejection of Satan, then, is an implicit denunciation of the Church of England and encouragement for persecuted Nonconformists of the 1670s. To fully appreciate the militancy of Milton's references to the church through his apocalyptic and astrological allusions in *Paradise Regained*, it is first necessary to clarify the meaning of "the kingdom of Christ" both in the Bible and in Milton's prose as he worked out the relationships between church and state under the changing conditions presented to him from 1640 to 1660.

Biblical scholars agree that the kingdom of God or, alternatively, the kingdom of heaven and Christ, is "the central theme of the mission of Jesus."[6] They do not agree, however, about what the phrase means, since "kingdom of God" is used in a perplexing variety of ways in the New Testament. The "kingdom" refers to the church (Matt. 16:19), Jesus himself (Matt. 16:28), Jesus' preaching (Mark 1:14) and a moral ideal of various descriptions (Matt. 5:3; Matt. 5:10; Rom. 14:17). The kingdom is not of this world (John 18:36–37) but is within each person (Luke 17:21); it is near (Matt. 4:17), here (Luke 11:10), in our midst (Luke 17:20) and to come (Luke 11:2), both during the millennium (Rev. 20:3) and after the final defeat of Satan (Rev. 20:10), when "a new heaven and a new earth" will be created (Rev. 21:1). It is a gift (Luke 12:32) and yet readers are urged to seek it (Matt. 6:33). The kingdom is an eschatological event at the end of time in which God intervenes in human history to invite the elect to a glorious banquet (Matt. 8:11), and also the historical church governed by Christ, separate from earthly political kingdoms, and often in open, militant conflict with them.

Nevertheless, despite the variety of references to the kingdom in Jesus' parables and in the New Testament generally, most scholars agree that there is one doctrine of the kingdom, although it takes different forms, depending on whether the writer is referring to the "incarnate, exalted or present Christ" embodied in the church.[7] Whether it is eschatological or moral, future or present, ecclesiastical or internal, the kingdom is an emergent reality, consisting of individuals transformed through their relationship to Christ and his Word, the fulfillment of which lies in an unknown future, both in Christ's triumphant return and in the heavenly banquet awaiting believers. The visible church is an imperfect image of the final kingdom since it includes members who will not be part of the final kingdom; at the same time, it *is* the kingdom since it extends Jesus' presence in time by embodying his Holy Spirit in its doctrine and discipline. Despite the unity of doctrine about the kingdom in the New Testament, the precise relationships between church members, between different churches, between civil society and the church, between models of civil and religious government in Scripture, and between the millennial kingdom and political authority are left open to debate and become flashpoints in the exercise of Christian liberty throughout the church's history.

If the biblical text is marked by a variety of interpretations of the kingdom of God, such variety virtually disappeared after Augustine identified the kingdom with the church, by which he meant both the invisible body of the elect, and the Roman Catholic church and its sacraments. The city of God included all of the elect and, technically, was distinguished from the visible church, which included reprobate as well as elect. However, because the Roman church was the only true, visible church for Augustine, he often identified the church with the "kingdom at hand" proclaimed by Jesus, making chiliasm, or millenarianism — the belief in Christ's imminent return before his 1,000 year reign — heretical.[8]

The churches of the Reformation also identified the church with the kingdom of God.[9] Calvin, like Augustine, rejected

chiliasm, especially when the identification of the church
with spiritual perfection led to the belief in the church's right
to civil power or, conversely, the church's right to avoid participation in the state altogether.[10] Throughout his *Institutes
of Christian Religion*, Calvin identifies the kingdom of Christ
with the visible church, the spiritual kingdom, and even more
specifically, with the Word, since the Word is the "power of
the keys" granted to the clergy.[11] Unlike Augustine, Calvin
argues that the church was not always visible, nor was it identical to the Roman church, but with "the pure preaching of
the Word."[12] Calvin attempts to correct what he considers to
be the abuses of the Roman church by separating the church
and the state. The church and state are "two [separate] kingdoms" since "man is under a twofold government," one internal and eternal, the other external and temporal. While church
government and discipline are not prescribed in Scripture, the
worldliness of bishops contradicts their spiritual purpose and,
therefore, episcopacy should be removed.[13]

At the same time, however, Calvin argues that the "two kingdoms" were not antithetical. The state is obligated to "protect the outward worship of God, [and] to defend sound doctrine"
as well as to "form our social behaviours to civil righteousness."[14] Thus, in his attempt to make God's will sovereign in
all aspects of life, and to find a middle position between the
Roman and Anabaptist churches — both of which identified
the visible and invisible church — Calvin conflates the
church and state. He separates "Christ's spiritual kingdom"
from the state, but allows the state the power of protection,
and encourages Christians to adopt public office.[15] This is the
position of the authors of the Westminster Confession (1648)
as well.[16]

The interrelationship of church and state in Calvin's ecclesiology, despite his separation of the two kingdoms, is especially apparent in his encouragement of Christians to take
public office. Calvin expected the civil state to be reformed by

individuals living out the Christian life in their day-to-day activities, leading to, in practice, if not theory, a Christian theocracy. Calvin's vision of the Christian life unified the church and state in the kingdom. As he explains in his discussion of the second petition of the Lord's Prayer: "God reigns where men, both by denial of themselves and by contempt of the world and of earthly life, pledge themselves to his righteousness in order to aspire to a heavenly life."[17] The church and the kingdom are in continual warfare with the world, the flesh, and the devil; therefore, "zeal for daily progress is not enjoined upon us in vain, for it never goes so well with human affairs that the filthiness of vice is shaken and washed away, and full integrity flowers and grows. But its fullness is delayed to the final coming of Christ when, as Paul teaches, 'God will be all in all' [1 Cor. 15:28]."[18] Although the state's authority is separate from the church's, here Calvin urges the moral reformation of the commonwealth in the image of Christ and his kingdom, a process of reform that unites civil and spiritual jurisdictions in the universal attempt to bring about Christ's kingdom.

Martin Bucer, the Strassburg reformer and advisor to Edward VI, was even more explicit than Calvin and not nearly as subtle. In *De Regno Christi* (1550), Bucer argued that both the church and state were subject to the law or kingdom of Christ, for, in his view, both church and state were means of bringing about Christ's will declared in Scripture. As Wilhelm Pauck remarks,

> Bucer linked the Kingdom of Christ, the Church, and the State . . . because they both, the Church and the State, are the instruments by which, under God, Christ exercises his rule, they cooperate with one another in pursuit of the same ultimate end. . . . In the understanding of Bucer, this Kingdom, we must note, is to be established here on earth. . . . Where such a community of love and mutual service exists, there is the Kingdom of Christ — and there also is the truly Christian Church and the Christian commonwealth.[19]

Thus, Bucer's program was designed to drive away "intemperance, wickedness, and luxury" in daily life through the reformation of all laws according to the Word of God. His treatise teaches how, by the "salutary Word of God," King Edward could restore "the blessed Kingdom of the Son of God, our only Redeemer, i.e., renew, institute, and establish the administration not only of religion but also of all other parts of the common life according to the purpose of Christ our Savior and supreme King."[20] The church, education, the use of material things, marriage and divorce, work and leisure, the appointment of judges, the punishment of criminals and many other aspects of everyday life should be reformed by the Word, creating the kingdom of the Word.

Even though Bucer, like Calvin, separates church and state, identifies the kingdom with the church, and defines the church as the gathering of the elect, the distinction between church and state virtually disappears. In fact, lay ministry and moral reform are necessary for salvation, as are church discipline and government. Bucer explains "how salutary it is for all men to have the Kingdom of Christ firmly restored among them and how necessary it is for salvation that every Christian, according to his place in the body of Christ and the gifts he has received from him, aim and work toward this with deepest concern."[21] Bucer's formal definition of the kingdom of Christ illustrates how the church as a spiritual community, and the state as a civil society, are essentially two expressions of Christ's kingdom: "The Kingdom of our Savior Jesus Christ is that administration and care of the eternal life of God's elect, by which this very Lord and King of Heaven by his doctrine and discipline, administered by suitable ministers chosen for this very purpose, gathers to himself his elect . . . . He incorporates them into himself and his Church and so governs them in it that purged more fully day by day from sins, they live well and happily both here and in the time to come."[22] Christ's kingdom, then, refers at the same time to the spiritual kingdom, consisting of the visible gathering of the church, the civil kingdom, transformed by the moral will of the elect, and the eschatological kingdom to come, when the communion of saints will enjoy union with God at the end of time. As in the New Testament, the kingdom is internal and external, moral and eschatological, present and still to come at the same time.

The Reformed Protestant view of the kingdom formulated by Calvin and Bucer is guided by two principles. On the one hand, because Christ is king in his mediatorial office, only he, not the Pope or the magistrate, can govern the church, his kingdom. Hence, it is necessary to separate religious and civil jurisdictions, leaving the church with spiritual, persuasive power and the state with physical, coercive power. On the other hand, both Calvin and Bucer believed that the state was subordinate to the church, and that the Christian commonwealth could be created by members of the internal kingdom inspired by the Word. In both principles, Scripture is the supreme law. Not only does Scripture supersede tradition, the Roman church, and the civil state, but it is by means of the Word that God calls the elect into communion with each other and Christ, opening the doors of the visible and spiritual kingdom of God until the eschatological kingdom is realized on earth as it is in heaven.

The doctrines of the first and second generation of Protestant reformers, including Luther, Calvin, Zwingli, and Bucer, were both adopted and transformed by English Protestants of the seventeenth century, including Milton. The doctrine of "sola scriptura," for example, was used to defend both the ordained ministry of the Presbyterian church as well as the lay ministry of sectarian churches. The interpretation of Christ's kingdom by Protestants from 1640 to 1660 followed a similar pattern. Bucer and Calvin's views of the relationship of church and state was far from unambiguous: on the one hand, the church and state have separate jurisdictions, each responding to one part of our twofold nature: body and soul, nature and grace, external and internal; on the other hand, they were convinced that God's sovereign will, as it is revealed in Scripture, should be made manifest throughout daily life, leading to social and political activism and, eventually, political leadership by the church.

This theocratic tendency in Calvin and Bucer's thought was developed by two distinct groups during the course of the Civil War in England: the Presbyterians and the millenarians.[23] For the Presbyterians, since God's will was revealed in Scripture and interpreted by the ordained ministry, the clergy was responsible for advising the king or Parliament, while the forms of civil government were "equally of God" and, therefore, indifferent to salvation.[24] Millenarian Fifth Monarchists like Henry Archer, however, rejected both the ordained clergy and the "indifferency" of political organizations; instead, they advocated setting up "by force a type of millennial government of Christ with his saints."[25] Not only was political leadership restricted to the "visible saints," but the forms of government had to resemble, if not duplicate, forms of government found in Scripture.[26] Despite their many differences, then, both Presbyterian and millenarian ecclesiologies emphasized the control of the state by the church.

Many others rejected the theocratic solution to the problem of the state's relationship to the church. The Erastians of the 1644 Parliament, whom Ernest Sirluck suggests had a significant influence upon the argumentation of Milton's *Areopagitica*, offered one answer to the problem: the church should not control the state; the state should control the church.[27] Indeed, many Anglicans, including Richard Hooker, argued that the church was not a society of the regenerate, visible saints but a "politic society" with the king as its head. More important for the later Milton, however, were the "segregationists," exponents of gathered church ecclesiology who argued that the church and state had absolutely separate jurisdictions. Segregationists rejected a national church in favor of the toleration of many separate churches whose worship was based on Scripture. This position became state policy under Cromwell's reign, but it first became prominent after the Westminster Assembly failed to satisfy Independent demands for liberty of worship in 1643. The majority of church leaders, however, including "Non-Separating Congregationalists, Independents, and most sectaries, distinguished to some degree between the laws and concerns of the two orders, and the functions of their institutions, but did not wholly segregate them."[28] Thus, leading Independents like John Owen could claim that the church and state ruled over separate spheres and by different methods, but still argue for state support of the church through tithes and still defend the state's right to use force to punish heresy.[29] Following Bucer and Calvin, Owen argued that the state and church were separate except when the state had to intervene to protect and promote the church and when the clergy could directly influence political affairs through spiritual counsel and ecclesiastical legislation.

It was this mainstream Puritan tradition, codified in the Westminster Confession and the Savoy Declaration (1659), that Milton adopted and transformed throughout his career. On the one hand, he rejected the theocratic pretensions of the Presbyterians, as well as the confusion of spiritual and civil jurisdictions implicit in their support of tithes and in their use of force to curtail aspects of worship which were "things indifferent" and left to the individual's conscience in the Scriptures. On the other hand, he assumed that each individual was responsible for the reformation of both the church and state in order to create the kingdom of the Word. By living the Christian life, each individual contributes to the growth of the kingdom of the Word throughout the state as well as the church, identifying the two orders through voluntary discipline rather than force.

It should also be noted, however, that despite his broad agreement with the Independents and more radical gathered churches on the separation of church and state, and his agreement with millenarians on the "rule of the virtuous," if not the regenerate, Milton also differed from these groups in some respects.[30] Although he insisted upon the separation of church and state, unlike all other separatists he continued to defend "the political wisdom of the ancients as directives to his Christian nation." Moreover, although he agreed that the worthiest should rule, he also insisted that "moral goodness and virtue (and thus worthiness to exercise political rule) though most fully enjoyed by the regenerate are not impossible to natural man." Political leadership, therefore, is the right of those who "manifest certain virtues and dispositions."[31] Based on revelation and reason, Scripture and the classics, the external and internal Word, Milton's literary ecclesiology distinguishes him from both moderate and radical Puritan ecclesiologies.

According to Michael Fixler, Milton's thought about the kingdom of Christ developed through four phases, each corresponding to a different meaning of the phrase, as he responded to changing political and religious conditions.[32] After briefly invoking the apocalyptic kingdom formed by the Spirit in *Of Reformation* and the ecclesiastical kingdom formed by the reading of Scripture in *The Reason of Church Government*, Milton then placed more emphasis on the transformation of church and state by liberated individuals and by the leadership of Parliament. At this more explicitly political stage in Milton's thinking, a stage encompassing his prose works from *The Doctrine and Discipline of Divorce, Areopagitica* and *The Tenure of Kings and Magistrates* to *The Readie and Easie Way to Establish a Free Commonwealth*, he assumed that Parliament could create the conditions under which the textual community might thrive. At first, as in *Areopagitica*, he assumed that the nation would accept the burden of Christian liberty, transforming the state and church from the ground up, but later, as in *The Readie and Easie Way*, he realized that the nation was as likely to choose idolatry and self-imposed slavery, providing justification for the authority of reformation being placed in the hands of only a few worthy individuals.

Despite Milton's firm belief in the possibility of building a Christian commonwealth and protecting the church through legislative means, he made "bewildering shifts of political allegiance among the various parties and models of government," especially in 1659–1660 but also from as early as 1644.[33] In *Areopagitica*, Milton calls upon Parliament to reject pre-publication censorship so that the church, conterminous with the nation, will be free to pursue truth and reformation. In 1649 Milton defended the regicide with a popular sovereignty argument, but in 1651 supported Pride's Purge and the right of a virtuous minority to govern without the support of the majority of people. In 1654, after the Rump failed to create the conditions under which Christ's kingdom might thrive, he approved of Oliver Cromwell, the Barebones Parliament, and Cromwell's Protectorate as he began to consider the separation of church and state. The separation of church and state is advocated in *A Treatise of Civil Power in Ecclesiastical Causes* and also in *Hirelings*, but Milton is also less enthusiastic about the Protectorate in 1659, now in Richard Cromwell's hands, because the implications of church/state separation were not pursued to their logical conclusion: the eradication of tithes and of the state-supported clergy.[34]

From August, 1659 to April, 1660, Milton proposed or supported no less than seven different political positions, many of which contradict the others.[35] In *Hirelings*, he accepts the authority of the Rump, vilified in 1654; in the "Letter to a Friend, Concerning the Ruptures of the Commonwealth" (October, 1659), written after the army had deposed the Rump, he proposes an interim government composed of army officers and members of the Rump; in "Proposalls of Certaine Expedients for the Prevention of a Civill War Now Feard" (October–December, 1659), he argues for the return and perpetual government of the Rump; in the first edition of *The Readie and*

Easie Way to Establish a Free Commonwealth (February, 1660), he advocates perpetual government by a "worthy minority" and "Councel of ablest men" derived from both the Rump and the Long Parliament, the latter denounced in 1651; in "The Present Means, and Brief Delineation of a Free Commonwealth" (March, 1660), he attempts to convince Monk to limit the vote to "the well affected," to provide for the rotation of elected officials rather than perpetual government, and to establish local committees with legislative power, rather than a monolithic central government; in "Brief Notes Upon a Late Sermon" (April, 1660), Milton admits that a "temporary king or protector" might be necessary and to prove it uses the popular sovereignty argument, abandoned since 1651, when he "defended the right of the worthy minority to impose their government upon the rest"; and finally, in the second edition of *The Readie and Easie Way* (April, 1660), he supports rule by a worthy minority, modifies proposals for perpetual government and local councils, and despairs of the inevitable return of tyranny with the restoration of Charles II. In the course of 20 years, Milton moved from a view of church and state united in Christ's kingdom by the nation responding to the Word and Spirit, to a view of the Christian commonwealth reformed by Parliament, to a view of the state as separate from Christ's kingdom, but led by its most worthy members.

In the last stage of his thought about Christ's kingdom, Milton increasingly emphasized the spiritual, inward kingdom of Christ, the possession of all individuals who are guided by the Holy Spirit in the reading of Scripture and which should not be overruled by the church or the state. This view is developed in *De Doctrina Christiana* (1650–1660), *A Treatise of Civil Power in Ecclesiastical Causes* (1659), and *Hirelings* (1659), but we can see its culmination in *Paradise Regained* (1671). The "divine excellence of his [Christ's] spiritual kingdom" is manifested in Christ's ability "to subdue the powers and kingdoms of this world, which are upheld by outward force only"

(*Civil Power, CPW* 7:255); therefore, "external force should never be used in Christ's kingdom, the Church (*Christian Doctrine, CPW* 6:436). The kingdom is synonymous with "the law of the kingdom, the gift of the spirit, [which] was given at Jerusalem on the fiftieth day after Christ's passion" (*CPW* 6:436).

The development of Milton's ecclesiology as it touched on church/state relationships and the kingdom of Christ is described by Fixler "as an evolution toward something like a vanishing point." It began with the apocalyptic kingdom of 1641–42, in which church and state were identical. It changed into the Christian commonwealth, in which individual church members and Parliament reformed the church and state in a Bucerian mode, first as identical and then as separate kingdoms. Finally, the visible church virtually disappeared in the inward, spiritual kingdom, in which each member is a "church of one man."[36]

Fixler's general account of the development of Milton's ecclesiology differs on two points from my own. First of all, Milton's view of Christ's kingdom, while shifting in some details to accommodate the changing political arrangements that should have guaranteed its essentials, remained remarkably consistent throughout his career.[37] Rather than fading to a vanishing point in the inner kingdom within each believer, Milton's visible church was associated with the kingdom within from the beginning. The inner kingdom of the Spirit is as crucial for Christ's apocalyptic kingdom in 1641, when Milton recommends "searching, trying, examining all things, and by the Spirit discerning that which is good" (*Of Reformation, CPW* 1:566), as it is in *Of Civil Power*, where he emphasizes the authority of "the illumination of the Holy Spirit within us" (*CPW* 7:242), the "inward Oracle" of *Paradise Regained* (1.463). Moreover, the differences between Milton's early apocalypticism and the Bucerian vision of Christ's kingdom implied in the works on domestic liberty from 1643 to

1645 can be exaggerated. The antiepiscopal tracts and the works on education, freedom of the press, and divorce share a vision of the church united in the textual body of Scripture. If the nation fails to respond collectively to God's call to build Christ's kingdom, and the national church also proves to be an obstacle for the kingdom of the Word, the nation must be led by its worthiest representatives in Parliament rather than in the official church. When the state continued to assert its power in ecclesiastical causes, it became necessary to separate church and state completely.

The bewildering shifts in Milton's thought about the kingdom of Christ can be clarified if we keep the dependence of religious settlement on the free encounter with Scripture in mind. Milton turned from apocalyptic expectations of Christ's Second Coming to a Bucerian model of Christ's kingdom, but Milton's vision of Bucerian activism, with his emphasis on human agency, is also present in his apocalypticism, as the English people must be worthy of Christ's return. Early apocalyptic expectations also survive in the general framework of the kingdom of Christ since the final representation of Christ's church can only occur when he returns as its prophet, priest, and king.[38] When church leaders failed to guarantee freedom of worship based on the Word, he argued that only Parliament, and then the separation of church and state, could ensure the freedom of interpretation upon which Christ's kingdom rested.

Milton adopted or discarded various political organizations from 1640 to 1660 based on their potential to bring about his vision of Christ's kingdom. His reasons for turning against the Presbyterians in 1649, then, were the same as his reasons for condemning the Independents in 1659: neither guaranteed the liberty of all Christians to gather to read and write about the Word granted by Scripture. "This liberty of conscience which above all other things ought to be to all men dearest and most precious" (*Readie and Easie Way, CPW* 7:456) was, in fact, not "most precious"; as a result, Milton supported any political organization led by those who seemed to possess it and to extend it to others. He was determined to defend the church with whatever political institutions were appropriate at the time so that he could contribute to its flourishing and growth.

Fixler also argues that Milton's assumptions about Christ's millennial kingdom, and preparation for it through political means, change dramatically in his late works. Milton is no longer interested in "the ideal of the Holy Community" or the visible church; instead, he emphasizes the reign of Christ within each person. After the Restoration, only "inward illumination," and personal "responsibility for righteousness regardless of outward circumstances" are necessary. [39] In fact, Milton envisioned church history in apocalyptic, not millennial terms from the beginning to the end of his career, even though the timing of a final victory for the church changed as the visionary hope of the 1640s became the sober resolution of the 1660s and 1670s. Milton also continued to engage in the reformation of the visible church throughout the Restoration. In *Paradise Regained* this becomes evident when the context of the poem's astrological and apocalyptic references are kept in mind.

As several scholars have shown, significant developments in English apocalyptic thought were introduced during the seventeenth century. [40] For most sixteenth century reformers, history was seen through the lens of The Revelation [Apocalypse] of St. John the Divine, the last book of the Protestant Bible. This resulted in the conviction that Antichrist — the Pope and some of the doctrines and practices of Catholicism — would soon be defeated, eventually leading to the Second Coming of Christ, the Last Judgment, and the new heaven and earth. Seventeenth century Puritans were less enthusiastic about this reading of Revelation and contemporary events, however, since many traces of Catholicism remained in the doctrine and discipline of the English church.

Antichrist for Puritans included the English church, or parts of it, making them more open to a reading that emphasized

the progressive nature of the Apocalypse. Despite the differences between the Anglicans' opponents that would surface
later in the century, as the nation approached civil war, and
especially after the fall of Laud and the bishops in the early
1640s, many felt that the Second Coming was imminent in
the newly reformed church. During this period a new emphasis on the literal reign of Christ and his saints also began to
emerge in English apocalyptic thought. Derived from Revelation
20:1–10 and the interpretations of Mede, Alsted, and others,
millenarianism was not uncommon among Independents and
various radical groups, one of which was later called the Fifth
Monarchists. Unlike Anglicans and Presbyterians, these radicals envisioned the beginning of a literal thousand-year period
of peace ruled by Christ and his saints after years of persecution by Antichrist, even though not all millenarians, and not
even all Fifth Monarchists, advocated the use of force to create the conditions for Christ's millennial reign. These expectations of Christ's return, whether spiritual or literal, turned
to bitter disappointment when first the Presbyterians, then the
Independents, and finally the return of Charles II and the
Anglican hierarchy made it clear that a state church would continue to delay the Apocalypse. While belief in a future millennial
kingdom persisted among Nonconformists after the Restoration,
Christ's return no longer seemed imminent as the saints
entered a new era of persecution. Passive millenarianism was
certainly one response to these new conditions, but for others, like Milton, standing and waiting — and especially writing — were defiant acts of resistance, as they continued to
call down Antichrist in their reading of scriptural and astrological signs.

Throughout his career Milton's political hopes were linked
to the Second Coming of Christ to defeat Antichrist and reign
with the saints in Judgment.[41] The identifying mark of
Antichrist is consistent, too. As Milton suggests in *Of
Reformation*, "Antichrist began first to put forth his horne"

during Constantine's reign because he encouraged the confusion of civil and religious authority, leading to the church's accumulation of wealth, its use of force in religious matters, and its alliance with the state (*CPW* 1:551). In *De Doctrina Christiana*, assembled throughout Milton's career but probably reaching the state in which we have it in the late 1650s, the Pope is identified as Antichrist for the same reasons the English church was in the antiepiscopal tracts. Arising within the church, Antichrist uses civil power to compel individuals in religious matters (*CPW* 6:604, 797–98). What changes in Milton's apocalyptic thought is the timing of Christ's return. Whereas in 1641 Christ's return seemed imminent, in the decade after the Restoration the continuing spiritual struggle with Antichrist is stressed. The turn to inwardness in the last stage of Milton's apocalyptic thought should not be confused with passivity, quietism, or indifference about the Apocalypse, however. Vigorous spiritual preparedness is never absent from Milton's early hope for a literal reign of Christ, but it receives special emphasis in the Restoration wilderness of persecution suffered by Nonconformists, republicans, and the hero of *Paradise Regained*.

The presence of apocalyptic imagery in a temptation narrative might have been expected by Milton's readers because the setting of Jesus' battle with Satan in the wilderness would have brought to mind not only the struggles between Israel and Egypt in the Old Testament but also the apocalyptic struggles of the end times.[42] In his opening speech in *Paradise Regained*, Satan boasts about ruling "th' affairs of Earth" but also reminds his colleagues of the "dread attending when that fatal wound / Shall be inflicted by the Seed of Eve / Upon my head" (*PR* 1.53–55). Satan refers here to the *protoevangelium* of Genesis 3:15, commonly read as a prophecy of the last battle between Christ and Satan. John Diodati suggests that this verse prophesies Satan's "deadly and continual war" with the church in which Christ and "his elect through his Spirit, shall destroy all . . . [Satan's] kingdom, power, and works by a compleat and everlasting victory."[43] As I pointed out in chapter 2, in his misuse of Scripture on the spire of the temple in book 4, Satan fails to refer to this prophecy in his citation of Psalm 91. He omits the second clause of verse 11 — "to keep thee in all thy ways" — and ignores references to the Apocalypse in verse 13 which refer to the messiah who will "Tread upon the lion and the adder: the young lion and the dragon shalt thou trample under feet" (Ps. 91:13). At the end of the poem, as the angelic chorus reminds us, Satan's fall from the pinnacle prefigures his more permanent overthrow when he "like an Autumnal Star / Or lightning [thou] shalt fall from Heav'n trod down / Under his feet" (PR 4.619–21). This reference conflates the Son's defeat of Satan in heaven, Jesus' defeat of Satan on the spire, and the Son's final defeat of Satan in Revelation 20. Isaiah 14:12 ("How art thou fallen from heaven, O Lucifer, son of the morning!"), Jesus' own report in Luke 10:18 ("I beheld Satan as lightning fall from heaven"), and Revelation 12:4, 9, when Satan is defeated and thrown to earth, were all read as evidence of the war in heaven. They were also seen as prophecies of the time when, according to the angels in the poem, Satan will receive his "last and deadliest wound" (PR 4.622), as in Revelation 20:10, before the appearance of a new heaven and earth.

The purpose for which Jesus has been sent to defeat Satan is announced in apocalyptic terms as well, this time in the allusion to the Old Testament apocalypse of Daniel (2:34–35).[44] Christ's kingdom, imperfectly shadowed in the earthly church, will have no end and "shall to pieces dash / All Monarchies besides throughout the world" (PR 4.149–50) without force of arms. At a time when the church was referred to as Christ's kingdom and when a monarchy was restored that did not hesitate to use force in spiritual matters, this strident prophecy was anything but quietist. Milton's Nonconformist readers probably expected these allusions and likely recognized in the temptations not just an ethical trial of a solitary individual, but an ongoing combat of the whole church against Satan. Their own struggles were inseparable from the continuous assaults suffered by the church militant and the last battle between the Son and Satan.

If Milton's readers expected this eschatological context, neither would they have found the association of the temptation narrative with the church unique. A long line of commentary on Revelation 12 shows that this association was quite common. In his 1548 exegesis of Revelation 12, John Bale identifies the woman clothed with the sun as the church, her crown as the 12 apostles and "all other godly ministers of the word," her child as faithful Christians of all times, the dragon as Antichrist, and the flight of the woman as the persecuted church fleeing Rome. Even during the apostolic period, the church had to flee persecution, seeking God "in the solitary heart" and hiding in the wilderness where she was "fed with the scriptures." Bale also links Revelation 12 with the temptations: "He that will live godly in Christ, and be a patient sufferer; he that will stand in Gods fear and prepare himself to temptation . . . let him give himself wholly to this prophecy."[45] Bale's advice was even more poignant 120 years later when the Nonconformist churches were suffering for their beliefs.

David Pareus, whose exegesis of Revelation Milton clearly knew, continued this tradition, although his interpretation of the historical sense of Revelation 12 is much more specific. The visions of St. John touch on "the present conflicts of the Christian Church, which already were in John's time." The battle in which Michael overthrows Satan is also explicitly linked to the temptation narratives of Luke and Matthew. "The first conflict," Pareus writes, "consisted in Satans temptations, the which Christ did often most stronglie sustaine and suppresse." The battle, however, does not end there. Verse 13 refers to the time when "the true church fled into the wilderness," leaving the visible church in

> that desolate and apostatical state brought in by Antichrist in
> which indeed there was a true Church, but not apparent to the
> view of men: like as of old in Israels apostacie, there was indeed
> a Church of 7,000, but unknown to Elias and others. It is, I say
> the spiritual confusion of the Papacie: like as the Prophet Isaiah
> calls the spiritual desolation of the Jewish Kingdom a wilderness. In this wildernesse or spiritual confusion of the Romish
> Church, John sees a woman riding on a scarlet Beast.

Pareus, then, has it both ways. The flight of the woman represents the invisibility of the true church and shows that "God will reserve and feed some remnants" of the true church, but it also foreshadows the spiritual desolation of the visible church prophesied in Revelation 17:1–5, where the whore of Babylon, another symbol of the Roman church, rides upon "a scarlet coloured beast" in the wilderness. This signifies the "ambition, covetousness, luxurie, and power of prelates and carnal priests" as well as their faith "not in the heart but in Creeds and paper."[46] For Pareus, Revelation 12 unfolds the persecution of the true church throughout history by the Roman Antichrist, and, by extension, for many English Puritans, the unreformed English church. Such persecution also offers hope, however, because it is a sign of the coming Apocalypse and the final defeat of Satan by the Son, whether this defeat brings about an imminent, earthly kingdom or not.

The historical interpretation of Revelation 12 became more and more specific in the years that followed. John Diodati identifies Michael with Jesus, the angels with "the Pastors and Ministers of his Word" and the Dragon's angels with "the Ministers of Satan, namely antichrist and his adherents."[47] The Westminster divines read the dragon as the "Roman Emperours," "the man child, who was to rule all nations with a rod of iron," as Constantine, and the persecuted woman in the wilderness as the Waldenses, the small Christian community that Milton believed had preserved apostolic Christianity in the isolated valleys of the French Alps.[48] Thomas Taylor also associates the woman with the church and links the church's battle with Satan to the temptations. The passage depicts the spiritual "state and condition of the church," "an afflicted, wasted, and solitary condition": "our Lord Jesus himselfe was content to to goe into the wildernesse unto us and indure al temptations, wants, and dangers, that he might sanctifie our wildernesse unto us, and . . . [drive] from us all the hostile powers which would hinder us in our translation to his heavenly kingdome."[49] Mary Cary also connects Daniel 7:26 and Revelation 12:14, implying that Charles I, the little horn that subdues three kings in Daniel 7:24, forced the church into the wilderness. The persecution, however, "is very neer come to a period," for once the kingdom of the beast is diminished, as it had been with the regicide, the saints can "go on in their work of breaking down the strength of the beast, and bringing it to nothing, that the Lord Christ may be all."[50]

In Christ's temptation in the wilderness, Milton's readers would have seen, with varying degrees of specificity, the persecution of the true church by Antichrist in the Roman and English church. For some the persecution was thought to have begun as early as the apostolic period, while for others it began during Constantine's reign or soon after. Reaching its height during the period of papal supremacy, the false church began to crumble with the onset of the Reformation, when the true church, the kingdom of Christ, began to emerge. When that kingdom failed to appear, especially after the Restoration, the timetable of the battle with Antichrist needed to be revised as Nonconformists such as Milton realized that the church was in a state of militancy and persecution for an indefinite period. The identity of Antichrist had to change as well, when it became clear that the kingdom of Christ was not being realized.

The Antichrist was, at different times, Satan himself, or, more often, one of his representatives, including the Pope, the Roman church and its government and ceremonies, the vestiges of the Roman church in the English church, Charles I, Cromwell, or the spiritual attributes that made such obstacles to Christ's kingdom possible.[51]

Milton identified the apocalyptic vision of Revelation 12 with the trials of the church in his prose. In 1641 he describes the dragon's "traine of error" sweeping "the Starres out of the Firmament of the *Church*" while the militant Protestant church scorns "the fiery rage of the old *red Dragon*" (*CPW* 1:524–25). In *The Reason of Church Government* he declares that "Christ by those visions of S. John foreshewes the reformation of his *Church*" (*CPW* 1:760). He cites the "general apostacy that was foretold and the Churches flight into the wildernes" (*CPW* 1:827) and claims in *Animadversions* that the church has been in "this our wildernesse since Reformation began" (*CPW* 1:703), identifying the church as the antitype of Israel and warning that Egypt might "destroy us in this Wildernesse though wee deserve" (*CPW* 1:706). He portrays the Waldenses as the true church persecuted in the wilderness of "Alpine mountains cold" in Sonnet 17 and shows in *Paradise Lost* that Christ's obedience throughout the temptations (*PL* 11.381–84) and Satan's persecution of the church in the wilderness are parallel events through which Jesus will defeat

> The adversary Serpent, and bring back
> Through the world's wilderness long wander'd man
> Safe to eternal Paradise of rest.
>
> (12.311–14)

In *De Doctrina Christiana*, Milton describes Antichrist as "the great enemy of the church" which "arises from the church itself," noting that "the revealing of antichrist" is a sign of Christ's Second Coming, as are persecutions, false prophets, and "an almost universal apostasy" (*CPW* 6:604, 617, 616).

In *The Tenure of Kings and Magistrates* he is more specific. Satan's offer of worldly power to Jesus in Luke 4 is linked to the dragon's empowering of the beast in Revelation 13 and marks tyrannical monarchy as satanic government (*CPW* 3:210). Milton shared with many radical Puritans the view that the Antichrist not only worked through Rome or the Pope, but any religious hierarchy or practice, including the church of England's, which confused civil and spiritual jurisdictions when they violated the freedom of individuals to understand God's will through the Word and Spirit. This is particularly important because Dissenters, often persecuted during the Restoration for precisely this religious freedom, defined themselves as "sufferers for truth in the wilderness" at the same time as Milton was composing *Paradise Regained*.[52]

The association of the temptation narrative with the Apocalypse and both with the church in a state of persecution would have had a special and precise resonance for Milton and the Nonconformist churches of the Restoration. The Cavalier Parliament's burning of the Solemn League and Covenant (May, 1661) set the tone for the 1660s and 70s. MPs were ordered to receive the Eucharist by the order of the *Book of Common Prayer*; the Act of 1641 excluding the bishops from the upper house was repealed; and the definition of treason was altered to include writing and speaking. To commemorate Charles I's execution, on 30 January 1661, the bodies of Bradshaw, Cromwell, and Ireton were disinterred, hung at Tyburn, and decapitated.[53] On 24 August 1662 more than 1,000 Nonconformist ministers were ejected from their churches for failing to give "unfeigned assent" to the Act of Uniformity. Prescribing the *Book of Commom Prayer* and the Thirty-Nine Articles throughout the realm, forcing members of the clergy to swear not to subvert church or state, and compelling all clergy to be ordained by a bishop, the Act set impossible conditions for Nonconformists. The Licensing Act of the same year virtually muzzled Dissenters as well, for it required the "censorship of all printed works by a panel of the most important government ministers and churchmen."[54]

The king was not altogether against some kind of reconciliation with the Nonconformists: his policy of toleration was designed for Roman Catholics and included Dissenters by default. Events such as Venner's Fifth Monarchist uprising of 1661 and the Yorkshire Plot of 1663, as harmless to the state as they were in themselves, gave hardliners in Parliament more evidence to support their view that harsh legislation against Nonconformists was necessary. A royal proclamation against all "seditious sectaries and other disloyal persons" was developed further in the Conventicle Act of 1664, culminating in the Second Conventicle Act of 1670. The 1664 Act threatened with deportation ministers who presided at prayer meetings of more than five people and gave sweeping powers to officials for the arrest of conventiclers, while the 1670 Act levied stiffer fines and held church wardens and court officials more accountable if they failed to administer the Act.[55] For a man who had fought for liberty of conscience and the spiritual kingdom of Christ's church for decades, this atmosphere of fear and persecution must have been oppressive to say the least. The Anglican church, in its support of the Conventicle Act and its antitolerationist outlook, supported the use of civil power to enforce conformity throughout the first decade of the Restoration and stands boldly condemned in *Paradise Regained*, its position on the relationship between church and state reflected in Satan's persecution of Jesus.

As Gary Hamilton has shown, The Conventicle Act was reinforced by a vigorous antitolerationist campaign sponsored by Archbishop Sheldon and spearheaded by Milton's former acquaintance and now bishop of Oxford, Samuel Parker.[56] Parker's *A Discourse of Ecclesiastical Politie* (1670), a defence of the King's absolute power over religious affairs and an attack on "The Mischiefs and Inconveniences of Toleration . . . And All Pretenses Pleaded in Behalf of Liberty of Conscience," was in its third edition when *Paradise Regained* was published in 1671. In his treatise, Parker advances two arguments to prove that it is justifiable to force Dissenters to comply with the discipline of the Church of England: first, discipline is "a thing indifferent," and since the King is the legally constituted head of the church of England, subjects are obligated to comply with his will; secondly, coercion is "a theologically justifiable and effective instrument of education and persuasion," as proof texts such as Proverbs 23:14, 1 Corinthians 1:10–13 and 1 Corinthians 3:3–4 indicate.[57] Later, Milton may have been dissuaded by Andrew Marvell or Edward Phillips from replying to Parker's *A Reproof to the Rehearsal Transprosed* (1673) and Samuel Butler's *The Transproser Rehears'd* (1673), but Parker's argument that the church should be subservient to civil power must have irked Milton even before Parker's personal attacks.[58] In this context, it is no wonder that Milton adopted an indirect, though effective strategy of opposition. In *Paradise Regained*, the arguments used by Parker and other Restoration apologists are also Satan's: he tries to compel Jesus to worship him and offers arms and civil power to establish his kingdom.

Milton's prophetic warning against the kind of idolatry suggested by Satan, and by analogy, the views of Parker and others who argued that the king is the head of the church, is also summarized in the closing paragraphs of *The Readie and Easie Way*: "if, lastly, after all this light among us, the same reason shall pass for current to put our necks again under kingship, as was made use of by the *Jews* to return back to *Egypt* and to the worship of their idol queen . . . our condition is not sound but rotten, both in religion and all civil prudence" (*CPW* 7:462). Ten years earlier, in *Eikonoklastes* (*CPW* 3:405, 404, 343), Milton condemned the idolatry of *Eikon Basilike*, especially in the comparison of Charles to Christ on the pinnacle of the temple and in the frontispiece to most editions of the tract. The process of canonization was revived in 1660 when Charles was praised as a "blessed saint and martyr," and when, two years later, an order of service commemorating his martyrdom was included in the *Book of Common Prayer*. In the portrayal of Christ's patient suffering in *Paradise Regained*, Milton reminds his readers of what a true martyr is — one who suffers for truth, not for worldly power — and underlines the sacrilege implied in the comparison of Charles with Christ in *Eikon Basilike*.[59] Since Jesus is the only head of the church, his kingdom, and since the kingdom is achieved by spiritual means, the professionally religious — primarily the bishops and hireling clergy — impose upon Christ and, in fact, are Antichristian, creating what Milton calls a "civil papacie" each time they use civil power to enforce an interpretation (*CPW* 7:244–45).

Idolatry was also a concern of special importance in the 1670s because of the debate about the toleration of Roman Catholicism.[60] Milton's last tract, *Of True Religion* (1673), was written to persuade Parliament to exclude Roman Catholics from the Declaration of Indulgence (1672), and to assert, once again, that Scripture is the foundation of the church. In this tract, Milton reiterates, as he did throughout his career, that all doctrines and disciplines based on Scripture should be tolerated (*CPW* 8:419), a view that by definition, according to Milton, excluded Catholicism because of its idolatrous worship of human tradition and its elevation of the Pope. In fact, Milton reiterates the first principle of his literary ecclesiology in a way that is reminiscent of similar statements in *Areopagitica*: "If it be asked how far they [dissenters] should be tolerated? I answer doubtless equally, as being all Protestants, that is on all occasions to give account of their Faith, either by Arguing, Preaching in their several Assemblies, publick wrting, and the freedom of Printing" (*CPW* 8:426).

In *Paradise Regained*, then, Jesus' apocalyptic battle is also a Restoration one and his arguments reflect Milton's earlier radicalism, suggesting that he was anything but withdrawn from the ongoing pursuit of Christ's kingdom in this world. In *A Treatise of Civil Power in Ecclesiastical Causes*, Milton argues that Christ's spiritual reign "show[s] us the divine excellence of [Jesus'] spiritual kingdom able without worldly force to subdue all the powers and kingdoms of this world" (*CPW* 7:255). In Jesus' defeat of Satan by patience, argument, and exegesis, Milton illustrates how Christ's kingdom will come about, condemning, in the process, the intrusion of the state in the church in legislation like the Conventicle Act; the state's persecution of Nonconformists; and the idolatry implied in works like Parker's *Ecclesiastical Politie* and his preface to *Bishop Bramhall's Vindication of Himself and the Episcopal Clergy, from the Presbyterian Charge of Popery* (1672), where he claims that God, priest, and king are so interwoven that one cannot be rejected without rejecting the others.[61] In addition, by emphasizing Jesus' refusal to act before his time, let alone to speculate about the time of his kingdom's arrival, Milton distances himself from those Fifth Monarchists who advocated the use of force to bring about the 1,000 year reign of the saints described in Revelation 20:1–10. Although Milton still seems to expect the coming of Christ in judgment, this part of the Apocalypse is no longer as imminent as it was for him in the 1640s. The nature of the kingdom Jesus will proclaim and for which he is being prepared by the temptations is identical to the one Milton had been advancing at least since the publication of *A Treatise of Civil Power* in 1659. The kingdom, or church, is a religious society ruled by Christ through Scripture, not a civil society ruled by the King through force. It will suffer persecution in its struggle against Antichrist and will ultimately prevail as the temptation narrative and Revelation disclose, but no one, not even Jesus, knows when this victory will occur. In the process, Milton rejects the Restoration Settlement, radical Fifth Monarchism, the Independents, and the Presbyterians — all of whom, at one time or another, used force to persecute Protestants who attempted to derive the principles of their churches from Scripture alone.

The temptation of the kingdoms is explicitly linked to the church. According to Lewalski, Satan first tempts Jesus in the banquet-wealth-glory sequence to abandon his spiritual reign in favour of the external, worldly trappings of kingship, including pleasure, ambition, and fame. When he fails, Satan invites Jesus to assume his public, kingly office by using the wrong means, acting at the wrong time, and forming the wrong kingdom. As a result, the sequence beginning with Satan's reference to Jesus' inheritance of David's throne "alludes frequently to the exposed position of the church in its encounters with the world throughout history, but also to its confident expectation of glorious triumph in the millennium."[62] In addition, "the exposed position of the church" is revealed in the banquet-wealth-glory sequence. This time Satan appears in courtly guise, chiding the Son for his harsh, otherwordly purity, just as members of Charles II's court and the religious establishment ridiculed Nonconformists for their unrealistic and hypocritical saintliness (*PR* 2.300, 324–36).[63]

Although several specific temptations are included under the heading of the kingdom here, ranging from the temptations to "worth, [of] honour, glory, and popular praise" (2.227) to the political kingdom of Rome and the intellectual kingdom of Greece, they are all temptations to idolatry, to worship the ruler of the kingdoms of the world as a ruler of the kingdom of God. The banquet scene, for example, could depict what Milton called the "paganisme of sensuall idolatry" in *Of Reformation* (*CPW* 1:520) — the external, worldly, carnal, and ceremonial aspects of worship introduced by Archbishop Laud and renewed during the Restoration. Milton could also be alluding to the "dissolute," "sumptuous," luxurious court devoted to "eating and drinking [of] excessive dainties" and to "deifying and adoring" the king as a "demigod" that Milton condemns in *The Readie and Easie Way* (7:425–26).[64]

The banquet, according to Satan, is a "thing indifferent," something that Jesus can enjoy and use without endangering his salvation.[65] He claims that Jesus has a "right to all Created things," just as Christians are not bound by dietary laws because of Christian liberty. Jesus answers as Puritans had argued since the sixteenth century: outward ceremonies, like the banquet, are not indifferent when they imperil the spiritual condition of Christ's kingdom; therefore, Jesus asks rhetorically, "who withholds my pow'r that right to use?" (*PR* 2.324, 380). In other words, who withholds his power of choice in things indifferent and uses civil power in the church but Satan himself? If things of the created world are indifferent, as Satan suggests, Christ can freely reject them as his conscience sees fit. Milton's audience, familiar with the arguments about discipline and ceremonies, would identify with Christ's choice not to participate in the banquet because ceremonies which are not scriptural cannot be forced onto the individual by the leader of the state or church, "unless," as Milton argues in *De Doctrina Christiana*, "he wants to be called antichrist as the Pope, chiefly for this reason, is" (*CPW* 6:797–98).

When the sacramental imagery of the banquet is considered, the meal is anything but indifferent. When Jesus replies that he would eat if he liked "the giver," he rejects the principle of sacramental theology that affirmed the efficacy of the sacrament regardless of the spiritual condition of the priest who administers it. Earlier, in a play for the Son's sympathy, Satan associated himself with just the kind of "Hypocrite or Atheous Priest," who frequents "Sacred Courts," "handling holy things" "about his [God's] Altar" (1.487–89), that Milton and his audience would have identified with the sacerdotal priesthood of Catholicism and Anglicanism. The conjunction of "sacred" and "court" also underlines the confusion of religious and civil jurisdictions that undermines the English Reformation in Milton's view. In addition, Satan's table resembles the altar of the Roman and English churches; it is "richly spread, in regal mode" (*PR* 2.340). The table's luxuriance, but also the corruption of ceremony by the state implied in the word "regal," make it clear that this is not an indifferent ceremony but a spiritually perilous one. To eat the meal is to worship Satan; therefore, Jesus is justified in refusing to participate in the meal, even though, in itself, it is a "thing indifferent."

Throughout the temptations of the kingdom, Jesus also redefines the nature of Christ's kingdom in ways suggested by Milton in *Areopagitica,* illustrating how "the true warfaring Christian" is purified by trial, "and triall is by what is contrary" (*CPW* 2:515).[66] The series of oppositions and contraries throughout the second temptation highlights the contrast between Satan's literal, external, and political interpretation of Christ's kingdom and Jesus' typological, internal, and spiritual interpretation. In his first speech, Satan refers to his rule of "th' affairs of Earth" since the Fall. To defend his "Empire," however, preparations must be made "Ere in the head of nations he [the Son] appear / Their King, their leader, and Supreme on Earth" (*PR* 1.50, 63, 98–99). Satan interprets Christ's kingship in the image of his own.

When Satan offers wealth as a means of acquiring his kingdom (2.406–31), Jesus responds by redefining a king as one who "reigns within himself" (2.466), reinforcing the connection among church discipline, temperance, and the struggles of the militant church that Milton made years earlier in his prose. Echoing arguments made in *Of Education* and *Of Civil Power,* Jesus asserts that "To know, and knowing worship God aright" (*PR* 2.475) is the path of self-kingship which "governs the inner man" (477). Kings and "headstrong Multitudes" (470) who do not acquire virtue and self-rule, can only govern and be governed "by force, which to a generous mind / So reigning can be no sincere delight" (479–80). The characterization of "the people" as "headstrong," "a herd confus'd," and a "miscellaneous rabble" (3.49–50) looks ahead to those "inward slaves" (4.145) who aren't worthy of freedom but also brings to mind the English people on the eve of the Restoration described by Milton in *The Readie and Easie Way.* They are "strangely infatuated," a "misguided," "inconsiderate multitude" ready to "put [their] necks again under kingship" (*CPW* 7:427, 463, 461). They ignore the prophet's advice offered years before in *The Second Defence of the English People*: "learn to obey

right reason, to master yourselves." For those who have freedom and abuse it, unable to rule themselves and likely to turn
freedom into license, "it is not meet, for such men to be free"
(*CPW* 4:1.684, 683).

On the other hand, the true king reigns within and is willing to take "each man's burden," accepting a "wreath of
thorns" rather than a "Crown, / Golden in show" (*PR* 2.
458–59). The crown of thorns grasped by Charles I on the frontispiece of *Eikon Basilike,* as well as its pairing with the secular crown, couldn't have been more ironic for Milton since
the conjunction of spiritual and political authority in the king
is the result of self-promotion rather than self-sacrifice. The
qualities of true kingship, originating in the self-rule of the inner
kingdom, are conspicuous by their absence from Milton's
description of kingship in *The Readie and Easie Way*. Rather
than sacrificing himself for the good of the people, the king
claims absolute power over them in order to be "adored like
a demigod." To secure such power and adoration, the king is
made a slave to passions; he is "pusillanimous, full of fears,
full of jealousies, startled at every umbrage" (*CPW* 7:458). The
true king, on the other hand, "reigns within himself, and rules /
Passions, Desires, and Fears" (*PR* 2.466–67). More importantly,
worship is due only to "our true and rightful and only to be
expected King" whose power is spiritual (*Readie and Easie Way,*
CPW 7:445 429). The spiritual kingdom of Christ in which each
member participates by ruling within and searching the
Scriptures, as Jesus models in *Paradise Regained,* thus stands
diametrically opposed to the rule of "a single person" who stands
above others as a secular ruler and "demigod" of the church.
The juxtaposition between the true kingdom in *Paradise
Regained,* a model of the church, and the false one described
in Milton's prose and reconfigured in Satan's offer of the kingdom of the world in all its forms, couldn't be more plain.

The inner kingdom of Christ is defined further when Satan
offers "Empire" as a means of attaining glory (3.45). Jesus

reclaims true glory as "deeds of peace" accomplished by "wisdom eminent, by patience, temperance" and suffering "for truth's sake" (3.91–92, 98). Satan's concept of glory is limited to the fame acquired by conquest, while the Son's heroic actions are meant to "show forth his [God's] goodness" and to glorify him (3.124). As a last resort, Satan turns to the kingdom that he thinks Jesus has come to claim, hoping to use the Son's compassion for his country and his people to convince him to acquire glory and begin his kingdom before his time. Once again Satan's interpretation of Christ's kingdom is literal. The Son's "Father" is not David, his "Throne" is not limited to the rule of Judaea, and his endless reign is not political or even earthly. Satan describes Judaea "under Roman yoke" and tempts Jesus to use political force to begin his "endless reign, / The happier reign the sooner it begins" (3.178–79). This dilemma parallels one faced by Fifth Monarchists, who hoped to prepare for the Second Coming by using force to gain political power before and shortly after the Restoration. Jesus rejects this temptation to act prematurely, opting to wait for God's time to reveal itself. He redefines action not as violence or military force but as suffering and trial: "who best / Can suffer, best can do; best reign, who first / Well hath obey'd" (3.194–96). The public form of the inner kingdom of the church, then, is not political action or force of any kind but patient waiting and the acceptance of trial. Like the Nonconformists of the Restoration, Jesus should be "quietly expecting / Without distrust or doubt" because along with suffering and trial will come release and triumph. As Jesus knows, suffering is necessary before he is exalted "without change or end." The "everlasting Kingdom" will arrive, but only the Father, "in whose hand all times and seasons roll" (3.192–93, 197, 187), knows exactly when.

Admitting that Jesus' inner character is superior, the temptations of the world's pleasure, wealth, glory and popularity failing dismally, Satan takes the Son to the mountain top and shows him the "Monarchies of th' Earth" (3.246), from Assyria to Rome. Jesus has already established the terms of his kingdom and of true heroic action, but Satan is unable to abandon the idea that Christ's kingdom must be material and political, convinced that the retired and private Jesus only needs some exposure to the world to be persuaded of the need to assume David's throne and begin his reign. Jesus is first shown the kingdoms of Assyria/Babylon, Persia, Greece, and Parthia, this last kingdom the culmination of the others and an impressive example of the military force that Satan argues Jesus will need in order to establish his kingdom and to free the ten tribes of Israel. As Lewalski suggests, "Parthia is symbolically the power of the civil state."[67] Jesus' rejection of arms to advance his kingdom restates Milton's rejection of the use of civil power in the church in *Of Civil Power,* and the idolatry of the ten tribes of Israel parallels the "perpetual bowings and cringings of an abject people, . . . deifying and adoring" their idol king condemned in *The Readie and Easie Way* (7:426). For many millenarians, the deliverance of the ten tribes of Israel was also a sign of the approaching Apocalypse. Jesus' decision to wait for God's deliverance by inward call in his "due time" parallels Milton's commitment to the spiritual means of Christ's kingdom and his rejection of the use of force advocated in different ways by Fifth Monarchists, Presbyterians, Anglicans, and some Independents before and after the Restoration.[68]

The suggestion of the apocalyptic new heaven and earth in the typological symbol of the "promised land" gained by the ancestors of the ten tribes is reversed in the temptation of Rome. In his portrayal of Rome, Milton includes references to the Antichrist, but also to the "extravagance of regal power in Restoration culture" and the confusion of church and state in the Anglican church.[69] As I have suggested, Rome was identified with the Antichrist by seventeenth century Puritans who turned to Revelation 17 and 18 for the imagery of beasts, fornication, luxury, and the corrupt city to describe papal power.

In *Paradise Regained*, Tiberius, like the apocalyptic beast, is a "brutish monster" (4.128), and Rome is called "Queen of the Earth" (4.45), an allusion to Revelation 17:5 and 18:7, and perhaps to the "idol queen" of *The Readie and Easie Way* (7:462). The Roman people are exhausted by "lust and rapine" (4.137) and like the English are "by themselves enslaved" (4.144). The corrupt luxury of the court, already denounced in the temptation to wealth, here reaches new depths: "Towers and Temples" are "proudly" elevated, buildings "more like / Houses of Gods" are adorned with "Cedar, Marble, Ivory, or Gold," and wine is served in "Gold, / Crystal and Murrhine cups emboss'd with Gems" (4.34, 55–56, 60, 118–19). Through these descriptions, Milton indirectly condemns the corruption of the church by wealth and luxury as well as by the confusion of civil and spiritual power in Roman and Anglican ecclesiology. The corruption of the false church is even more apparent when we compare the "Queen of the Earth" with its opposite. Mary, "the Virgin pure," dwells in simplicity and obscurity like the true church, teaches Jesus about his kingdom, and provides an unassuming house to which Jesus returns before he begins his ministry.

Jesus' most definitive rejection of Rome and the kingdoms of the world, however, comes when he interprets the apocalyptic texts of Daniel as foreshadowing his everlasting kingdom of glory after the final defeat of Antichrist. According to many Protestant readers, the book of Revelation showed that the defeat of the Roman church and Antichrist must precede the beginning of the millennium. This reading was supported by Protestant interpretations of Daniel 2 in which Rome, the fourth monarchy represented by iron, had to be defeated before "the God of heaven set up a kingdom, which shall never be destroyed" (Daniel 2:44).[70] Alluding to Daniel 2:35, Jesus predicts that "All Monarchies" will be dashed to pieces by a stone which will become a mountain. Of his kingdom, like a "tree / Spreading and overshadowing all the Earth," "there shall be no end" (*PR* 4.146–51). Jesus models the church as a textual community illuminating Scripture; he redefines in its spiritual sense Satan's literal interpretation of his kingship and his claim to "David's throne." The Restoration church and the English people are put on notice as well. By associating them with Rome and looking forward to the Apocalypse when Rome will fall, Milton enacts imaginatively what he predicts will happen in history.

Finally understanding that Jesus is not inclined to wear "a worldly crown" or rule the "Kingdoms of the world," Satan begins a series of temptations, leading up to the temptation of the tower, in which corrupt forms of spiritual wisdom are offered. I have already discussed the relationship between church discipline and the temptation of classical wisdom, but it is important to point out again that it is not classical wisdom in itself that is rejected in this temptation, but classical wisdom offered by Satan as a source of fame and as a spiritual kingdom superior to Christ's. Even though Jesus is well versed in the classics, he redefines wisdom as having its source in "Light from above, from the fountain of light" (4.289), the only source of wisdom needed by the church and its ministers, and in the "God inspir'd" (4.350) authors of Scripture, the only text necessary to "best form a King" (4.364). After tempting Jesus' spiritual kingship with a night of terrors, literal signs of the suffering and passion that Jesus must undergo before his kingdom begins, Satan places Jesus on the pinnacle of Jerusalem's temple, a symbol of spiritual authority, but an authority he has come to fulfill in the spiritual kingdom of the church.

In the final temptation of the tower, the first temptation is repeated but in reverse: whereas the first temptation was to distrust God's providence, here the temptation is to tempt or try God by presuming his protection. Whereas in the first temptation Jesus was tempted to use material things for spiritual purposes, here he is tempted to use spiritual things for material purposes by using the Word for his personal gain. By presuming God's protection and casting himself from the pinnacle, Jesus is also being tempted to exalt himself as the spiritual head of his kingdom, symbolized by his position on the spire of Jerusalem's temple. By obeying the Word and refusing to act before his time, Jesus fulfills his kingly office and proves that he is ready to proclaim the kingdom to the world.

After Satan falls from the pinnacle of the Temple, Jesus is presented with "A table of Celestial Food" (4.588) in a lush, pastoral setting. The garden is often an image of the church in Nonconformist writing and here it represents the "Recover'd Paradise" of collective salvation — the church triumphant — promised in the poem's third line. The meal, the antithesis of the debased banquets offered by Satan, foreshadows the eternal kingdom of glory after the Apocalypse, when the church will sit at the Lord's Table in God's presence. A worthy communicant who has demonstrated his faith, Jesus sits down to a sacramental meal, but the meal also symbolizes the everlasting kingdom at the end of time.[71] It was this communal, eschatological sense of the Lord's Supper that often prevailed in Nonconformist churches and in their sacramental theologies. The Westminster *Directory for the Public Worship of God* (1645), even though too prescriptive for many Nonconformists like Milton, still anticipates this view in its directive "that the communicants may orderly sit about it, or at it" [the Lord's Table] in anticipation of the time when they "are admitted to eat and drink at his own Table."[72] The food imagery of *Paradise Regained*, then, develops the theme of the kingdom. Whereas Satan offers a demonic sacramental meal associated with the churches of England and Rome, Christ's victory over Satan on the pinnacle and the celebration of that victory in the celestial meal that follows it are associated with the persecuted Nonconformist church. The celestial banquet foreshadows the revelation of Christ's everlasting kingdom of glory, "the marriage supper of the Lamb" (Rev. 19:9) in which the church will participate.

Before Jesus returns to his "Mother's house private" to begin the process of regaining paradise and forming his kingdom, the angelic choir provides a glimpse of another feature of the Apocalypse: the judgment of Satan and his followers. After falling from the spire of the Temple, the choir proclaims that Satan will again "Rule in the clouds," but "not long": "like an Autumnal Star / Or Lightning thou shalt fall from Heav'n trod down / Under his feet" (*PR* 4.619–21). I have already alluded to the biblical texts that illuminate Satan's fall from the pinnacle, particularly Isaiah 14:12 and Luke 10:18, but verses such as Revelation 12:4, 9; 19:20; 20:3; and 20:10, depicting Satan or his followers falling from the sky or being thrown down, are important in establishing the apocalyptic context of these lines as well. To these should be added passages such as Matthew 24:29, Mark 13:25, and Luke 21:25, in which signs in the heavens and stars falling to the earth are associated with the effects of Satan's influence or signs of the approaching Last Judgment. Since Satan will fall like an "Autumnal Star," well-known images of judgment as a harvest of God's wrath might be recalled, too. Like weeds at harvest time and the tares that he has sown (Matt. 13:38–40), Satan will be harvested and thrown in the fire at the end of the world; he and his followers will be reaped with a sharp sickle and thrown "into the great winepress of the wrath of God" (Rev. 14:19). The reference to the winepress in *Paradise Regained* (4.15–16), then, is more menacing than might appear at first glance. Satan, returning to his assault on Jesus like a mindless fly to a winepress "in vintage time," does not recall this image of Judgment even though he is more than capable of quoting Scripture. Readers, on the other hand, understand that this image is proleptic, anticipating the apocalyptic, autumnal harvest of Satan as well as his fall from the pinnacle of the Temple.

Milton must also have known that autumnal stars were associated with comets in handbooks of astronomy and astrology. Although the debate about the origins of comets and their significance was still ongoing and would not be settled until Halley and others proved that comets had their own orbits, most seventeenth century readers of the stars believed that comets were generated when hot, dry vapors coagulated in the upper atmosphere during the autumn. As John Gadbury, an important astrologer of the 1660s, explains: "although the Comets that appeared in the years 1618 and 1652 and now in 1664 with us, have bin in the Winter-season; yet are divers Astronomers and Philosophers of opinion, that they are generated in Autumn or Summer but mostly in Autumne."[73] Gadbury goes on to explain with some skepticism that spring has too much moisture and too little heat, while winter has too little heat and summer too much to properly explain the appearance of comets; therefore, autumn, with the right combination of heat and dryness, is the only season in which comets could be produced. Milton's "Autumnal Star" simile, then, is one of his most extraordinary, drawing upon both scriptural and astrological signs of the end times. It condenses the charged, dramatic context of the Apocalypse with the visual power of the comet while reinforcing the contrast in the poem between Jesus, "our Morning Star then in his rise" (*PR* 1.294; Rev. 22:16) who stands on the spire, and Satan, the "Autumnal Star," or comet who falls from it.

Astrological tracts and almanacs were still very popular in the seventeenth century and contributed to Protestant eschatology becoming "an amalgamation of Christian and astrological speculation."[74] John Bainbridge, Oxford professor of astronomy, considered the comet of 1618 a sign of the fall of Antichrist and a portent of the Second Coming.[75] John Booker, republican licenser of almanacks and mathematics texts during the civil war, linked the prophecies of John Napier to contemporary events, noting "strange wonders in the Ayre" and proclaiming the downfall of monarchy, the defeat of Antichrist, and the spread of Christ's Kingdom.[76] William Lilly, "Parliament's unabashed apologist," argued that eclipses, comets, and conjunctions proclaimed God's displeasure with "Monarchicall Pomp" and "Popery" and associated the appearance of the 1618 comet in Scorpio with the scorpions of Revelation 19 and the "legates of the Pope."[77] Black Monday — the solar eclipse of 29 March 1652 — created the biggest stir, primarily because of its closeness to 1656, the date that many chose for the defeat of Antichrist and the beginning of the end.[78] For Nicholas Culpepper, the eclipse and the comet that appeared after it seemed to confirm the justice of the fall of monarchy and to portend that "the Fifth Monarchy of the world is coming." John Durant, in *A Set Time for Judgement* (1656), clearly identifies the signs of Apocalypse with the natural phenomena observed by astrologists: "by the signs that shall appear in Heaven as the darkening of the Sun, obscuring the moon, and shaking or falling of stars, I understand the debasing, dethrowning, and destroying of the Kings, Princes, and powers of this world."[79] Milton, then, could have counted on his readers to recognize allusions to comets, the fall of monarchy, and the Apocalypse in his description of Satan as an "Autumnal Star."[80]

Before the Restoration countless almanacs and astrological tracts routinely associated comets with contemporary events, including the fall of Charles I. Several even cite Du Bartas's *Divine Weekes and Workes* (1592), where comets portend "To Princes death, to Kingdomes many crosses."[81] After the king's return, however, it became more difficult for Nonconformists and Republicans to make these associations openly. Many turned from domestic politics to foreign policy — especially the Dutch wars — in their predictions about comets, resigning themselves to monarchy and episcopacy.[82] But tales of comets, fiery dragons, prodigies, wonders, and judgments upon enemies of Nonconformists persisted in works such as *Mirabilis Annus* (1661), *Mirabilis Annus Secundus* (1662), and Henry Jessey's *The Lords Loud Call to England* (1660). These narratives of signs and wonders "encourage the Godly, to hope and rejoyce in the Lord," for they are "praeludiums to that signal and last revelation which makes way for the new Heavens and the new Earth."[83] Through the Licensing Act the government quickly censored this popular genre because of its support of "the Good Old Cause" but also, more generally, because a prophecy could influence the course of events, whether it was true or not. As Thomas suggests, the Royalists sensed that the predictions were self-fulfilling to some extent because "nothing is more likely to bring about the success of an enterprise than the conviction of those who undertake it that they are predestined to succeed."[84]

Interpretations of comets were especially suspect because a long tradition of commentary associates them with "unusual calamities [such] as the death or deposition of princes, &c. Destruction and Ruine of Kingdomes, Empires, States, and Governments."[85] The return of monarchy and the failure of earlier prophecies did not deter later Republicans and Nonconformists from reading the comets of November–December 1664 and those of January and March–April 1665 as signs of God's displeasure and the approaching fall of monarchy. Many post-Restoration references are vague, however, leaving open the possibility that if monarchy did not fall immediately, it would eventually. In 1668 William Lilly commented on the connection between comets and the death of princes, reminding his readers of "some dreadful matter at hand," but "a prediction of the fall of kings and tyrants" was removed from a draft of his 1670 almanack by Roger L'Estrange.[86]

Once monarchy was restored, some astrologers looked to 1666 as the date of the defeat of Antichrist, even though Lilly seemed to backtrack on his earlier apocalyptic predictions for the year.[87] Thomas Trigge was a Royalist who still hoped to avoid "the many vials of wrath, threatened to be poured upon them, by the apparition of these Celestial Ministers, the Comets."[88] But as that date passed, it became clear that the battle with Antichrist was to last much longer than expected. After quoting Matthew 24:7 one author urges his readers to "see that you be not troubled (saith our blessed Saviour) for all these [signs] must come to pass, but the End is not yet. There will doubtless, after these grand revolutions, be a time of tranquility and peace, but it cannot yet be expected."[89]

Most Royalists refuted the traditional association of comets with the death of kings and the ruin of kingdoms, claiming that the signs were far too indeterminate in meaning to be read accurately, but offering their own readings anyway. One author suggests that the comet of 1652 was a sign of Charles II's return: "this Comet. . . hath a signification of a great man to arise, and this man is King Charles." He will be a man "guided by God's speciall providence," "a man deprived of all his just rights."[90] John Gadbury supports Charles II by rewriting the discourse of comets, asserting that "this Comet had a principle signification of his said Majesty King Charles, and . . . he is that Man, who shall act his part on the stage of Europe with so much divine assistance, that it will not be in the power of any Prince, King, or Nation to resist him."[91] After noting that the comet of 1652 could be read in at least two contradictory ways, the author of *The Blazing Star: or, A Discourse of Comets* points out that "a sign signifieth; and what signifieth is known and how little understood or known any Meteor, Exhalation, Comet, Apparition is." He finds "in reason no ground" for "political effects that are ascribed to them [comets] by those that would arouse and deceive the World," but goes on to suggest that the comet of 1664 portends "that a Kingdom or Dominion shall remain a long time" and that the king will "be active, and freely forward in good things."[92] Another tract of the same title condemns those who associate the comet of 1664 with "the grand Revelation of the world [in] the Year 1666, wherein they expect the down-fall of the Pope, and other strange and wonderful businesses."[93] John Spencer's sustained attack on the Nonconformist discourse of prodigies, including comets, particularly in the *Mirabilis Annus* tracts, reduces all prophetic discourses to party interests: "each party superstitiously interprets all accidents in favour of it self." If God "intended these portentous occurences as his trumpets to alarm a drowzy world," he asks, why are they so obscure that no one can understand them? Comets are not signs of evil, nor do they portend the deaths of princes, argues Spencer. The deaths of many princes have not been accompanied by comets, while malignant influences have not followed when they have appeared: "Almost four years and an half are past from us, since the Nation was first alarm'd with the dreadful news of strange Sights in Heaven and Earth, and yet (with all due thankfulnes to God be it spoken) never did those three National Felicities, Peace, Health, Plenty, more bless our habitations."[94]

Milton appears to share Spencer's skepticism since Jesus rejects "false portents" in *Paradise Regained* and Satan remarks that "turbulencies" in the air "*seem* to point " [my emphasis] to the "affairs of men" (4.491, 462, 463, 462). It is, admittedly, hazardous to infer an author's specific beliefs or ideas from literary works, but we can assume that Milton would have rejected the signs of providence in such works as *Mirabilis Annus*. Monsters, toads and frogs, armies in battle, fields of corn being reaped in the air, people dying in wondrous ways after cursing Nonconformists: these are unscriptural visions and stories that parallel too conveniently Nonconformist interpretations of contemporary events, enacting thinly disguised revenge fantasies.[95] In fact, critics of judicial or predictive astrology often claimed that prophecies of the future based on the stars and other natural signs are "heathen" at best and ultimately the "work of the devil." Readers are reminded of Matthew 24:24, which cites false prophets and signs.[96] Milton, too, must have been wary of natural signs or prodigies that had no scriptural basis, but as the defenders of astrology pointed out, numerous verses could be read to justify astrology, including the Gospel of Matthew's account of the nativity and the earthquakes, comets, and eclipses of the Apocalypse. As one defender of astrology argued, "though Comets . . . do not *make* [my emphasis] future events uncontroulably legible, yet when

they are placed in Conjunction with Sacred Script, they are not
without their proper Instruction, but foretell singular things
provided the word of God (who is the creator of Comets) be
the rule of that Interpretation."[97]

A similar, conservative acceptance of natural signs based on
Scripture seems to inform the passage from *Paradise Regained*
in which Jesus rejects "false portents." He rejects them because
they are sent from Satan, have no basis in Scripture, and imply
a belief in Fate rather than God (*PR* 4.491, 490). Satan reads in
the stars what Fate has in store for Jesus and, ironically, he is
right. Jesus will suffer violence and "cruel death," but Satan
is unable to understand the importance of suffering for Christ's
kingdom to come. He is also unable to distinguish between
the real and figurative characteristics of the kingdom, and is
reduced to feeble puns about the nature of the kingdom's eternal presence. Since his reading of the stars is based on fatal-
ism — Satan is the only character to use the word "dismal" with
its connotations of astrological determinism (1.101; 4.452) —
the meaning of the stars is beyond his grasp. No date is "prefixt"
in the "Starry Rubric" for the beginning of the kingdom, leaving Satan perplexed about what is meant by "eternal" and
"without end" (4.382–93). Satan then sends storms, thunder,
lightning, and dreams as signs of that cruel, uncertain future
to frighten Jesus into submission and to urge him to begin his
kingdom before the time set by God. Such signs "seem to
point" to "turbulencies in the affairs of men." Once again, Satan
is partly right, but to accept Satan's reading of the storms is
to accept Satan himself rather than Scripture. Instead Jesus
asserts his freedom of choice. Refusing to be compelled by the
signs and prodigies that "oft fore-signify and threaten ill"
(4.482, 464), Jesus rejects the "portents" not because signs are
inherently false but because they are "not sent from God." He
remains steadfast in his belief in his Father's eternal kingdom
as it has been revealed to him in Scripture.

More importantly, Milton counters the Royalist reading of

comets and signs with his apocalyptic one, prophesying the fall of monarchy and its anti-Christian reign. Regardless of the truth or falsity of the reports of lightning striking conformist churches, of meteors in the shape of fiery dragons falling to the ground, or of comets portending the fall of princes, Milton could be certain that the apocalyptic tenor and meaning of his autumnal star would be recognized. Whether or not he expected Christ's kingdom in England anytime soon, his readers could appreciate the Apocalypse in his poem and learn how to prepare for the kingdom's arrival. Milton could draw on both scriptural and astrological discourses, creating a powerful image and signaling once again his continuing commitment to reformation in England. Knowing that comets were associated with the fall of princes, he associates both with Satan's apocalyptic downfall in order to condemn the Stuart monarchy, especially its confusion of spiritual and civil authority and its use of civil power to force free consciences. When Jesus denounces Satan's astrological "false portents" (4.382–93), rejects his interpretation of the storm's significance (4.462–64), and refuses his temptation to name the precise date of his kingdom's inception, Milton indirectly condemns both the Restoration settlement and Fifth Monarchist radicalism.

Royalists often compared Charles II to David and to Christ, turning the star that appeared on the day of Charles's birth into a sign of the messianic Restoration of 1660.[98] Jesus, Milton reminds his readers, sits on "David's throne" not Charles II, the god-like new Augustus, and Satan's fall to the earth proclaims the authority of Scripture and the nature of Christ's spiritual kingdom, both of which, according to Milton, were corrupted by Satan in the poem and the Stuart regime in Restoration England. Through Jesus' refusal to act before his time or to name the date of his Second Coming, Milton also distances himself from enthusiasts like Thomas Venner and his congregation of Fifth Monarchists, who attempted to usher in Christ's kingdom on earth by seizing political power in

January 1661. He even might have had in mind his own suggestions of an imminent Apocalypse in the 1640s. Not force of arms, he suggests, but patience and scriptural combat will lead to Christ's kingdom.

The epic "battle of the Book," the "hermeneutic contest" between Satan and Jesus throughout *Paradise Regained*, then, prefigures the apocalyptic battle at the end of history and is informed by both scriptural and astrological imagery.[99] By associating with Satan views of corrupt religious and, there-fore, political life that he fought against earlier in his career and continued to fight against during the Restoration, Milton shows his readers what must be accomplished before Satan is defeated forever and Christ's kingdom can begin. The sources of corruption are the same in 1671 as they were in 1640: the confusion of religious and civil authority, the persecution of those who seek God's will through the Word and Spirit alone, and the idolatry implied in not following Scripture. That Milton would engage in such a polemic against the Restoration church in the 1660s and 1670s, when the persecution of Nonconformists was at its height, speaks clearly, albeit qui-etly and figuratively, of his ongoing commitment to this embat-tled minority community and to the militant church more generally. Despair, quietism, and conformity may have been possibilities for some defenders of the Good Old Cause after the failure of the revolution, but not for Milton. He created a hero whose patience, endurance, and faith were the condi-tions for Nonconformity's survival in the Restoration wilder-ness, giving it a strategy for resistance and a hope for renewal until the kingdom of glory arrived.[100]

NOTES

Notes to Preface

1. *Paradise Regained* first appeared in *Paradise Regain'd. A Poem. In IV Books. To which is added Samson Agonistes*. Printed by "J. M." (John Macock); the book was advertised by John Starkey in a catalog of 29 May 1670, but the date on all of the title pages I've seen is 1671. On 2 July 1670 it was licensed by Thomas Tomkyns, on 10 September it was entered in the *Stationers' Register*, and in November it was cited in the term catalog for Michaelmas. The delay in publication raises many questions, especially given the persecution of Nonconformists, the publication of Samuel Parker's *A Discourse of Ecclesiastical Politie* in 1670 (entered in the *Stationers' Register* in September 1669), and the passing of the Second Conventicle Act in 1670. These events will be discussed in more detail in chapter 5. See Barbara K. Lewalski, *The Life of John Milton*, rev. ed. (Oxford: Blackwell, 2003), 494 and 692–93 n. 21–22, for further discussion of the delay in publication.

2. See the following: William Bouwsma, *Calvinism as Theologica Rhetorica* (Berkeley: The Center for Hermeneutical Studies in Hellenistic and Modern Culture, 1987); Marjorie O'Rourke Boyle, *Erasmus on Language and Method in Theology* (Toronto: University of Toronto Press, 1977); Brian Cummings, *The Literary Culture of the Reformation: Grammar and Grace* (Oxford: Oxford University Press, 2002); Manfred Hoffman, *Rhetoric and Theology* (Toronto: University of Toronto Press, 1994); Lewis J. Spitz, *Luther and German Humanism* (Aldershot: Variorum, 1996); Charles Trinkaus, *In Our Image and Likeness: Humanity and Divinity in Italian Humanist Thought* (London: Constable, 1970).

3. According to Lakoff and Johnson, foundational metaphors structure the experiences that we have and the conceptual systems that

we live by. See *Metaphors We Live By* (Chicago: University of Chicago Press, 1980).

4. Fredric Jameson, "Religion and Ideology: A Political Reading of *Paradise Lost*," in *Literature, Politics, and Theory*, ed. Francis Barker et al. (London: Metheun, 1986), 37, 50. See Joan Bennett's more detailed analysis in *Reviving Liberty: Radical Christian Humanism in Milton's Great Poems* (Cambridge: Harvard University Press, 1989), 2–6.

5. Andrew Milner, *John Milton and the English Revolution* (London: Macmillan, 1981), 168, 174.

6. By reducing religion to its material or ideological conditions, Marxist approaches have failed to appreciate the radicalism of Milton's poems. For Milton, forms of political authority follow from the knowledge claims about God's being and will that characterize religious discourse. This is not to say that what we mean by "religious" — and Milton is primarily a religious poet — is apolitical, divorced from the power struggles within political and religious institutions. Nothing could be further from the truth in Milton's time or our own. Rather, by denying that transcendent value is possible and reducing religious experience to a function of political struggles, we ignore the unique claims of religious experience and discourse and fail to account for their importance in culture generally.

7. Barbara Lewalski, *Milton's Brief Epic* (Providence: Brown University Press, 1966).

8. Bennett, *Reviving Liberty*, 162–85. Barbara Lewalski and Howard Schultz also acknowledge Milton's interest in the church. For Schultz, the poem is an allegory, while for Lewalski, Milton engages in the "learned ministry controversy" and in anti-Anglican and Roman Catholic commentary, but only in passing since Milton's main interest is the identity of the Son. See Howard Schultz, "Christ and Antichrist in *Paradise Regained*," *PMLA* 67 (1952): 790–808; and Lewalski, *Milton's Brief Epic*, 283–302.

9. In *Writing the English Republic: Poetry, Rhetoric and Politics, 1627–1660* (Cambridge: Cambridge University Press, 1999), David Norbrook suggests that "dissent in the 1660s was not always as subdued as has sometimes been thought" and that "far from retiring into political resignation, Milton made every effort to intercede in the now-diminished public sphere as far as he possibly could" (434). I disagree, however, that "for all his championing of an open religious public sphere, Milton saw it as a means to an end" (480). Two other significant works are David Loewenstein's *Representing Revolution in Milton and His Contemporaries* (Cambridge: Cambridge University Press, 2001) and John King's *Milton and Religious Controversy* (Cambridge: Cambridge University Press, 2001). Loewenstein argues that Milton's radicalism continues in *Paradise Regained*, linking him with Quakerism (243), while King, after emphasizing Milton's use of

vituperation and satire against the false church in *Paradise Lost,* concludes that *Paradise Regained* and *Samson Agonistes* "fail to match the deeply embedded engagement of *Paradise Lost* with religious polity . . . or other polemical issues that embroiled seventeenth-century British public life" (189). I agree with King that religious satire and polemic are not as strident in the brief epic, but this does not mean that Milton is disengaged from the ecclesiological issues that surface so often in *Paradise Lost.* Simply put, in *Paradise Lost* the church is torn down while in *Paradise Regained* it is rebuilt in the image of the Son; as a result, satire and vituperation, although not absent in the later poem, are not as appropriate.

10. Gary Hamilton, "*Paradise Regained* and the Private Houses," in *Of Poetry and Politics: New Essays on Milton and His World,* ed. P. G. Stanwood (Binghamton, N. Y.: Medieval and Renaissance Texts and Studies, 1995), 240, 248.

11. Ashraf Rushdy, *The Empty Garden* (Pittsburgh: University of Pittsburgh Press, 1992), 118; Laura Knoppers, *Historicizing Milton* (Athens, Ga.: University of Georgia Press, 1994), 141.

12. Stephen Honeygosky provides a thorough analysis of Milton's ecclesiology, but he considers only the prose works and ignores the influence of literary humanism on Milton's theology. George McLoone does examine the ecclesiology of Milton's poems, but in the process, ignores details that contradict the depiction of Milton as a doctrinaire Independent, especially the emphasis on reason and the church as an ongoing interpretive activity. See Stephen Honeygosky, *Milton's House of God* (Columbia: University of Missouri Press 1993), and George McLoone, *Milton's Poetry of Independence* (Lewisburg: Bucknell University Press; Associated University Presses, 1999).

13. The term "textual community" is borrowed from Brian Stock who uses it to describe the textual practices, both oral and written, which create and are created by a distinct and clearly identifiable social organization. Small, isolated groups, such as constituted the early church and various Christian communities of medieval Europe, formed their identities in response to the "experience of the text" as they gathered to read and listen to others read: "the ritual of reading recapitulates the primal experience of speaking and hearing the word of God. Each reading is a speaking anew." This sense of the textual community captures the presence of the Word in Milton's church. I would only add that, for Milton, the real presence of a body of listeners was unnecessary; to participate in the church's communal life, it was sufficient for a reader to listen to the text. See Brian Stock, *Listening for the Text* (Baltimore: Johns Hopkins University Press, 1990), 149–51, and *The Implications of Literacy: Written Language and Models of Interpretation in the Eleventh and Twelfth Centuries* (Princeton: Princeton University Press, 1983).

Notes to Chapter One

1. On Milton and vocation see John S. Hill, *John Milton: Poet, Priest and Prophet* (London: Macmillan, 1979); and Lewalski, *Brief Epic*, 219–321. I am grateful to the editors of *Studies in Philology* for permission to reprint in this chapter a slightly different version of "Rhetoric and Revelation: Milton's Use of *Sermo* in *De Doctrina Christiana*," *Studies in Philology* 96 (1999): 334–47.

2. I refer to "Elegia Tertia" (Elegy 3), "In Quintum Novembris" (On the Fifth of November), "The Passion," and "Il Penseroso" respectively. From this point forward, references to Milton's poetry will be noted parenthetically and will cite *John Milton: Complete Poems and Major Prose*, ed. Merritt Hughes (Indianapolis: The Odyssey Press, 1957) unless otherwise stated. References to Milton's prose will also be noted parenthetically, but will cite *The Complete Prose Works of John Milton* (*CPW*), ed. D. Wolfe et al., 8 vols. (New Haven: Yale University Press, 1953–1982). Parenthetical references to *De Doctrina Christiana* in this chapter will cite this edition first and then the Latin text in *The Works of John Milton* (*CE*), ed. Frank A Patterson et al., 20 vols. (New York: Columbia University Press, 1931–40). Latin quotations provided in square brackets are from the Columbia edition and have been checked against the manuscript, SP 9/61, in the Public Record Office, London. In subsequent chapters I refer only to the Yale edition of *Christian Doctrine*. All works are cited in the text by volume and page number. References to *The Second Defence of the English People* include the part of the volume after the volume number as follows: 4:1.169.

3. For two useful suggestions about the significance of Milton's metrical psalms see William B. Hunter, "Milton Translates the Psalms," *Philological Quarterly* 28 (1949): 125–44; and Regina M. Schwartz, *Remembering and Repeating: Biblical Creation in Paradise Lost* (Cambridge: Cambridge University Press, 1988), 87.

4. See Esther Gilman Richey, *The Politics of Revelation in the English Renaissance* (Columbia: University of Missouri Press, 1998), 142.

5. Arthur Barker, *Milton and the Puritan Dilemma* (Toronto: University of Toronto Press, 1942), 17, 19–21.

6. Michael Fixler, "Ecclesiology," in *A Milton Encyclopedia*, ed. W. B. Hunter et al. (Lewisburg, Pa.: Bucknell University Press, 1978–83), 2:190, 192; Michael Fixler, *Milton and the Kingdoms of God* (London: Faber and Faber, 1964), 9; Fixler, "Ecclesiology," 192.

7. See Thomas N. Corns, *John Milton: The Prose Works* (New York: Twayne Publishers, 1998); and Reuben Sanchez, Jr., *Persona and Decorum in Milton's Prose* (London: Associated University Presses, 1997), 11. The rhetorical approach yields valuable insights, especially because Milton was familiar with the rhetorical arts, but it often

overlooks the continuity of the author and his views when it is used too exclusively.

8. Despite fascinating biographical evidence, Hunter's view that Milton did not write *De Doctrina Christiana* is unconvincing. It is probably an unfinished work by Milton that he worked on for many years and that he continued to revise until his death. There are too many parallels between the treatise and other works by Milton, no more plausible author has been suggested, and differences between the treatise and other prose works are exaggerated. Hunter also claims that Milton alludes to the "Anglican communion" when he refers to "Our church" in *Of True Religion*, but the context and other references in the tract suggest that he is referring to the Protestant church generally rather than a particular national church. See *Visitation Unimplor'd: Milton and the Authorship of De Doctrina Christiana* (Pittsburgh: Duquesne University Press, 1998), 15. This is part of an ongoing debate on the subject of Milton's authorship of the treatise that began at the 1991 Milton Symposium in Vancouver and continues in print. See William B. Hunter, "The Provenance of the *Christian Doctrine*," *Studies in English Literature* [*SEL*] 32 (1992): 129–42. For rebuttals by John Shawcross and Barbara Lewalski see "Forum: Milton's *Christian Doctrine*," *SEL* 32 (1992): 143–62. See also W. B. Hunter, "The Provenance of the *Christian Doctrine*: Addenda from the Bishop of Salisbury," *SEL* 33 (1993): 191–207, as well as responses to Hunter by Maurice Kelley and Christopher Hill and Hunter's reply to them in "Forum II: Milton's *Christian Doctrine*," *SEL* 34 (1994): 153–203. Other significant studies include the following: Paul R. Sellin, "John Milton's *Paradise Lost* and *De Doctrina Christiana* on Predestination," *Milton Studies* 34 (1996): 32–61; Gordon Campbell, Thomas N. Corns, John K. Hale, David I. Holmes and Fiona J. Tweedie, "The Provenance of *De Doctrina Christiana*," *Milton Quarterly* 31, no. 3 (1997): 67–121; Barbara K. Lewalski, "Milton and *De Doctrina Christiana*: Evidences of Authorship," *Milton Studies* 36 (1998): 203–28; Stephen M. Fallon, "Milton's Arminianism and the Authorship of *De Doctrina Christiana*," *Texas Studies in Literature and Language* 41 (1999): 103–27; William B. Hunter, "Responses," *Milton Quarterly* 33, no. 2 (1999): 31–37; Paul R. Sellin, "Further Responses," *Milton Quarterly* 33, no. 2 (1999): 38–51.

9. See especially the works by Loewenstein and King mentioned above.

10. Milton used many Bibles during his career, including a 1612 Authorized Version, a Geneva Bible, a Junius-Tremellius translation, and Brian Walton's *Biblia Sacra Polyglotta*, but used the Junius-Tremellius Latin text most frequently in *De Doctrina Christiana*. For a brief overview of the topic see John Shawcross, "Bibles," in *A*

Milton Encyclopedia, ed. W. B. Hunter et al. (Lewisburg, Pa.: Bucknell University Press, 1978–83), 1:163. Unless otherwise stated, I refer to the King James Version.

11. I refer to the logical, not the chronological relationship between the two works. From the chronological point of view, Milton begins by asserting the sufficiency of Scripture in the antiepiscopal tracts and later explores Christian liberty in *Areopagitica*. I discuss Scripture's authority for the church in *De Doctrina Christiana* rather than in the earlier tracts because the logical implications of Milton's view of Scripture for the church are more fully developed in the later work.

12. See the following: W. H. Schmidt, "dabhar," in *Theological Dictionary of the Old Testament*, ed. G. J. Botterweck and H. Ringgren; trans. J. T. Willis, G. W. Bromiley, and D. E. Green (Grand Rapids: Eerdmans, 1978), 3:84–125; G. Kittel et al., "*Logos*," in *Theological Dictionary of the New Testament*, ed. G. Kittel and trans. G. W. Bromiley (Grand Rapids: Eerdmans, 1967), 4:69–143; J. L. McKenzie, S. J., "Word of God," in *Dictionary of the Bible* (New York: Macmillan, 1965), 938–41; H. Stephan, "Word of God," in *Sacramentum Mundi*, ed. Karl Rahner, S. J. (Montreal: Palm Publishers, 1970), 6:362–67.

13. Schmidt, *Old Testament*, 101.

14. The first edition, *Novum Instrumentum*, was published by Froeben in Basel in 1516. The second, *Novum Testamentum*, was published by Froeben in 1519. References in the text are to *Desiderii Erasmi Roterdami Opera Omnia*, ed. J. Leclerc, 10 vols. (Leiden, 1705; reprint, London: Gregg Press, 1962).

15. Boyle, *Language and Method*, 5. I am indebted to Boyle's study throughout this section on Erasmus. On *sermo* see also J. Bentley, *Humanists and Holy Writ* (Princeton: Princeton University Press, 1983), 170; C. A. L. Jarrott, "Erasmus' *In Principio Erat Sermo:* A Controversial Translation," *Studies in Philology* 61 (1964): 35–40; Werner Schwartz, *Principles of Biblical Translation: Some Reformation Controversies and Their Background* (Cambridge: Cambridge University Press, 1955), 146; G. H. Williams, *The Radical Reformation* (London: Weidenfeld and Nicolson, 1962), 25.

16. Erika Rummel, *Erasmus and His Catholic Critics* (Nieuwkoop: De Graaf Publishers, 1989), 2:122–27. See also Boyle, *Language and Method*, 151 n. 34.

17. Boyle, *Language and Method*, 8–12 passim.

18. Boyle, *Language and Method*, 25.

19. Erasmus, *Paraphrasis in Evangelium Joannis*, in *Opera Omnia* 7:499E, 499C; Erasmus, *Paraphrase on John*, trans. Jane E. Phillips, in *The Collected Works of Erasmus* (Toronto: University of Toronto Press, 1991), 46:16.

20. Charles Trinkaus uses "rhetorical theology" to describe the

thesis, shared by early humanists and reformers in their opposition to scholastic methodology, that "since matters of faith cannot be proved by logic, they must be induced by rhetoric — the word of man in the service of the Word of God." The commitment to the *studia humanitatis* and the application of the "new philology" to the Bible led to the emergence of a shared textual practice in which Scripture was viewed as the rhetoric and Word of God. As a result, a new emphasis was placed on evangelical preaching, on the original languages and textual sources of Scripture, on the literary merits of the Bible, and on rhetorically effective as well as grammatically accurate translations. Moreover, in the process of defending the value of poetry and rhetoric by citing the Word as God's speech to the church, early humanists like Ficino elevated the Bible almost to the status of a sacrament by insisting on the immediacy and real presence of the written Word: "the entire Holy Scriptures speaking of Christ through the Holy Spirit, is as if it is Christ Himself, living everywhere and breathing into all who ever reads, hears, and meditates by a more powerful affection. Therefore Paul seems secretly to warn that we should approach the Evangel with the highest reverence, almost as if to the Eucharist." See Trinkaus, *In Our Image and Likeness,* 2:611, 745–46. For Ficino's text see "In Epistolas Pauli," in *Opera Omnia* (Basel, 1576; reprint, Torino: Bottega d'Erasmo, 1959), 1:1.435.

21. Trinkaus, *In Our Image and Likeness,* 2:564, 611; Hoffman, *Rhetoric and Theology,* 5; Peter Matheson, "Humanism and Reform Movements," in *The Impact of Humanism on Western Europe,* ed. A. Goodman and A. McKay (London: Longman, 1990), 34–38; Bouwsma, *Calvinism as Theologica Rhetorica,* 1–12.

22. Erasmus, *Lingua,* in *Opera Omnia* 4:696; Erasmus, *The Tongue,* trans. Elaine Fantham, in *The Collected Works of Erasmus* (Toronto: University of Toronto Press, 1974), 29:323.

23. For patristic and Reformed contexts respectively see W. B. Hunter, "Milton's Arianism Reconsidered," in *Bright Essence: Studies in Milton's Theology,* ed. W. B. Hunter, C. A. Patrides, and J. H. Adamson (Salt Lake City: University of Utah Press, 1971), 29–51, and Maurice Kelley, "Milton's Debt to Wolleb's *Compendium Theologicae Christianae,*" *PMLA* 55 (1940): 156–65.

24. As Kelley notes, Milton adapts but does not transcribe the Junius-Tremellius text of John 1:1, but Kelley, quoting G. H. Williams, also refers to *sermo* as "*merely* the voice of God" (my emphasis), indicating his failure to fully appreciate the implications of this translation for Milton's later arguments (*CPW* 6:239). Williams also refers to *sermo* as "theologically neutral." See Williams, *Radical Reformation,* 10. William Shullenberger, on the other hand, rightly emphasizes the importance of the *sermo* or "speech of God" in the antitrinitarian doctrine of *De Doctrina Christiana,* but his suggestion

that Milton conceived "the creative structure of the Deity in the same
pattern which Saussure found to obtain between language and speech"
ignores a more plausible and historically concrete analogy which
shapes Milton's theology of the Word. See William Shullenberger,
"Linguistic and Poetic Theory in Milton's *De Doctrina Christiana*,"
English Language Notes (March, 1982), 268. See also his "The Omnific
Word: Language in Milton" (Ph.D. diss., University of Massachusetts,
1982).

25. Erasmus, *Lingua*, in *Opera Omnia* 4:691; Erasmus, *The Tongue*,
314–15. For language as mediation in Erasmus's rhetorical theology
see Hoffman, *Rhetoric and Theology*, 6.

26. Sir Philip Sidney, *The Defence of Poesie*, in *Prose of the English
Renaissance*, ed. J. W. Hebel et al. (New York: Appleton-Century-
Crofts, 1952), 271. For the theological use of this Renaissance commonplace by a writer who had a tremendous influence on Milton in
De Doctrina Christiana see William Ames, *The Marrow of Sacred
Divinity* (London, 1642), 27: "In every artificer, or one that workes
by counsell *ad extra*, outwardly, there is a platforme afore hand in
the mind which when he is about to worke hee lookes into . . . so
also in God, seeing he worketh not naturally, nor rashly, nor by con-
straint, but with greatest perfection of reason, such a platforme is to
be conceived to preexist in his mind as the exemplary cause of all
things to be done. . . . The platforme of all things is the Divine
Essence."

27. Implied here, of course, is Milton's Arianism. See Shullenberger,
"The Omnific Word," 167–85 and John P. Rumrich, *Milton Unbound*
(Cambridge: Cambridge University Press, 1996), 40–47 for concise sum-
maries of the problem.

28. Erasmus, *Paraphrasis In Evangelium Joannis*, in *Opera Omnia*
7:499E; Boyle, *Language and Method*, 28–29; 173 n. 171. The possible misuse of *logos* theology and the analogy of the preexistent Word
and human speech was also anticipated by Athanasius and other
Nicene theologians long before Erasmus, but they reached different
conclusions: *logos* language was excluded from the Nicene Creed (325)
to avoid the suggestion, possibly useful to their enemies, the Arians,
that temporality was introduced into the Trinity by the Word. Calvin
saw potential problems as well: he defended Erasmus's translation,
but carefully qualified his approval so that antitrinitarians would not
jump to the conclusion that the Son was not equal to the Father just
because the Word follows the speaker of the Word. Milton was not
the only one to ignore the warnings of the orthodox. The *Racovian
Catechism*, published in 1651 and known by Milton, also capitalizes
on the antitrinitarian implications of the speech metaphor, taking
the central metaphor of rhetorical theology to its logical conclusion
just as Milton does in *De Doctrina Christiana*. See the following:

J. N. D. Kelly, *Early Christian Creeds* (London: Longmans, 1950), 217–18; H. A. Wolfson, *The Philosophy of the Church Fathers*, 2d ed. (Cambridge: Harvard University Press, 1964), 227–30; John Calvin, *The Gospel According to St. John, 1–10*, trans. T. H. L. Parker (Edinburgh: Oliver and Boyd, 1959), 6–7; *The Racovian Catechism*, ed. and trans. Thomas Rees (London, 1818), 139–40.

29. For the doctrine of rhetorical decorum see the following: Aristotle, *Rhetoric*, trans. W. R. Roberts, in *The Rhetoric and the Poetics of Aristotle* (New York: Random House, 1954), 178; Quintillian, *The Institutio Oratoria of Quintillian*, trans. H. E. Butler (Cambridge: Harvard University Press, 1980), 4:155–87; Cicero, *De Oratore*, trans. E. W. Sutton and H. Rackam (Cambridge: Harvard University Press, 1942), 2:31–211.

30. See Paul M. Dowling, "*Areopagitica* and *Areopagiticus:* The Significance of the Isocratic Precedent," *Milton Studies* 21(1986): 50; and John M. Steadman, "The Dialectics of Temptation: Milton and the Idealistic View of Rhetoric," in *The Hill and the Labyrinth: Discourse and Certitude in Milton and His Near-Contemporaries* (Berkeley: University of California Press, 1986), 71.

31. See Christopher Hill, *The World Turned Upside Down* (Harmondsworth: Penguin, 1972), 395–96.

32. See Ernest Sirluck, Introduction to Vol. 2 of *The Complete Prose Works of John Milton* (New Haven: Yale University Press, 1959), 140–44, 169–71.

33. Although he mistakes progressive revelation for interpretive indeterminacy see Stanley Fish, "Driving From the Letter: Truth and Indeterminacy in Milton's *Areopagitica*," in *Re-membering Milton: Essays on the Texts and Traditions*, ed. Mary Nyquist and Margaret W. Ferguson (New York: Methuen, 1988).

34. See Christopher Hill, *The Experience of Defeat: Milton and Some Contemporaries* (London: Faber and Faber, 1984), 300.

35. See Lana Cable, *Carnal Rhetoric: Milton's Iconoclasm and the Poetics of Desire* (Durham, N. C.: Duke University Press, 1998); and Michael Lieb, "Milton and the Organicist Polemic," *Milton Studies* 4 (1972): 79–94.

Notes to Chapter Two

1. Calvin, *The Gospel According to St. John, 1–10*, 7. I am grateful to the University of Pittsburgh Press for permission to reprint in chapter 2 an altered version of "Lingering Voices, Telling Silences: Silence and the Word in *Paradise Regained*," *Milton Studies* 35 (1997): 179–95.

2. John Goodwin, *The Divine Authority of the Scriptures Asserted* (London, 1648), 16–17, 20.

3. John Owen, "Of the Divine Originall, Authority, Self-evidencing Light, and Power of the Scriptures," in *The Works of John Owen*, ed. W. H. Goold (Edinburgh: Johnstone and Hunter, 1853), 16:305.

4. John Owen, "Of the Integrity and Purity of the Hebrew and Greek Text of Scripture," in *The Works of John Owen*, 16:350.

5. Owen, "Integrity and Purity," 16:348, 353.

6. John Owen, "Pro Sacris Scripturis Exercitationes Adversus Fanaticos," in *The Works of John Owen*, 16:427–29.

7. Samuel Fisher, *Rusticus Ad Academicos in Exercitationibus Expostulatoriis. Apologeticis Quator. The Rustics Alarm to the Rabbies* (1660), A2v.

8. William Erbery, *The Testimony of William Erbery* (1658), 8.

9. See Hugh MacCallum, "Jesus as Teacher in *Paradise Regained*," *English Studies in Canada* 14 (1988): 146–47.

10. For this literal translation of "kol demamah dakkah" in 1 Kings 19:12 see Aharon Wiener, *The Prophet Elijah in the Development of Judaism* (London: Routledge and Kegan Paul, 1978), 14. For Diodati's view of this passage see John Diodati, *Pious Annotations of the Holy Bible*, 3d ed. (London, 1651), 1 Kings 19:11–12.

11. Cf. Abraham Cowley, "Upon His Majesties Restoration and Return," in *The Works of Mr. Abraham Cowley* (London, 1668), 137–40; and Richard Baxter, *An Apology for the Nonconformist Ministry* (1668), 7. For Cowley, the Puritans misread God's providence, finding it in the "fierce thunder" and "violent wind" of the Civil War rather than "the still voice of peace" of the Restoration. According to Baxter, the Nonconformists have "patiently waited on Gods Providence, in silence as to the pleading of our cause . . . whilest Volume after Volume hath been published against us." Baxter's reading is closest to Milton's since Satan and the established church are more voluble than Jesus and the Nonconformists.

12. For Milton, many of God's attributes must be stated negatively to "show God is not imperfect as created things are" (*Christian Doctrine, CPW* 6:149; *CE* 14:52–54). He also notes that eternity "is expressed in the Hebrew language by inference rather than by distinct words" (*CPW* 6:144; *CE* 14:44–46), indicating a possible textual strategy of his own.

13. Two exceptions include Georgia Christopher, "The Secret Agent in *Paradise Regained*," *Modern Language Quarterly* 41 (June, 1980): 137; and Leonard Mustazza, "Language as Weapon in Milton's *Paradise Regained*," *Milton Studies* 18 (1983): 214. Silence has fared better in the following studies of other works by Milton: Ronald B. Bond, "God's 'Back Parts': Silence and the Accommodating Word," in *Silence, the Word and the Sacred*, ed. E. D. Blodgett and H. G. Coward (Waterloo: Wilfrid Laurier University Press, 1989), 169–87;

Gregory F. Goekjian, "Deference and Silence: Milton's Nativity Ode," *Milton Studies* 21(1986): 119–35; and Shirley Sharon-Zisser, "Silence and Darkness in *Paradise Lost,*" *Milton Studies* 25 (1989): 191–211.

14. Stanley Fish, "Inaction and Silence: the Reader in *Paradise Regained,*" in *Calm of Mind,* ed. J. A. Wittreich, Jr. (Cleveland: The Press of Case Western Reserve University, 1971), 42.

15. Steven Goldsmith, "The Muting of Satan: Language and Redemption in *Paradise Regained,*" *Studies in English Literature* 26 (1986): 125.

16. Fish, "Inaction and Silence," 27.

17. For the view that Christ's divinity in *Paradise Regained* consists in his unity with the Father's will see Hugh MacCallum, *Milton and the Sons of God: the Divine Image in Milton's Epic Poetry* (Toronto: University of Toronto Press, 1986), 240.

18. James M. Pearce, "The Theology of Representation: the Meta-Argument of *Paradise Regained,*" *Milton Studies* 24 (1988): 277–96; Ashraf H. A. Rushdy, "Standing Alone on the Pinnacle: Milton in 1752," *Milton Studies* 26 (1990): 193–218. I agree with Rushdy that the mystery of the Incarnation is not revealed by the miracle of Jesus standing on the pinnacle; on the other hand, the "identity test" is central to the action of the poem and leads to a restatement of the mystery of the Son's nature in the coexistence of silence and the Word.

19. Pearce, "The Theology of Representation," 290.

20. Rushdy, *The Empty Garden,* 317, 316, 270–71.

21. Rushdy, *The Empty Garden,* 317; "Standing Alone," 197.

22. Mark 1:14. All scriptural references in this chapter are to *The Holy Bible* [King James Version] (London, 1612) unless otherwise noted. Subsequent citations will appear in the text.

23. Douglas Lanier suggests that Jesus' use of silence in *Paradise Regained* reveals Milton's "fear of the independent interpretive afterlife of the written word." Jesus refuses to say what his identity or kingdom are because he knows Satan will misrepresent the radically interior nature of the kingdom and the irreducible mystery of his identity. Jesus' "controlled indeterminacy," in my view, is the silence that reminds the reader of the divine, unrepresentable source of his identity and his ministry of the Word. See Douglas Lanier, "'Unmarkt, unknown': *Paradise Regained* and the Return of the Expressed," *Criticism* 33 (Spring, 1995): 187–212.

24. Erich Auerbach, *Mimesis: The Representation of Reality in Western Literature,* trans. W. R. Trask (Princeton: Princeton University Press, 1968), 11.

25. Pseudo-Dionysius, "Letter Nine," in *Hierarchy and the Definition of Order in the Letters of Pseudo-Dionysius,* trans. R. F. Hathaway (The Hague: Nijhoff, 1969), 154. Hereafter, I will include references to *Patrologia Graeca,* ed. J.-P. Migne (Paris, 1857), and

Patrologia Latina, ed. J. -P. Migne (Paris, 1853). I will cite volume and column number as follows: *PG,* 3:1105D; *PL,* 122:1113A.

26. Pseudo-Dionysius, *The Divine Names,* in *PG,* 3:588C; *PL,* 122:1113A. This is my translation of Erigena's Latin translation in *PL.*

27. Pseudo-Dionysius, *The Divine Names,* in *The Divine Names and Mystical Theology,* trans. and intro. J. D. Jones (Milwaukee: Marquette University Press, 1980), 177; *PG,* 3:869A; *PL,* 122:1154B.

28. Pseudo-Dionysius, *The Divine Names,* 179; *PG,* 3:871A; *PL,* 122:1155B–C.

29. Pseudo-Dionysius, *Mystical Theology,* trans. Jones, 217, 218; *PG,* 3:1033B, C; *PL,* 122:1175B, C.

30. Jones, Introduction to *Divine Names,* 22–25.

31. For the complicated development of the *Logos* in early Christian thought, see Wolfson, *The Philosophy of the Church Fathers,* 141–372 passim, and J. N. D. Kelly, *Early Christian Doctrines,* 3d ed. (Longmans: London, 1965), 83–338 passim. For a lucid account of the Word and early Christian mystical theology, see A. Louth, *The Origins of the Christian Mystical Tradition* (Oxford: Oxford University Press, 1981).

32. St. Ignatius, "Letter to the Magnesians," trans. R. M. Grant, in *The Apostolic Fathers: A New Translation and Commentary* (Toronto: University of Toronto Press, 1966), 4:63; *PG,* 5:669B. As Grant indicates on page 62, most modern translators think that the Latin and Greek texts, which state that the Word does *not* proceed from silence, reflect anti-Gnostic emendation.

33. St. Augustine, *The Christian Doctrine,* trans. D. W. Robertson (New York: Macmillan, 1958), 11; *PL,* 34:21. See also *Corpus Christianorum Series Latina,* ed. J. Martin (Turnhout: Brepols, 1962), 32:9–10.

34. Robert Barclay, *An Apology for the True Christian Divinity . . . [of the] Quakers* (London, 1678), 249.

35. Alexander Parker, *Letters, &c. of Early Friends,* ed. A. R. Barclay (London, 1841); Isaac Penington, *The Works of Isaac Penington* (Philadelphia, 1863); Charles Marshall, *An Epistle to Friends Coming Forth in the Beginning of a Testimony* (n. p., 1677). Cited in Richard Bauman, *Let Your Words Be Few: Symbolism of Speaking and Silence Among Seventeenth-Century Quakers* (Cambridge: Cambridge University Press, 1983), 121, 122, 127.

36. For many Quakers, silence was a symbol of crucifixion and mortification as well. William Britten writes of the "pure silencing of the flesh" while Richard Farnsworth praises those who have "crucified the flesh" and are able to "wait upon God in silence from the fleshly birth." See William Britten, *Silent Meeting, A Wonder to the World* (London, 1660), 11; and Richard Farnsworth, *The Spirit of God Speaking in the Temple of God* (London, 1663), 4, 11.

37. Lewalski, *Milton's Brief Epic*, 157. For an account of the development of orthodox Christology, formulated at the Council of Chalcedon in 451 and adopted in The Thirty-Nine Articles of Religion and The Westminster Confession, see Kelly, *Early Christian Creeds*, 205–62. For a detailed discussion of Milton's doctrine of the Incarnate Son and its relationship to Reformed formulations, see chapter 6 of MacCallum, *Milton and the Sons of God*.

38. MacCallum, *Sons of God*, 218.

39. I call these liturgical sabbath hymns (*PL* 7.565–73; 602–32) not because Milton approved of such forms in his own worship, but because they occur on the seventh day (7.592, 634), they offer praise in song to the "great Creator" (7.567), and they ritualize a divine event by referring to liturgical forms such as choral music, incense, scriptural reference, and schemes of repetition (7.601, 599, 565, 591–93).

40. A full discussion of the interplay of silence and speech in Milton's poetry before *Paradise Regained* could include a comparison of the following: *PL* 4.598; *PL* 8.3; *A Mask*, 560; *PR* 4.601 and Jesus' stillness throughout the pinnacle scene. In each case, stillness, silence and speech or singing are linked. In *A Mask* (548–64), the Attendant Spirit describes how silence overcomes "barbarous dissonance" and then, in turn, is overcome by "a soft and solemn-breathing sound" to the point where

> even Silence / Was took ere she was ware, and wished she
> might / Deny her nature and be never more, / Still to be so displaced.
> (557–60)

Listening in silent entrancement, "amaz'd" (565) like Satan in the pinnacle scene of *Paradise Regained*, he later discovers the origin of the sound: the voice of the Lady.

41. A similar sequence is found in Rev. 5:1–11. No angels volunteer to open the sealed book, the Lamb steps forward, and "the voice of many Angels round about the Throne" is heard in heaven.

42. For a concise overview and analysis of the criticism see MacCallum, *Sons of God*, 230–38.

43. Erasmus, *The first tome or volume of the Paraphrase of Erasmus upon the Newe Testamente* (London, 1548), sig. Cii.

44. Lancelot Andrewes, *Ninety-Six Sermons* (Oxford, 1843), 5:483, 503, 482.

45. William Perkins, *The Workes of that Famous and Worthie Minister of Christ . . . William Perkins* (London, 1612–1613), 3:371–72.

46. James H. Sims, "Jesus and Satan as Readers of Scripture in *Paradise Regained*," *Milton Studies* 32 (1995): 194, 209–11.

47. Perkins, *Workes*, 3:394.

48. See the following: *The Bible and the Holy Scriptures Conteyned in the Olde and Newe Testament* (Geneva Bible, 1560; facsimile

reprint, Madison: University of Wisconsin Press, 1969), Matt. 4:6–7; John Calvin, *A Harmony of the Gospels: Matthew, Mark, and Luke,* trans. A. W. Morrison and ed. D. W. Torrance and T. F. Torrance (Grand Rapids: Eerdmans, 1972), 1:140; Diodati, *Pious Annotations,* Luke 4:10; John Downame et al., *Annotations Upon all the Books of the New and Old Testament,* 2d ed. (London, 1651), Matt. 4:6; William Fulke, *The Text of the New Testament of Jesus Christ Translated out of the Vulgar Latin by the Papists of the traiterous Seminarie of Rheims. With Arguments of Books, Chapters, and Annotations* (London, 1601), Luke 4:8; John Lightfoot, *The Works of John Lightfoot* (London, 1684), 1:498; Matthew Poole, *A Commentary on the Holy Bible* (London, 1683–1685; reprint, 2 vols. in 3, London: Banner of Truth Trust, 1963), 3:17.

49. Downame et al., *Annotations,* Matt. 4:6.

50. See the following: Lancelot Andrewes, *Ninety-Six Sermons,* 5:522; John Calvin, *Calvin: Commentaries,* ed. and trans. J. Haroutunian and L. B. Smith (Philadelphia: Westminster Press, 1958), 166; Downame et al., *Annotations,* Matt. 4:6–7; Erasmus, *Paraphrase of Erasmus upon the Newe Testamente,* sig. Cii^v; Geneva Bible, Ps. 91:11; Martin Luther, *Lectures on the Psalms 2,* ed. Hilton C. Oswald and trans. Herbert J. Bouman, in *Luther's Works,* gen. ed. Jaroslav Pelikan (St. Louis: Concordia, 1976), 11:107–08; William Perkins, *Workes,* 3:393.

51. For the same evidence with a different emphasis see Goldsmith, "The Muting of Satan," 131–36.

52. Thomas Wilson, *The Arte of Rhetorique* (London, 1553; facsimile reprint, Gainesville, Florida: Scholars' Facsimiles and Reprints, 1962), 9.

Notes to Chapter Three

1. Malcolm Ross, *Poetry and Dogma* (New Brunswick, N. J.: Rutgers University Press, 1954), 189. I am grateful to Medieval and Renaissance Texts and Studies for their permission to reprint in chapter 3 an altered version of "'That Sovran Book': The Discipline of the Word in Milton's Anti-Episcopal Tracts," in *Of Poetry and Politics: New Essays on Milton and His World,* ed. P. G. Stanwood (Binghamton, N.Y.: Medieval and Renaissance Texts and Studies, 1994), 313–25.

2. This translation is from Merritt Hughes, ed., *John Milton,* 819.

3. A. S. P. Woodhouse, *The Poet and His Faith* (Chicago: University of Chicago Press, 1965), 105.

4. William Kerrigan, *The Prophetic Milton* (Charlottesville: University Press of Virginia, 1974), 41. For Milton's vocational development, see also John S. Hill, *Poet, Priest, and Prophet.* I am indebted

to both Hill and Kerrigan throughout this chapter, but I argue that prophecy occurs within a coherent ecclesiological context in Milton's works rather than in isolation.

5. Desiderius Erasmus, "The Antibarbarians," trans. Margaret Mann Phillips, in *The Collected Works of Erasmus* (Toronto: University of Toronto Press, 1978), 23:64.

6. John Calvin, *Institutes of the Christian Religion*, trans. Ford Lewis Battles and ed. John T. McNeill (Philadelphia: Westminster Press, 1960), 1:93 n. 1.

7. See the following: Henry Ainsworth, "A True Confession of the Faith . . . which we hir Maiesties Subjects, falsely called Brownists, doo hould towards God" (1596), in *The Creeds and Platforms of Congregationalism*, ed. Williston Walker (Philadelphia: Pilgrim Press, 1960), 65; Henry Jacob, *A Confession and Protestation of the Faith* (London, 1616), B4–B6; "The Cambridge Synod and Platform" (1648), in *The Creeds and Platforms of Congregationalism*, 211; "The Westminster Confession" (1646), in John H. Leith, ed., *Creeds of the Churches*, 3d ed. (Louisville: John Knox Press, 1982), 222–25; "The Savoy Declaration" (1658), in *The Creeds of Christendom*, ed. P. Schaff, 6th ed. (New York: Harper, 1877), 3:725.

8. See "The Savoy Declaration," 3:726, sec. 13–14. For a comprehensive view of the relationship between the Word and Spirit in Puritan theology, see Geoffrey Nuttall, *The Holy Spirit in Puritan Faith and Experience* (Oxford: Basil Blackwell, 1946).

9. John Goodwin, *Pleroma to Pneumatikon, or A Being Filled with the Spirit* (London, 1670), 240, 4, 3.

10. John Owen, "A Discourse Concerning Liturgies" (1661), in *The Works of John Owen*, 15:62, 65.

11. See William Erbery, *Testimony of William Erbery*, 4–8.

12. For a summary of the doctrines of poetic inspiration, see Kerrigan, *The Prophetic Milton*, 47–51.

13. Erasmus, "The Antibarbarians," 74. See also Charles Trinkaus, *In Our Image and Likeness*, 2:565.

14. Kerrigan, *The Prophetic Milton*, 47–54.

15. Bernard Weinberg, *The History of Literary Criticism in the Italian Renaissance* (Chicago: University of Chicago Press, 1961), 1:259–62, 347–48. See also Kerrigan, *The Prophetic Milton*, 47–61. For Plato's and Aristotle's views see the following: Plato, "Phaedrus," in *Plato: The Collected Dialogues*, ed. Edith Hamilton and Huntington Cairns, Bollingen Series 71 (Princeton: Princeton University Press, 1961), 491–92, 244a–245a; Aristotle, "Poetics," in *The Rhetoric and Poetics of Aristotle*, 222–26, 1447a–1448b.

16. For Castelvetro's suspicion of inspiration theories see his "The Poetics of Aristotle Translated and Annotated," in *Literary Criticism: Plato to Dryden*, ed. Allan H. Gilbert (New York: American

Book Company, 1940), 310–11. For Ben Jonson's view see *Timber: or Discoveries Made Upon Men and Matter* (1640–41), ed. Israel Gollancz (London: Dent, 1951), 116–19. See also Francis Bacon, "The Advancement of Learning" (1605) in *The Philosophical Works of Sir Francis Bacon*, ed. John Robertson (London: George Routledge and Sons, 1905), 88–89; and George Puttenham, *The Arte of English Poesie* (1589) (Menston: Scolar Press, 1968), 1.

17. Sir Philip Sidney, "The Defence of Poesie," 294.

18. Ibid., 296, 273.

19. Ibid., 270.

20. Stephen Gosson, "The Schoole of Abuse" (1579), in *Prose of the English Renaissance*, ed. J. W. Hebel et al. (New York: Appleton-Century-Crofts, 1952), 258–67.

21. See Courtland D. Baker, "Certain Religious Elements in the English Doctrine of the Inspired Poet During the Renaissance," *English Literary History* 6 (1939): 308–11. In his sermons Donne makes more strident claims. For example, he argues that "in a Sermon God speaks to the Congregation" even though he distinguishes between the "spirit of the Minister" and "the spirit of God." Cited in P. G. Stanwood and Heather Ross Asals, eds., *John Donne and the Theology of Language* (Columbia: University of Missouri Press, 1986), 39, 13. Cf. also 59, 63.

22. Joshua Sylvester, trans., *Du Bartas His Divine Weekes and Works*, 4th ed. (London, 1613), 1.

23. Baker, "Certain Religious Elements," 315.

24. Ibid., 311, 319, 321.

25. Kerrigan confirms that the devaluation of inspiration in critical theory of the late seventeenth century was due to its association with the Puritan preachers. See Kerrigan, *The Prophetic Milton*, 70–71.

26. William D'Avenant, "The Author's Preface to his much honour'd friend, Mr. Hobbes," in *The Works of Sr. William D'Avenant* (London, 1673), 10.

27. Ibid.

28. Ibid.

29. Thomas Hobbes, "The Answer of Mr. Hobbes to Sir William D'Avenant's Preface Before *Gondibert*," in *The Works of Sr. William Davenant* (London, 1673), 23.

30. Abraham Cowley, *Davideis* (1656), in *The Works of Mr. Abraham Cowley* (London, 1668), 24.

31. Samuel Butler, *Hudibras* (London, 1663).

32. As early as the second half of the sixteenth century, however, Protestant poets such as D'Aubigne in France were asserting their independent authority. See Daniel Menanger, "Calvin et d'Aubigne: vocation prophetique et vocation poetique,"*Renaissance and Reformation* 11 (1987): 24.

33. Giovanni Boccacio, "The Life of Dante" (1363–64), in *Literary Criticism: Plato to Dryden*, ed. Allan Gilbert (New York: American Book Company, 1940), 208; cf. Castelvetro, "The Poetics of Aristotle," 310–11.

34. Poetry and prophecy also had common etymological origins as Sidney and many others pointed out. See Sidney, "The Defence of Poesie," 270.

35. See William Perkins, "A Treatise of Vocations," in *Workes*, 1:760. Cf. *Christian Doctrine, CPW* 6:455.

36. According to Article 34 of the 1604 ecclesiastical canons, a priest had to be "four and twenty years complete" before taking orders. Milton was eligible in December 1632, just months after completing his M. A. His decision to postpone ordination until his private studies were complete is not a sign of his rejection of the ministry but of his serious attitude toward it. See Hill, *Poet, Priest, and Prophet*, 28–49.

37. William Prynne, *Lord Bishops None of the Lords bishops* (London, 1640), 66; Edmund Calamy, *Gods Free Mercy to England* (London, 1642), 2, cited in Hill, *Poet, Priest, and Prophet*, 91.

38. Louis Martz, "Milton's Prophetic Voice: Moving Toward Paradise," in *Of Poetry and Politics: New Essays on Milton and his World*, ed. P. G. Stanwood (Binghamton, N. Y.: Medieval & Renaissance Texts & Studies, 1994), 5–6.

39. Kerrigan, *The Prophetic Milton*, 11–46 passim.

40. For further references to divine inspiration in Milton's prose see the following: *First Defence, CPW* 4:1.536; *Second Defence, CPW* 4:1.557, 590; *Defence of Himself, CPW* 4:2.735; *Hirelings, CPW* 7:278.

41. Recent critical discussions of Milton's references to prophecy, influenced by new historical preoccupations with self-fashioning, often emphasize Milton's prophetic "stance," "posture," or "strategy," as if he refers to the prophets only to get the upper hand in an argument. For an example of this tendency in Milton criticism, see Reuben Sanchez, "From Polemic to Prophecy: Milton's Uses of Jeremiah in *The Reason of Church Government* and *The Readie and Easie Way*," in *Milton Studies* 30 (1993): 27–44.

42. Hill, *Poet, Priest, and Prophet*, 106–13.

43. See Richard Hooker, *Of the Laws of Ecclesiastical Polity: Preface, Books I to IV*, ed. Georges Edelen, in *The Folger Library Edition of the Works of Richard Hooker* (Cambridge: Belknap Press of Harvard University Press, 1977), 1:151–71. See also Jeremy Taylor, *The Liberty of Prophesying* (London, 1647), 170–71.

44. See Erbery, *Testimony of William Erbery*, 21, 4.

45. Leith, ed., "The Westminster Confession," 217–18, 227–28, 224, 195–96.

46. Schaff, ed., "The Savoy Declaration," 724; Owen, "A Discourse Concerning Liturgies," 65–67; "The Savoy Declaration," 724, 726, 725.

47. See Robert Funk, *Language, Hermeneutic, and Word of God* (New York: Harper and Row, 1966), 140.

48. See J. B. Webster, *Eberhard Jungel, An Introduction to his Theology* (Cambridge: Cambridge University Press, 1986), 8; and Eberhard Jungel, *Theological Essays,* trans. and ed. J. B. Webster (Edinburgh: T. & T. Clark, 1989), 16–94.

49. For the concept of *kenosis* see Phil. 2:7 and *The Christian Doctrine, CPW* 6:419, 438; *CE* 15:261, 303–07.

50. The source of the shepherd/flock image is biblical but see also Richard Baxter, *The Reformed Pastor,* ed. Hugh Martin (London: SCM Press, 1956), 50, 57, 61–71. Baxter emphasizes that "every minister should be a man that hath much insight into the Tempter's wiles."

51. See Howard Schultz, *Milton and Forbidden Knowledge* (New York: MLA, 1955; reprint, New York: Kraus Reprint Co., 1970), 184–226; and Barbara K. Lewalski, "Milton on Learning and the Learned-Ministry Controversy," *Huntington Library Quarterly* 24 (1961): 267–81. I discuss this issue in more detail in chapter 5.

52. H. R. MacCallum, "Jesus as Teacher in *Paradise Regained,*" 135–51.

53. Although most clergy agreed that, by the time of Elizabeth's reign, the Church of England's doctrine was sufficiently reformed, the discipline of the church still came under attack from the 1550s onward. The Puritan critique of discipline developed through four phases: the critique of vestments and images (1550, 1563–1568), government (1572–1600), ceremonies (1603–1638), and episcopal jurisdiction (1638–1644). Although aspects of each phase are present in the others, sufficient thematic emphasis exists at each stage to justify these generalizations. For a more detailed discussion of the two reformations of the church see Patrick Collinson, *From Iconoclasm to Iconophobia: The Cultural Impact of the Second English Reformation* (Reading: University of Reading Press, 1986) and "With a small 'r'," *The Times Literary Supplement,* 22 October 1993, 14–15. According to W. J. Torrance Kirby, Richard Hooker argued that Puritan theologians such as Thomas Cartwright and Walter Travers violated the ecclesiological doctrine of the magisterial reformers, especially Calvin, when they insisted that discipline was a sign, with the Word and sacraments, of the true church and was prescribed in Scripture. See *Richard Hooker's Doctrine of the Royal Supremacy* (Leiden: Brill, 1990), 80–89. The Puritans failed to distinguish carefully enough between the internal and external kingdoms of Christ, pillars of orthodox Reformed ecclesiology, and ended up "spirtualising . . . the external Church" (79).

54. The general details of Milton's participation in the Smectym-nuuan controversy are outlined by D. M. Wolfe in *CPW* 1:76–86, 107–28.

55. Arthur Barker, *Milton and the Puritan Dilemma*, 17; Stanley Fish, *Self-Consuming Artifacts: The Experience of Seventeenth-Century Literature* (Berkeley: University of California Press, 1972), 270.

56. Keith Stavely, *The Politics of Milton's Prose Style* (New Haven: Yale University Press, 1975), 29.

57. See William B. Hunter, "Milton and the Presbyterians," in *The Descent of Urania: Studies in Milton, 1946–1988* (London and Toronto: Associated University Presses, 1989), 93–95. Milton's Presbyterianism is general enough to be shared by Congregationalists and Independents within the Church of England in the early 1640s. See also the following: George Yule, *The Independents in the English Civil War* (Cambridge: Cambridge University Press, 1958), 12; C. G. Bolam and Jeremy Goring, *The English Presbyterians* (London: Allen and Unwin, 1968), 40; Murray Tolmie, *The Triumph of the Saints: The Separate Churches in London, 1616–1644* (Cambridge: Cambridge University Press, 1977), 116.

58. For a concise analysis of church discipline in the Jacobean and Caroline periods see J. P. Somerville, *Politics and Ideology in England, 1603–1640* (London: Longman, 1986), 189–240. See also Kirby, *Richard Hooker's Doctrine of the Royal Supremacy*, 80–89.

59. *OED*, s.v. discipline.

60. See Calvin, *Institutes*, 2:1232.

61. Richard Hooker used similar imagery when he argued that "in harmonie the verie image and character even of virtue and vice is perceived." Richard Hooker, *Of the Laws of Ecclesiastical Polity: Book V*, ed. W. Speed Hill, 2:151 (5.16.8). See also Hooker, *Of the Laws of Ecclesiastical Polity: Preface, Books I to IV*, ed. Edelen, 1:142 (1.16.8). Despite their different views of discipline, Milton and Hooker both used these images of music, possibly because of the common influence of Plato, to convey the individual's embodiment of the natural law.

62. Arnold Stein, *Heroic Knowledge* (Minneapolis: University of Minnesota Press, 1957), 17–35.

63. Ibid., 28.

64. For the theme of Jesus' self-kingship see Lewalski, *Milton's Brief Epic*, 219–55.

Notes to Chapter Four

1. Edward Muir, *Ritual in Early Modern Europe* (Cambridge: Cambridge University Press, 1997), 7. On ritual in this period see also John Bossy, *Christianity in the West, 1400–1700* (Oxford: Oxford

University Press, 1985); John Bossy, "Blood and Baptism: Kinship, Community and Christianity in Western Europe from the Fourteenth to the Seventeenth Centuries," in *Sanctity and Secularity: The Church and the World*, ed. D. Baker (Oxford: Blackwell, 1973), 129–43; Peter Burke, "The Repudiation of Ritual in Early Modern Europe," in *The Historical Anthropology of Early Modern Italy: Essays on Perception and Communication* (Cambridge: Cambridge University Press, 1987), 223–38; David Cressy, *Birth, Marriage, and Death: Ritual, Religion, and the Life-Cycle in Tudor and Stuart England* (Oxford: Oxford University Press, 1997); John Harper, *The Forms and Orders of Western Liturgy from the Tenth to the Eighteenth Century* (Oxford: Clarendon Press, 1991); David I. Kertzer, *Ritual, Politics, and Power* (New Haven: Yale University Press, 1988); and R. W. Scribner, *Popular Culture and Popular Movements in Reformation Germany* (London: Hambleton, 1987). I use "ritual" to refer to all forms of symbolic actions, both verbal and nonverbal, sacred and secular which, when repeated, unite a group of people in a common purpose. A "liturgy" is a form of public, Christian ritual sanctioned by a specific church for the worship of God, while a "rite" is a specific liturgical ritual such as baptism. For ritual theory and the problem of definition, see Catherine Bell, *Ritual Theory, Ritual Practice* (Oxford: Oxford University Press, 1992); Ronald L. Grimes, *Ritual Criticism: Case Studies in Its Practice, Essays on Its Theory* (Columbia: University of South Carolina Press, 1990); and Ronald L. Grimes, *Beginnings in Ritual Studies*, rev. ed. (Columbia: University of South Carolina Press, 1995). I am grateful to Benwell-Atkins Press for permission to reprint in this chapter a slightly different version of "The Rituals of Presence in *Paradise Regained*," in *Wrestling with God: Literature and Theology in the English Renaissance*, ed. M. Henley and W. Speed Hill, and assisted by R. G. Siemens (Vancouver: Benwell-Atkins, 2000), 213–32.

2. Thomas Greene, "Ritual and Text in the Renaissance," *Canadian Review of Comparative Literature* 19, no. 2 (1992): 195. See also Muir, *Ritual in Early Modern Europe*, 186.

3. Muir, *Ritual in Early Modern Europe*, 8.

4. For Mircea Eliade, religion consists of just this human response, in the form of rituals and sacred objects, to the manifestation of the sacred in the world. See *Patterns of Comparative Religion* (New York: Harper and Row, 1958), 2.

5. Cressy, *Birth, Marriage, and Death*, 182, 189. See "Constitutions and Canons Ecclesiasticall" (1640) in *CPW* 1:990 for Laudian references to the Puritan emphasis on sermons in worship.

6. See Horton Davies, *Worship and Theology in England: From Andrewes to Baxter and Fox, 1603–1690* (Princeton: Princeton University Press, 1975); Horton Davies, *The English Free Churches*,

2d ed. (London: Oxford University Press, 1963); Horton Davies, *The Worship of the English Puritans* (Westminster: Dacre Press, 1948); Patrick Collinson, *From Iconoclasm to Iconophobia: the Cultural Impact of the Second English Reformation* (Reading: University of Reading Press, 1986); Bryan D. Spinks, *Freedom or Order? The Eucharistic Liturgy in English Congregationalism, 1645–1980* (Allison Park, Pa.: Pickwick Publications, 1984); Barker, *Milton and the Puritan Dilemma;* Christopher Hill, *Milton and the English Revolution* (London: Faber and Faber, 1977).

7. Muir, *Ritual in Early Modern Europe,* 181.

8. Ibid., 187; Scribner, *Popular Culture,* 51. Scribner refers to the German Reformation here, but a similar elevation of the Word can be seen in England much later as well.

9. Greene, "Ritual and Text," 192.

10. A. B. Chambers, *Transfigured Rites in Seventeenth-Century English Poetry* (Columbia: University of Missouri Press, 1992), 3–5, 126.

11. P. G. Stanwood, "Liturgy, Worship, and the Sons of Light," in *New Perspectives on the Seventeenth-Century English Religious Lyric,* ed. John R. Roberts (Columbia: University of Missouri Press, 1994), 123, 106.

12. Georgia Christopher refers to Milton as a "minimal mystic" in "The Secret Agent in *Paradise Regained,*" *Modern Language Quarterly* 41 (1980): 146. Christopher refers, as I do, to the quiet but important role played by the Holy Spirit in *Paradise Regained* and distinguishes Milton's views from those of the Ranters and Quakers, on the one hand, and the Cambridge Platonists, on the other. Her study of the Word as a sacrament in Milton's work is important too. See *Milton and the Science of the Saints* (Princeton: Princeton University Press, 1982).

13. Mircea Eliade, *The Myth of the Eternal Return,* trans. W. R. Trask (Princeton: Princeton University Press, 1954), 20–25, 35–36.

14. Thomas Goodwin et al., *An Apologetical Narration* (London, 1644), 12.

15. John Cotton, *The Way of the Churches of Christ in New England* (London, 1645), 66.

16. William Erbery, *The Testimony of William Erbery,* 272. According to Geoffrey Nuttall, the relationship between Word and Spirit dominated theological controversy in the 1650s as scriptural precedents were found for conflicting church polities and forms of worship. See *The Holy Spirit in Puritan Faith and Experience* (Oxford: Basil Blackwell, 1946), 28, 66–73.

17. As Secretary of Foreign Tongues, Milton was ordered to answer the "King's Book" on 15 March 1649. Milton assumes that the author of *Eikon Basilike* (1649) is King Charles but also suspects that someone

else might be responsible. The author was probably John Gauden, future bishop of Exeter and Worcester. For the textual history of *Eikon Basilike* and the occasion of *Eikonoklastes* see *CPW* 3:149–59.

18. See Desiderius Erasmus, "The Ciceronian: A Dialogue on the Ideal Latin Style" (1528), trans. Betty I. Knott, in *The Collected Works of Erasmus* (Toronto: University of Toronto Press, 1986), 28:407. Erasmus attacks the slavish imitators of Cicero and proposes constructive imitation in which models are used, not copied, to assist the natural genius of the author in adapting words to the subject and occasion of the speech in order to achieve eloquence, the principle of *decorum* underlying Cicero's own rhetorical theory. See Cicero, *De Oratore*, 2:31–211. Milton seems to echo Erasmus and Cicero, especially when Erasmus emphasizes that "a speech comes alive only if it rises from the heart, not if it floats on the lips." See Erasmus, *The Ciceronian*, 402. Milton's preference for the constructive, creative use of models is made explicit in *The Reason of Church Government* when he contrasts "the rules of Aristotle" with "nature . . . which in them that know art and use judgement, is no transgression but an enriching of art" (*CPW* 1:811). This is a clear example of rhetoric and theology, literature and liturgy, supporting each other. Just as God's Word is made eloquent by the Holy Spirit, so the human word is made eloquent by inspiration, the gift of the Holy Spirit. In fact, liturgy and literature are closely connected for Milton, although he would reject the term "liturgy," for the Holy Spirit is the true author of both. The eloquence of the Holy Spirit can be heard in preaching and prayer as well as poetry and prose. For the interplay of classical and Christian traditions of eloquence in Milton's prose I am indebted generally to Joseph A. Wittreich Jr., "The Crown of Eloquence: The Figure of the Orator in Milton's Prose," in *Achievements of the Left Hand: Essays on the Prose of John Milton*, ed. Michael Lieb and John Shawcross (Amherst: University of Massachusetts Press, 1974), 3–54.

19. The phrase is Edward Phillips's, Milton's nephew, student, and biographer, but Milton would have shared the sentiment. See "The Life of Milton," in *The Early Lives of Milton*, ed. Helen Darbishire (London: Constable, 1932), 69. The plain style of *Eikonoklastes* is a result of Milton's distrust of images, according to Corns, and his lack of confidence in his audience, according to Stavely. See Thomas Corns, *The Development of Milton's Prose Style* (Oxford: Oxford University Press, 1982), 57–65; Keith Stavely, *Politics of Milton's Prose Style*, 93–95.

20. *A Modest Confutation of A Slanderous and Scurrilous Libell, Entitled, Animadversions* (London, 1642), 2.

21. See the following for other examples of invocations in Milton's prose: *Second Defence*, *CPW* 4:1.553, 557 (thanksgiving); *CPW* 4:1.558

(petition); *Hirelings, CPW* 7:321 and *Second Defence, CPW* 4:1.587–88 (oaths); *Reason of Church Government, CPW* 1:820 and *Martin Bucer, CPW* 2:433 (vows). Interestingly, in *Second Defence, CPW* 4:1.587–88, Milton alludes to the prayer following the greeting in the *Book of Common Prayer.*

22. James F. White, *Protestant Worship: Tradition in Transition* (Louisville: Westminster/John Knox Press, 1989), 81.

23. The most detailed study is Lana Cable's *Carnal Rhetoric: Milton's Iconoclasm and the Poetics of Desire* (Durham, N.C.: Duke University Press, 1995). See my "'That Sovran Book': The Discipline of the Word in Milton's Anti-Episcopal Tracts," in *Of Poetry and Politics: New Essays on Milton and his World,* ed. P. G. Stanwood (Binghamton, N.Y.: Medieval and Renaissance Texts and Studies, 1995), 313–25.

24. Samuel Johnson, "Milton," in *Lives of the English Poets,* ed. G. B. Hill (Oxford: Clarendon Press, 1905), 1:92.

25. John Toland, "The Life of John Milton," in *The Early Lives of Milton,* 195. For evidence that Milton's family attended a particular church see W. R. Parker, *Milton: A Biography* (Oxford: Clarendon Press, 1968),1:651; 2:1091. See also Geoffrey F. Nuttall's intriguing suggestions about Milton's association with "a French church in Westminster" in 1659 in "Milton's Churchmanship in 1659: His Letter to Jean de Labadie," *Milton Quarterly* 35, no. 4 (December 2001): 227–31. I agree that *"De Doctrina Christiana* contains what reads remarkably like a blueprint for Congregational ecclesiology" (227), but I emphasize "like" because Milton's humanism and his poetic vocation influence his ecclesiology, distinguishing it from other Independent "blueprints." Nevertheless, he still could have been a member of this church, and worshipped with this congregation, since it appears he was charged with the responsibility of persuading Jean de Labadie to be its new minister.

26. William Ames, "Conscience with the Power and Cases Thereof," in *The Workes of the Reverend and Faithful Minister of Christ William Ames* (London, 1643), 4:39, 7–8, 62.

27. See Timothy C. Miller, "Milton's Religion of the Spirit and 'the state of the Church' in Book XII of *Paradise Lost," Restoration: Studies in English Literary Culture* 13 (Spring 1989): 7–16.

28. Christopher, "Secret Agent," 134.

29. Muir, *Ritual in Early Modern Europe,* 176.

30. Christopher, "Secret Agent," 135–36.

31. For the poem as a hermeneutic "Battle of the Book" see the following: Christopher, "Secret Agent," 131–50; Mary Ann Radzinowicz, *"Paradise Regained* as Hermeneutic Combat," *University of Hartford Studies in Literature* 16, no. 1 (1984): 99–107; James H. Sims, "Jesus and Satan as Readers of Scripture," 187–215.

32. Victor Turner, *The Ritual Process: Structure and Anti-Structure* (Chicago: Aldine Press, 1969). See also Arnold van Gennep, *The Rites of Passage*, trans. Monika B. Vizedom and Gabrielle L. Caffee (Chicago: University of Chicago Press, 1960).

33. See Horton Davies, *Worship and Theology in England*, 138–39, 287; Geoffrey Nuttall, *The Holy Spirit*, 98, 21–22.

34. See Lee Sheridan Cox, "Food-Word Imagery in *Paradise Regained*," *English Literary History* 28 (1961): 225–43.

35. According to Henry Ainsworth in the "seales of his Covenant . . . he inviteth all me[n] to his supper, his marriage feast." See *A True Confession* (1596), in *The Creeds and Platforms of Congregationalism*, 64–65. John Cotton defends sitting at the Lord's Table by claiming that it symbolizes how the Last Supper was administered and how the saints will sit "as cosessors with him at the last judgement." See *The Way of the Churches of Christ in New England* (London, 1645), 68. Neither of these figures writes in the free church tradition, but there was broad agreement on the meaning of the sacrament across the spectrum of Puritanism despite disagreement about polity and administration. For the eschatological dimension of the Eucharist see William R. Crockett, *Eucharist: Symbol of Transformation* (New York: Pueblo, 1989), 5–8, 206.

36. For the Reformed liturgies see Bard Thompson, *Liturgies of the Western Church* (Cleveland: World Publishing, 1961), 147–48, 197–202, 167–71, 245–300, 322–34, 356–67, 385–93. In the absence of guidelines for worship in the free church tradition, comparisons with this more conservative tradition should be made with caution, but considering that worship in the Spirit was often predictable, it is not impossible that Milton may have had some experience with a liturgy of this type. The liturgy of the Word could have been remembered from his worship in the Anglican church as well, or from occasional worship at St. Margaret's, the church of Parliament while he was Latin Secretary.

37. Thompson, *Liturgies of the Western Church*, 209.

38. A "gospel harmony" attempts to resolve all conflicting textual details about an event that is narrated in more than one gospel. See John Lightfoot, *A Harmony of the Gospels* (1654), in *The Works of John Lightfoot* (London, 1684).

39. Jackson Cope, "*Paradise Regained*: Inner Ritual," *Milton Studies* 1 (1969): 63.

40. Ashraf Rushdy, *The Empty Garden*, 193–94. See Mircea Eliade, *The Sacred and the Profane*, trans. W. R. Trask (San Diego: Harcourt Brace and Company, 1959), 68, 72.

41. Eliade, *Myth of Eternal Return*, 20–25, 35–36.

42. Chambers, *Transfigured Rites*, 132, 134.

43. See Schwartz, *Remembering and Repeating*, 6, 91–110.

44. For the view that there is no narrative progress in the poem, see Fish, "Inaction and Silence," 42. For the view that Jesus undergoes a process of self-definition, see Barbara Lewalski, *Milton's Brief Epic*, 162. I agree with Fish, not because Milton creates a text that consumes itself in order to disclose a Neoplatonic reality, but because repetition is meant to draw the reader into the ritual order of time.

Notes to Chapter Five

1. See the following: Augustine, *The City of God*, Books 17–22, trans. G. G. Walsh and Daniel J. Honan, in *The Fathers of the Church* (New York: The Fathers of the Church, 1954), 24:169; bk. 18, ch. 49; John Calvin, *Institutes*, 2:1022; bk. 4, ch. 1, pt. 7–8. Many thanks to Cambridge University Press for permission to reprint in this chapter an altered version of *"The Apocalypse in Paradise Regained,"* in *Milton and the Ends of Time*, ed. J. Cummins (Cambridge: Cambridge University Press, 2003), 202–23.

2. Richard Hooker, *Of the Laws of Ecclesiastical Polity: Preface, Books I–IV*, bk. 3 passim. According to Kirby, Hooker was defending the doctrine of the magisterial reformers when he claimed that the Elizabethan "Disciplinarians," like the separatists, made the mistake of spiritualizing the church. Their insistence that discipline was a necessary feature of a true church arose from their confusion of the "two realms" and the two churches, one internal, invisible, and governed by Christ, the other external, visible, and governed by people. See Kirby, *Hooker's Doctrine of the Royal Supremacy*, 62, 22, 56–57, 67–69. See also P. G. Stanwood, "Of Prelacy and Polity in Milton and Hooker," in *Heirs of Fame: Milton and Writers of the English Renaissance*, ed. Margo Swiss and David A. Kent (Lewisburg, PA: Bucknell University Press, 1995), 66–84.

3. John Cotton, *The Way of the Churches of Christ in New England* (London, 1645), 54–55, 1; Augustine, cited in Jaroslav Pelikan, *The Growth of Medieval Theology, 600–1300*, vol. 3 of *The Christian Tradition: A History of the Development of Doctrine*, (Chicago: University of Chicago Press, 1978), 303.

4. Calvin, *Institutes*, 2:1016, 1022.

5. Throughout this chapter "Apocalypse" refers primarily to the allegories, visions, and signs about the end of the world and the beginning of a new heaven and earth outlined in The Revelation of St. John the Divine 4–20 and the "little" apocalypses of Matthew 24, Mark 13, and Luke 21. The Bible also includes many different examples of the apocalyptic genre, including Daniel 7–12, several apocryphal works, and many texts like 2 Thessalonians 2 that include apocalyptic features. I use "apocalyptic" rather than "millennial" or "millenarian" to refer to Milton's views of the end of the world. See

John Shawcross, "Confusion: The Apocalypse, the Millennium," in *Milton and the Ends of Time*, 106–19. Essentially, Milton held a broadly apocalyptic view of history throughout his career and continued to refer to a literal Second Coming and reign of Christ even when Christ's imminence was unlikely, but remained circumspect about a 1,000 year reign of Christ and the saints preceding or separate from the Last Judgment.

6. J. L. Mackenzie, S. J., "Kingdom of God," 479. See also Kittel, *Theological Dictionary of the New Testament*, 1:583; C. H. Dodd, *The Parables of the Kingdom* (New York: Scribner's, 1961); and Robert Funk, *Language, Hermeneutic, and Word of God*, 140.

7. Kittel, *Theological Dictionary of the New Testament*, 1:589; Mackenzie, "Kingdom of God," 481.

8. Augustine, *City of God*, 24:265–66; bk. 20, ch. 7; Pelikan, *Medieval Theology*, 3:303–04.

9. See Howard Schultz, *Milton and Forbidden Knowledge* (New York: MLA, 1955; reprint, New York: Kraus Reprint Co., 1970), 228–35.

10. Calvin, *Institutes*, 2:911, 944, 1487.

11. Ibid., 2:1046, 1486, 1034.

12. Calvin, Preface to *Institutes*, 1:24.

13. Calvin, *Institutes*, 2:1485.

14. Ibid., 2:1487.

15. For an example of the Anabaptist position, see Leith, ed., "Schleitheim Confession" (1527), 287–88.

16. Leith, ed., "The Westminster Confession," 219–20. The Westminster divines also identify the visible church with the kingdom of Christ. See Leith, ed., "The Westminster Confession," 222.

17. Calvin, *Institutes*, 2:905.

18. Ibid.

19. Wilhelm Pauck, Introduction to "The Kingdom of Christ," in *Melanchthon and Bucer*, ed. and trans. W. Pauck and P. Larkin (Philadelphia: Westminster Press, 1969), 169.

20. Martin Bucer, "The Kingdom of Christ," in *Melanchthon and Bucer*, 384.

21. Ibid., 225.

22. Ibid., 384.

23. A. S. P. Woodhouse, Introduction to *Puritanism and Liberty*, 3d ed. (London: Dent, 1986), 33–35.

24. See Michael Fixler, *Milton and the Kingdoms of God*, 34–36. Walter Travers, for example, claimed that magistrates must "submitt themselves and be obedient to the just and lawfull authoritie off the Officers off the churche." See *A Full and Plaine Declaration of Ecclesiastical Discipline Out off the Word off God*, trans. Thomas

Cartwright (Zurich, 1574), 185. For the Presbyterian view during the 1640s, see the preface to Samuel Rutherford, *Lex, Rex: The Law and the Prince* (London, 1644), 8. Both Travers and Rutherford follow Calvin, *Institutes*, 2:1493–95; bk. 4, ch. 20, pt. 9.

25. Barbara Lewalski, "Milton: Political Beliefs and Polemical Methods, 1659–60," *PMLA* 74 (1959): 193–94. I am indebted to Lewalski's work throughout this section on Milton's view of the relationship between Christ's kingdom and the political order. See also Henry Archer, *The Personal Reign of Christ upon Earth* (London, 1642). The title "Fifth Monarchists" is derived from Daniel 2:44 and the belief that, after the "monarchies" of Assyria, Persia, Greece and Rome, the fifth monarchy, or the reign of Christ and his saints would begin and continue for 1,000 years. Some Fifth Monarchists also advocated the seizure of political power in anticipation of Christ's reign. See Christopher Hill, *Milton and the English Revolution* (London: Faber and Faber, 1979), 95.

26. See the following: Lewalski, "Milton," 194; Hill, *English Revolution*, 283–84; Barker, *Milton and the Puritan Dilemma*, 270–71.

27. Sirluck, Introduction to Vol. 2 of *CPW*, 176.

28. See Lewalski's summary of Woodhouse's view in Lewalski, "Milton," 200 n. 51.

29. For Owen's position see Austin Woolrych, Introduction to Vol. 7 of *The Complete Prose Works of John Milton* (New Haven: Yale University Press, 1980), 39–40, 44–45, 80.

30. Lewalski, "Milton," 200.

31. Lewalski, "Milton," 201.

32. Fixler, *Kingdoms of God*, 77–78.

33. Lewalski, "Milton," 191.

34. See Lewalski's summary of Sirluck's view of Milton's shifts in political allegiance in "Milton," 191.

35. Lewalski, "Milton," 192–98.

36. Fixler, "Ecclesiology," 2:190, 192.

37. I agree with Lewalski's view that for Milton religious liberty is "the most important good for the state to achieve." The shifts in Milton's political allegiances, then, are best understood as practical decisions based on "principle, not mere expediency." The question was what structure of political authority would best defend religious liberty at the time. See Lewalski, "Milton," 198, 202.

38. For the activism of Milton's apocalypticism and his view that the English people must be worthy of Christ's return see Janel Mueller, "Embodying Glory: The Apocalyptic Strain in Milton's *Of Reformation*," in *Politics, Poetics, and Hermeneutics in Milton's Prose*, ed. David Loewenstein and James Grantham Turner (Cambridge: Cambridge University Press, 1990), 10.

39. Fixler, *Kingdoms of God*, 217.

40. My brief synopsis is based on the following: B. W. Ball, *A Great Expectation: Eschatological Thought in English Protestantism to 1660* (Leiden: Brill, 1975); Bernard Capp, "The Political Dimension of Apocalyptic Thought," in *The Apocalypse in English Renaissance Thought and Literature*, ed. C.A. Patrides and Joseph Wittreich (Manchester: University of Manchester Press, 1984), 93–124; Norman Cohn, *Cosmos, Chaos and the World to Come: the Ancient Roots of Apocalyptic Faith* (New Haven: Yale University Press, 1993); Katharine R. Firth, *The Apocalyptic Tradition in Reformation Britain, 1530–1645* (Oxford: Oxford University Press, 1975); and Christopher Hill, *Antichrist in Seventeenth-Century England* (Oxford: Oxford University Press, 1971).

41. See Stella Revard's analysis of the link between politics and the Apocalypse throughout Milton's career in "Milton and Millenarianism: From the Nativity Ode to *Paradise Regained*," in *Milton and the Ends of Time*, ed. Juliet Cummins (Cambridge: Cambridge University Press, 2003), 42–81.

42. For further discussion of the wilderness image in Puritan texts, see Christopher Hill, *The Experience of Defeat: Milton and Some Contemporaries* (London: Faber and Faber, 1984), 47, 72, 77, 122–23, 300–03, 359; and William Haller, *The Rise of Puritanism* (New York: Columbia Univ. Press, 1938), 131. See also Samuel Smith, "'Christ's Victorie Over the Dragon': The Apocalypse in *Paradise Regained*," *Milton Studies* 24 (1993): 59–82. According to Smith, *Paradise Regained* and Thomas Taylor's *Christs Victorie Over the Dragon or Satans Downfall* (1633) share the apocalyptic subtext of the temptation and wilderness narrative, but the immediate political and religious contexts of the poem are not discussed.

43. John Diodati, *Pious Annotations*, D2.

44. See Revard's analysis of references to Daniel in *Paradise Regained* in "Milton and Millenarianism," 62–68.

45. John Bale, *The Image of Both Churches, Being an Exposition of the Most Wonderful Book of Revelation*, in *Select Works of John Bale* (Cambridge, 1849), 401–10, 252.

46. David Pareus, *A Commentary upon the Divine Revelation of the Apostle and Evangelist John*, trans. Elias Arnold (Amsterdam, 1644), 16, 266, 272, 275, 265, 272.

47. Diodati, *Pious Annotations*, Xxx4.

48. John Downame, et al., *Annotations*, Rev. 12:14–17. For Milton's references to the Waldenses as the true church hidden in the wilderness see *The Tenure of Kings and Magistrates* (*CPW* 3:227), *Eikonoklastes* (*CPW* 3:514) and *Considerations Touching the Likeliest Means to Remove Hirelings Out of the Church* (*CPW* 7:291, 306, 308, 311).

49. Thomas Taylor, *Christs Victorie Over the Dragon or Satans Downfall* (London, 1633), 293, 305.

50. Mary Cary, *The Little Horns Doom and Downfall* (London, 1651), 8, 39–41, 171.

51. Christopher Hill, *Antichrist,* passim. The many forms of Antichrist, however, are not merely matters of political expediency and rhetoric as Hill suggests.

52. See J. R. Knott, Jr., "'Suffering for Truth's Sake': Milton and Martyrdom," in *Politics, Poetics, and Hermeneutics in Milton's Prose,* ed. David Loewenstein and James Grantham Turner (Cambridge: Cambridge University Press, 1990), 153–70; and Mark Goldie, "The Theory of Religious Intolerance in Restoration England," in *From Persecution to Toleration,* ed. O. P. Grell, J. I. Israel, and N. Tyacke (Oxford: Oxford University Press, 1991), 332.

53. See Knoppers, *Historicizing Milton,* 110–15.

54. Ronald Hutton, *The Restoration* (Oxford: Oxford University Press, 1985), 156. See also John Spurr, *The Restoration Church of England, 1646–1689* (New Haven: Yale University Press, 1991), 39–72.

55. Hamilton, "*Paradise Regained* and the Private Houses," 241–42.

56. Hamilton, "*Paradise Regained* and the Private Houses," 244–45. The following were also published at about the same time as Parker's treatise: N. Estwick, *A Dialogue Betwixt a Conformist and a Non-conformist Concerning the Lawfulnes of Private Meetings* (London, 1668); Simon Patrick, *A Friendly Debate between a Conformist and a Nonconformist* (London, 1669), and *An Appendix to the Third Part of the Friendly Debate* (London, 1670); Roger L'Estrange, *Toleration Discuss'd* (London, 1670); and William Assheton, *Toleration Disapprov'd and Condemn'd* (London, 1670).

57. Goldie, "Theory of Religious Intolerance," 334.

58. According to Phillips, Milton prepared, but didn't publish, an answer to the "scribing Quack" who attacked him, and he may have had Butler or Parker in mind. Milton was set to engage in controversy after *Paradise Regained* was published, and quite possibly before, since he knew Parker personally and, therefore, might have taken a special interest in early editions of his *Ecclesiastical Politie.* See Parker, *Milton: A Biography,* 1:629–31. See also Lewalski, *The Life of John Milton,* 498–501; 696–97 n. 54–66.

59. See Knott, "Suffering for Truth's Sake," 159–64.

60. See Keith W. F. Stavely, Preface to *Of True Religion,* in *CPW* 8:410–12, 418.

61. Samuel Parker, Preface to *Bishop Bramhall's Vindication of Himself and the Episcopal Clergy, from the Presbyterian Charge of Popery* (London, 1672), e2. Parker's preface has a separate title, *A*

Preface Shewing what Grounds there are of fears and Jealousies of Popery.

62. Lewalski, *Milton's Brief Epic*, 227, 257.

63. See Simon Patrick, *A Friendly Debate between a Conformist and a Non-Conformist;* and Samuel Butler, *Hudibras* (London, 1663), 1.1.221–28. See also Howard Schultz, "Christ and Antichrist in *Paradise Regained,*" *PMLA* 67 (1952): 798.

64. Loewenstein, *Representing Revolution,* 249. See also Schultz, "Christ and Antichrist," 799.

65. For a similar argument with a different emphasis see Michael Fixler, "The Unclean Meats of the Mosaic Law and the Banquet Scene in *Paradise Regained,*" *MLN* 70 (1955): 573–77.

66. MacCallum, "Jesus as Teacher," 135–51. MacCallum emphasizes Jesus' use of contraries as a teaching method in the poem.

67. Lewalski, *Milton's Brief Epic,* 268–69.

68. Revard, "Milton and Millenarianism," 65–66.

69. Loewenstein, *Representing Revolution,* 250.

70. See Revard, "Milton and Millenarianism," 66–68.

71. The eschatological dimension of the Eucharist is based on Luke 14:15–24, 13:29, Matthew 8:11, Mark 14:25 and other texts, including several parables of the kingdom. For further discussion see William R. Crockett, *Eucharist: Symbol of Transformation* (New York: Pueblo, 1989), 5–8, 206; and Davies, *Worship and Theology in England,* 13, 208, 323, 415.

72. Thompson, *Liturgies of the Western Church,* 369–70.

73. John Gadbury, *De Cometis* (London, 1665), 13.

74. Bernard S. Capp, *Astrology and the Popular Press* (London: Faber and Faber, 1979), 170. For the popularity of almanacs see Keith Thomas, *Religion and the Decline of Magic* (Harmondsworth: Penguin, 1971), 360–61.

75. Cited in Capp, *Astrology,* 168.

76. John Booker, *The Bloudy Almanack, for this present Jubilee* (London, 1647), frontispiece, 3. For Napier's views see Revard, "Milton and Millenarianism," 43–44.

77. Ann Geneva, *Astrology and the Seventeenth-Century Mind: William Lilly and the Language of the Stars* (Manchester: Manchester University Press, 1995), 56, and William Lilly, *England's Propheticall Merlin* (London, 1644), 25, 44.

78. Capp, *Astrology,* 164–65.

79. Nicholas Culpepper, *Catastrophe Magnatum: or, The Fall of Monarchie* (London, 1652), 68, 40; John Durant, *A Set Time for Judgement* (London, 1656), cited in Ball, *A Great Expectation,* 110.

80. In addition to remembering the comets of 1660, 1664, 1665, and 1667, some readers might have recalled a "fiery dragon," a type of comet known to be especially menacing because of its long tail,

seen 15/16 November 1656. See *Miraculum Signum Coeleste: A Discourse of Those Miraculous Prodigies that have been seen since the Birth of our blessed Lord and Saviour Jesus Christ* (London, 1658), 24–25. See also *Samson Agonistes*, line 1692 for a similar image of scriptural and astrological judgment.

81. Cited in *Miraculum Signum Coeleste*, 23; John Gadbury, *Natura Prodigiorum: or, A Discourse Touching the Nature of Prodigies* (London, 1665), 38; and Samuel Danforth, *An Astronomical Description of the Late Comet or Blazing Star* (London, 1666), frontispiece.

82. *Mr Lillyes Prognostications of 1667* (London, 1667), 1; Vincent Wing, *An Almanack and Prognostication for the Year of Our Lord, 1670* (London, 1669), C2; *The Bloody Almanack For the Year, 1666. And the Fiery Trigon* (London, 1666), 4–5; and William Lilly, *Astrological Judgements for the Year 1668* (London, 1667), A3–A4.

83. *Mirabilis Annus, or The Year of Prodigies and Wonders* (London, 1661), A4v.

84. Thomas, *Decline of Magic*, 409, 501.

85. Gadbury, *De Cometis*, 18.

86. William Lilly, *Astrological Judgements, 1668*, A3; Capp, *Astrology*, 48.

87. Capp, *Astrology*, 173–74.

88. Thomas Trigge, *Calendarium Astrologicum: or, an Almanack For . . . 1666* (London, 1666), C2.

89. *The Bloody Almanack*, 4.

90. *King Charles his Starre* (London, 1654), 4, 35, 36.

91. John Gadbury, *Britains Royal Star* (London, 1660), 41.

92. S. D., *The Blazing Star: or, A Discourse of Comets* (London, 1665), 12–13, 42.

93. *The Blazing Star: or, A Discourse of Comets* (London, 1664), 5.

94. John Spencer, *A Discourse of Prodigies* (Cambridge, 1665), 16, 102.

95. *Mirabilis Annus*, 26, 37, 16, 18, 69.

96. See John Allen, *Cases of Conscience Concerning Astrologie* (London, 1659), 8; John Spencer, A *Discourse of Prodigies*, 20.

97. Christopher Ness, *A Full and True Account of the Late Blazing Star* (London, 1680), 7.

98. See David Gay, "Astrology and Iconoclasm in Milton's *Paradise Regained*," *Studies in English Literature* 41 (2001): 181. Gay explores a different astrological phenomenon — the appearance of "Charles Wain" at the birth of Charles II — but also shows how it was used by Royalists to construct Charles's identity as David before and during the Restoration.

99. Georgia Christopher, "The Secret Agent in *Paradise Regained*,"

Modern Language Quarterly 41 (1980): 131, and Mary Ann Radzinowicz, *Milton's Epics and the Book of Psalms* (Princeton: Princeton University Press, 1989), 26.

100. For the suggestion that defeat and persecution were conditions that consolidated Nonconformist literature and culture, see Neil Keeble, *The Literary Culture of Nonconformity in Later Seventeeth-Century England* (Athens: University of Georgia Press, 1987). Keeble also suggests that for Nonconformists, writing was crucial in forming a collective identity during the Restoration, and Milton's literary ecclesiology in *Paradise Regained* confirms this. See Keeble, *Literary Culture*, vii.

BIBLIOGRAPHY

Editions of Milton's Works

Milton's English prose is cited from *The Complete Prose Works of John Milton,* ed. D. Wolfe, et al., 8 vols. (New Haven: Yale University Press, 1953–1982). When appropriate, Milton's Latin prose is cited from *The Works of John Milton,* ed. Frank A. Patterson, et al., 20 vols. (New York: Columbia University Press, 1931–1940). References in parentheses will include the abbreviated title, volume, and page number of the Yale edition (*CPW*). In some cases, the reference to the Yale edition is followed by a reference to the Columbia edition (*CE*) as in the following example: (*Christian Doctrine, CPW* 6:124; *CE* 14:12). Milton's poetry is cited from Merritt Hughes, ed., *John Milton: Complete Poems and Major Prose* (Indianapolis: Odyssey Press, 1957).

Editions of the Bible

The Bible and Holy Scriptures Conteyned in the Olde and Newe Testaments. Geneva Bible, 1560. Facsimile reprint, Madison: University of Wisconsin Press, 1969.

Biblia Sacra Polyglotta . . . Edidit Brianus Waltonus. 6 vols. London, 1657.

Biblia sacra, sive, Testamentum Vetus ab Im. Tremellio & Fr. Junio . . . et Testamentum Novum a Theod. Beza e Graeco in Latinum vers. London, 1656.

The Holy Bible [King James Version]. Nashville: Thomas Nelson, 1984.
The Holy Bible, Containing the Old and New Testaments. [King James Version]. London: Robert Barker, 1612.
The New Oxford Annotated Bible With the Apocrypha. [Revised Standard Version]. Ed. Herbert G. May and B. M. Metzger. New York: Oxford University Press, 1977.

Primary Sources

A Declaration of Several of the Churches of Christ . . . Concerning the Kingly Interest of Christ. London, 1654.
Ainsworth, Henry. *The Communion of Saints.* Amsterdam, 1607.
Allen, John. *Cases of Conscience Concerning Astrologie.* London, 1659.
Ames, William. *The Marrow of Sacred Divinity.* London, 1642.
———. *The Workes of . . . William Ames.* London, 1643.
Andrewes, Lancelot. *Ninety-Six Sermons.* 5 vols. Oxford: Parker, 1861–1863.
Archer, John. *The Personal Reign of Christ upon Earth.* London, 1642.
Aristotle. *The Rhetoric and the Poetics of Aristotle.* Trans. W. R. Roberts and I. Bywater. New York: Random House, 1954.
Aspinwall, William. *A Brief Description of the Fifth Monarchy.* London, 1653.
Assheton, William. *Toleration Disapprov'd and Condemn'd.* London, 1670.
Augustine, St. *The City of God*, Books 17–22. *The Fathers of the Church.* Trans. G. G. Walsh and Daniel J. Honan. Vol. 24. New York: Fathers of the Church, 1954.
———. *De Doctrina Christiana. Corpus Christianorum Series Latina.* Ed. J. Martin. Vol. 32. Turnhout: Brepols, 1962.
———. *On Christian Doctrine.* Trans. D. W. Robertson, Jr. New York: Macmillan, 1958.
Bacon, Francis. *The Philosophical Works of Francis Bacon.* Ed. John Robertson. London: Routledge and Sons, 1905.
Baillie, Robert. *A Dissuasive from the Errours of the Time.* London, 1645.
Bale, John. *The Image of Both Churches, Being an Exposition of the Most Wonderful Book of Revelation.* In *Select Works of John Bale.* Cambridge, 1849.
Barclay, Robert. *An Apology for the True Christian Divinity . . . [of the] Quakers.* London, 1678.
Barton, John. *The Art of Rhetorick Concisely and Compleatly Handled, Exemplified out of Holy Writ.* London, 1634.
Baxter, Richard. *An Apology for the Nonconformist Ministry.* London, 1668.

———. *A Holy Commonwealth*. London, 1659.

———. *The Reformed Pastor*. Ed. Hugh Martin. London: SCM Press, 1956.

Beard, Thomas. *The Theatre of Gods Judgements*. London, 1631.

Benbrigge, John. *God's Fury, England's Fire*. London, 1646.

Bilson, Thomas. *The Perpetual Government of Christes Church*. London, 1593.

The Blazing Star: or, A Discourse of Comets. London, 1664.

The Bloody Almanack For the Year 1666, And the Fiery Trigon. London, 1666.

Blount, Thomas. *The Academie of Eloquence*. London, 1654.

———. *Rhetorick Restrained*. London, 1660.

Bolton, Robert. *The Saints Sure and Perpetuall Guide. Or, A Treatise Concerning the Word*. London, 1634.

The Book of Common Prayer, 1559. Ed. John Booty. Charlottesville: University Press of Virginia, 1976.

Booker, John. *The Bloudy Almanack, for this present Jubilee. . . .* London, 1647.

Bramhall, John. *Bishop Bramhall's Vindication of Himself and the Episcopal Clergy, from the Presbyterian Charge of Popery*. London, 1672.

Brightman, Thomas. *A Revelation of the Revelation*. Amsterdam, 1615.

Britten, William. *Silent Meeting, A Wonder to the World*. London, 1660.

Bucer, Martin. *The Kingdom of Christ*. In *Melanchthon and Bucer*. Ed. Wilhelm Pauck and trans. W. Pauck and P. Larkin. Philadelphia: Westminster Press, 1969.

Bullinger, Heinrich. *A Most Godly and Learned Discourse of the Worthynesse, Authoritie, and Sufficiencie of the Holy Scripture*. Trans. J. Tomkys. London, 1557.

———. *Of the Holy Catholic Church*. In *Zwingli and Bullinger*. Ed. and trans. G. W. Bromiley. Philadelphia: Westminster Press, 1953.

Burroughs, Jeremiah. *The Excellency Of a Gracious Spirit*. London, 1638.

Burton, Henry. *The Protestation Protested*. London, 1641.

———. *A Vindication of Churches, Commonly Called Independent*. London, 1644.

Butler, Samuel. *Hudibras. The First Part. Written in the time of the late Wars*. London, 1663.

———. *Hudibras. The Second Part*. London, 1664.

———. *Hudibras. The Third and last Part*. London, 1678.

Byfield, Nicholas. *Directions for the Privat Reading of the Scriptures*. London, 1618.

Cabala, or, an Impartial Account of the Non-conformists Private

Designs, Actings, and Ways. From August 24, 1662 to December 25 in the same year. London, 1663.

Calvin, John. *Calvin: Commentaries*. Ed. and trans. Louise P. Smith and Joseph Haroutunian. Philadelphia: Westminster Press, 1958.

———. *The Gospel According to St. John, 1–10*. Ed. D. W. Torrance and T. F. Torrance and trans. T. H. L. Parker. Edinburgh: Oliver and Boyd, 1959.

———. *A Harmony of the Gospels: Matthew, Mark, and Luke*. Ed. D. W. Torrance and T. F. Torrance and trans. A. W. Morrison. 3 vols. Grand Rapids: Eerdmans, 1972.

———. *Institutes of the Christian Religion*. Ed. John T. McNeill and trans. Ford Lewis Battles. 2 vols. Philadelphia: Westminster Press, 1960.

Canne, John. *The Time of the End*. London, 1657.

Cartwright, Thomas. *A Replye to An Answer Made of M. Doctor Whitgifte. Agaynste the Admonition*. Wandsworth [?], 1574.

Cary, Mary. *The Little Horns Doom and Downfall*. London, 1651.

Chappell, William. *The Preacher, Or the Art and Method of Preaching*. London, 1656.

Cicero. *De Oratore*. Trans. E. W. Sutton and H. Rackam. 2 vols. Cambridge: Harvard University Press, 1942.

Cosin, John. *A Collection of Private Devotions*. Ed. P. G. Stanwood. Oxford: Clarendon Press, 1967.

Cotton, John. *The True Constitution of A Particular Visible Church*. London, 1642.

———. *The Way of the Churches of Christ in New England*. London, 1645.

Cowley, Abraham. *The Works of Mr. Abraham Cowley*. London, 1668.

Craddock, Walter. *Gospel-Libertie*. London, 1655.

Crisp, Samuel. *An Epistle to Friends, Concerning the Present and Succeeding Times*. London, 1666.

Culpepper, Nicholas. *Catastrophe Magnatum: or, The Fall of Monarchie*. London, 1652.

Danforth, Samuel. *An Astronomical Description of the Late Comet or Blazing Star*. London, 1666.

D'Avenant, Sir William. *The Works of Sr. William Davenant*. London, 1673.

Dell, William. *The City-Ministers Unmasked*. London, 1649.

———. *The Tryall of Spirits Both in Teachers & Hearers . . . With a Brief Testimony Against Divinity Degrees in the Universities . . . .* London, 1699.

Diodati, John. *Pious Annotations of the Holy Bible*. 3d ed. London, 1651.

Dolittle, Thomas. *A Treatise Concerning the Lord's Supper*. London, 1665.

Donne, John. *The Complete Poetry*. Ed. John T. Shawcross. Garden City, N. Y.: Doubleday, 1967.

Downame, John et al. *Annotations Upon All the Books of the Old and New Testament*. 2d ed. London, 1645.

Dryden, John. *Annus Mirabilis: The Year of Wonders 1666*. London, 1667.

———. *Astrea Redux: A Poem on the Happy Restoration and Return of his Sacred Majesty Charles the Second*. London, 1660.

Eachard, John. *The Grounds & Occasions of the Contempt of the Clergy and Religion*. London, 1670.

Edwards, Thomas. *Gangraena*. London, 1646.

———. *Reasons Against the Independent Government of Particular Churches*. London, 1641.

Eikon Basilike. Ed. Philip A. Knachel. Folger Library Edition. Ithaca: Cornell University Press, 1966.

Ellwood, Thomas. *The History of the Life of Thomas Ellwood*. London, 1714.

Erasmus, Desiderius. *The Antibarbarians. The Collected Works of Erasmus*. Trans. R. A. B. Mynours and ed. C. R. Thompson. Vol. 23. Toronto: University of Toronto Press, 1978.

———. *The Ciceronian. The Collected Works of Erasmus*. Trans. B. I. Knott and ed. C. R. Thompson. Vol. 26. Toronto: University of Toronto Press, 1986.

———. *Copia: Foundation of the Abundant Style. The Collected Works of Erasmus*. Trans. B. I. Knott and ed. C. R. Thompson. Vol. 24. Toronto: University of Toronto Press, 1978.

———. *Desiderii Erasmi Roterdami Opera Omnia*. Ed. J. Leclerc. 10 vols. Leiden, 1705; rpt. London: Gregg Press, 1962.

———. *The first tome or volume of the Paraphrase of Erasmus upon the Newe Testamente*. London, 1548.

———. *On the Method of Study. The Collected Works of Erasmus*. Trans. B. McGregor and ed. C. R. Thompson. Vol. 24. Toronto: University of Toronto Press, 1978.

———. *Paraphrase on John. The Collected Works of Erasmus*. Trans. Jane E. Phillips and gen. ed. Robert D. Sider. Vol. 46. Toronto: University of Toronto Press, 1991.

———. *The Tongue. The Collected Works of Erasmus*. Trans. Elaine Fantham and ed. C. R. Thompson. Vol. 29. Toronto: University of Toronto Press, 1974.

Erbery, William. *The Testimony of William Erbery*. London, 1658.

Estwick, Nicolas. *A Dialogue Betwixt a Conformist and a Non-conformist Concerning the Lawfulnes of Private Meetings in the Time of Publick Ordinances. . . .* London, 1668.

Farnsworth, Richard. *The Spirit of God Speaking in the Temple of God*. London, 1663.

Feake, Christopher. *The Fifth Monarchy, or Kingdom of Christ, in Opposition to the Beast's, asserted.* London, 1659.

Featley, Daniel. *The Embleme of the Church Militant.* In *Clavis Mystica: A Key Opening Divers Difficult and Mysterious Texts of Holy Scripture.* London, 1636.

Fenner, Dudley. *The Artes of Logike and Rethorike.* . . . Middelburg, 1584.

Field, John and Thomas Wilcox. *An Admonition to Parliament.* London, 1572.

Firth, C. H. and R. S. Rait, eds. *Acts and Ordinances of the Interregnum, 1642–1660.* 3 vols. London, 1911.

Fisher, Samuel. *Rusticus Ad Academicos in Exercitationibus Expostulatriis. Apologeticis Quator. The Rustics Alarm to the Rabbies.* London, 1660.

Fox, George. *The Journal of George Fox.* Ed. Norman Penney. Toronto: J. M. Dent, 1924.

Foxe, John. *Acts and Monuments.* 7th ed. London, 1641.

Fulke, William. *The Text of the New Testament of Jesus Christ Translated out of the Vulgar Latin by the Papists . . . of Rheims. With Arguments of Books, Chapters, and Annotations.* London, 1601.

Gadbury, John. *Britains Royal Star.* London, 1660.

——. *De Cometis.* London, 1665.

——. *Natura Prodigiorum: or, A Discourse Touching the Nature of Prodigies.* London, 1665.

Gilbert, Alan, ed. *Literary Criticism: Plato to Dryden.* New York: American Book Company, 1940.

Goodwin, John. *The Divine Authority of the Scriptures Asserted.* London, 1648.

——. *Pleroma to Pneumatikon, or A Being Filled with the Spirit.* London, 1670.

——. *Right and Might Well Met.* London, 1644.

Goodwin, Thomas et al. *An Apologeticall Narration.* London, 1643.

——. *A Glimpse of Sions Glory.* London, 1641.

Granger, Thomas. *The Application of Scripture. Or, The Maner How to Use the Word to most Edifying.* London, 1616.

Hall, Joseph. *Episcopacie by Divine Right Asserted.* London, 1640.

——. *An Humble Remonstrance to the High Court of Parliament.* London, 1641.

——. *A Modest Confutation of a Slanderous and Scurrilous Libel, Entitled, Adimadversions upon the Remonstrants Defense Against Smectymnuus.* London, 1642.

Haller, William. *Tracts on Liberty in the Puritan Revolution, 1638–1647.* 3 vols. New York: Columbia University Press, 1934.

Hebel, J. W. et al., eds. *Prose of the English Renaissance*. New York: Appleton-Century-Crofts, 1952.

Herbert, George. *The Works of George Herbert*. Ed. F. E. Hutchinson. Oxford: Clarendon Press, 1941; 2d ed., 1945.

Homes, Nathanael. *The Resurrection Revealed, or, The Dawning of the Day-Star, About to rise and radiate a visible incomparable Glory, far beyond any, since the Creation, upon the Universal Church on Earth, For a Thousand yeers. . . .* London, 1654.

Hooker, Richard. *The Folger Library Edition of the Works of Richard Hooker*. Ed. W. Speed Hill et al. Vols. 1–5. Cambridge, Mass.: Belknap Press of Harvard University Press, 1977–90.

How, Samuel. *The Sufficiency of the Spirits Teaching Without Humane Learning. Or a Treatise tending to prove Humane Learning to be no help to the Spiritual Understanding of the Word of God*. London, 1655.

Ignatius, St. "A Letter to the Magnesians." Trans. R. M. Grant. In vol. 4. of *The Apostolic Fathers: A New Translation and Commentary*. Toronto: Nelson and Sons, 1966.

Jacob, Henry. *A Confession and Protestation of the Faith*. London, 1616.
———. *The Divine Beginning and Institution of Christs True or Visible Ministeriall Church*. Leiden, 1610.

Jasper, R. C. D. and G. J. Cuming. *Prayers of the Eucharist: Early and Reformed*. 3d ed. New York: Pueblo Publishing Company, 1987.

Jessey, Henry. *The Lords Loud Call to England*. London, 1660.

Jewel, John. *A Treatise of the Holy Scriptures*. In vol. 4 of *The Works of John Jewel*. Ed. John Ayre. Cambridge, 1845–1850.

Johnson, Samuel. *Lives of the English Poets*. Ed. G. B. Hill. 3 vols. Oxford: Clarendon Press, 1905.

Jonson, Ben. *Timber: or Discoveries Made Upon Men and Matter*. Ed. Israel Gollancz. London: Dent, 1951.

Jungel, Eberhard. *Theological Essays*. Ed. and trans. J. B. Webster. Edinburgh: T. & T. Clark, 1989.

King Charles his Starre. London, 1654.

Laud, William. *The Works of . . . William Laud. . . .* 7 vols. Oxford, 1847–1860.

Lee, Samuel. *The Visibility of the True Church*. In vol. 6 of *Puritan Sermons, 1659–1689*. Ed. J. Nichols. Wheaton, Illinois: Richard Owen Roberts Publishers, 1981.

Leighton, Alexander. *An Appeal to Parliament or, Sions Plea against Prelacie*. London, 1628.

Leith, John, ed. *Creeds of the Churches*. 3d ed. Louisville: John Knox Press, 1982.

L'Estrange, Roger. *Toleration Discuss'd, in Two Dialogues. 1. Betwixt a Conformist and a Non-conformist. 2. Betwixt a Presbyterian and an Independent* . . . London, 1670.

Lightfoot, John. *The Works of* . . . *John Lightfoot.* 2 vols. London, 1684.

Lilburne, John. *England's New Chains Discovered.* London, 1648.

―――. *The Legall Fundamentall Liberties of the People of England.* London, 1649.

Lily, William. *Astrological Judgements for the Year 1668.* London, 1667.

―――. *England's Propheticall Merlin.* London, 1644.

Lloyd, David. *Cabala: or, The Mystery of Conventicles Unvail'd.* London, 1664.

Lockyer, Nicholas. *Some Seasonable and Serious Queries Upon the late Act Against Conventicles.* London, 1670.

Luther, Martin. *Luther's Works.* Ed. Jaroslav Pelikan et al. 55 vols. St. Louis: Concordia Publishing House, 1958–86.

Marshall, Stephen. *Meroz Cursed.* London, 1641.

―――. *Reformation and Desolation.* London, 1642.

Marvell, Andrew. *The Poems and Letters of Andrew Marvell.* Ed. H. M. Margoliouth. Oxford: Oxford University Press, 1927; 2d ed., 1952.

Mason, Francis. *The Authoritie Of The Church in making Canons and Constitutions Concerning Things Indifferent, and the Obedience Thereto Required.* London, 1607.

Mayer, John. *Ecclesiastica Interpretatio, Or the Expositions Upon the Difficult and Doubtful Passages of the Seven Epistles called Catholike, and the Revelation.* London, 1627.

Mede, Joseph. *The Key of the Revelation.* Trans. R. More. London, 1643.

Migne, J.-P., ed. *Patrologia Graeca.* Paris, 1857.

―――. *Patrologia Latina.* Paris, 1853.

Mirabilis Annus, or The Year of Prodigies and Wonders. London, 1661.

Mirabilis Annus Secundus: or, The Second Year of Prodigies. London, 1662.

Miraculum Signum Coeleste. . . . London, 1658.

Montague, Richard. *Appello Caesarem. A Just Appeal from Two Unjust Informers.* London, 1625.

Mr. Lillyes Prognostications of 1667. London, 1667.

Ness, Christopher. *A Full and True Account of the Late Blazing Star.* London, 1680.

Norton, John. *An Humble Apology for Non-conformists: with modest and serious reflections on the Friendly debate.* . . . London, 1669.

Owen, John. *A Brief Instruction in the Worship of God* . . . *By Way of Question and Answer.* London, 1667.

―――. *A Discourse Concerning Liturgies, and Their Imposition.* London, 1662.

———. *Pneumatologia, or A Discourse Concerning the Holy Spirit.* London, 1674.

———. *The True Nature of a Gospel Church and its Government.* London, 1689.

———. *Unto the Questions Sent Me Last Night . . . About Tythes, Proposed and Resolved.* London, 1659.

———. *The Works of John Owen.* Ed. W. H. Goold. 24 vols. Edinburgh and London: Johnstone and Hunter, 1850–1855.

Pareus, David. *A Commentary upon the Divine Revelation.* Trans. E. Arnold. Amsterdam, 1644.

Parker, Samuel. *A Discourse of Ecclesiastical Politie.* London, 1670.

———. *A Preface Shewing what Grounds there are of fears and Jealousies of Popery. . . .* [a preface to *Bishop Bramhall's Vindication of Himself and the Episcopal Clergy, from the Presbyterian Charge of Popery*]. London, 1672.

Patrick, Simon. *A Continuation of the Friendly Debate.* London, 1669.

———. *A Friendly Debate between a Confomist and a Non-conformist.* London, 1669.

———. *A Further Continuation and Defence, or, A Third Part of the Friendly Debate.* London, 1670.

Peacham, Henry. *The Garden of Eloquence.* London, 1593.

Perkins, William. *The Art of Prophecying.* Cambridge, 1609.

———. *The Combate Betweene Christ and the Devill.* In vol. 3 of *The Workes.* London, 1612–13.

———. *The Workes of . . . William Perkins.* 3 vols. London, 1612–13.

Petto, Samuel. *The Preacher Sent; or, A Vindication of the Liberty of Publick Preaching.* London, 1658.

———. *The Voyce of the Spirit.* London, 1654.

Plato. *The Collected Dialogues.* Ed. Edith Hamilton and Huntington Cairns. Trans. F. M. Cornford et al. Princeton: Princeton University Press, 1961.

Plutarch. "Isis and Osiris." Trans. F. C. Babbitt. In vol. 5 of *Moralia.* Loeb Classical Library. 15 vols. Cambridge: Harvard University Press, 1936.

Poole, Matthew. *A Commentary on the Holy Bible.* 2 vols. 1683–1685. Reprint (2 vols. in 3), London: Banner of Truth Trust, 1963.

Powell, Gabriel. *De Adiaphora.* London, 1607.

Prynne, William. *A Briefe Survay and Censure of Mr. Cozens his Couzening Devotions.* London, 1628.

———. *The Church of Englands Old Antithesis To New Arminianisme.* London, 1629.

———. *Lord Bishops None of the Lords Bishops.* London, 1640.

Pseudo-Dionysius. *The Divine Names and Mystical Theology.* Trans. J. D. Jones. Milwaukee: Marquette University Press, 1980.

———. *Hierarchy and the Definition of Order in the Letters of*

Pseudo-Dionysius. Trans. R. F. Hathaway. The Hague: Nijhoff, 1969.

Puttenham, George. *The Arte of English Poesie*. London, 1589; reprint, Menston: Scolar Press, 1968.

Quintillian. *The Institutio Oratoria of Quintillian*. Trans. H. E. Butler. 4 vols. Cambridge: Harvard University Press, 1980.

The Racovian Catechism. Trans. and ed. Thomas Rees. London, 1818.

Ramus, Peter. *The Logicke of the Most Excellent Philosopher P. Ramus Martyr*. Trans. Roland MacIlmaine (1574). Reprint, ed. Catherine M. Dunne. Northbridge, California: San Fernando State College, 1969.

Rolle, Samuel. *A Sober Answer To the Friendly Debate Betwixt a Conformist and a Nonconformist*. London, 1669.

Rutherford, Samuel. *Lex Rex: The Law of the Prince*. London, 1644.

———. *A Survey of the Spirituall Antichrist*. London, 1648.

S. D. *The Blazing Star: or, A Discourse of Comets*. London, 1665.

Saltmarsh, John. *Dawnings of Light*. London, 1645.

———. *Sparkles of Glory*. London, 1647.

Saravia, Hadrian. *Of the Diverse Degrees of the Ministers of the Gospell*. London, 1591.

Schaff, Phillip, ed. *The Creeds of Christendom*. 6th ed. 3 vols. New York: Harper, 1877.

Smectymnuus. *An Answer to a Book Entitled An Humble Remonstrance*. London, 1641.

———. *A Vindication of the Answer to the Humble Remonstrance*. London, 1641.

Spelman, Henry. *The Larger Treatise Concerning Tithes*. London, 1647.

Spencer, John. *A Short Treatise Concerning the Lawfullnesse of Every Man's Exercising His Gift*. London, 1641.

Spencer, John. *A Discourse of Prodigies*. Cambridge, 1665.

Sprigge, Joshua. *The Ancient Bounds, or Liberty of Conscience*. London, 1645.

———. *A Testimony of Approaching Glory*. London, 1649.

Simpson, Sidrach. *The Judgement of the Reformed Churches . . . concerning . . . Preaching by those who are not Ordained*. London, 1644.

Stanwood, P. G. and Heather Ross Asals, eds. *John Donne and the Theology of Language*. Columbia: University of Missouri Press, 1986.

Stewart, Adam. *Some Observations and Annotations upon the Apologeticall Narration*. London, 1644.

Stillingfleet, Edward. *A Discourse Concerning Idolatry Practised in the Church of Rome*. London, 1671.

Sylvester, Joshua, trans. *Du Bartas His Divine Weekes and Works.* 4th ed. London, 1613.

Taylor, Jeremy. *An Apologie for Authorized and Set Forms of Liturgie.* London, 1644.

———. *The Liberty of Prophesying.* London, 1647.

———. *Of the Sacred Order and Offices of Episcopacy.* London, 1642.

———. *The Worthy Communicant.* London, 1667.

Taylor, Thomas. *Christs Victorie Over the Dragon or Satans Downfall.* London, 1633.

Thompson, Bard, ed. *Liturgies of the Western Church.* Cleveland: World Publishing Co., 1961.

Toland, John. *Christianity not Mysterious. . . .* London, 1696.

———, ed. *A Complete Collection of the Historical, Political, and Miscellaneous Works of John Milton. . . .* 3 vols. Amsterdam, 1698.

Travers, Walter. *A Full and Plaine Declaration of Ecclesiastical Discipline Out off the Word off God.* Zurich, 1574.

Trigge, Thomas. *Calendarium Astrologicum: or, an Almanack For . . . 1666.* London, 1666.

Ursinus, Zacharius. *The Summe of Christian Religion.* Trans. Henrie Parrie. Oxford, 1587.

Vane, Sir Henry. *The Retired Mans Meditations.* London, 1655.

Vaughan, Henry. *Henry Vaughan: The Complete Poems.* Ed. Alan Rudrum. New Haven: Yale University Press, 1976.

———. *The Works of Henry Vaughan.* Ed. L. C. Martin. 2d ed. Oxford: Clarendon Press, 1957.

Vickers, Brian, ed. *English Renaissance Literary Criticism.* Oxford: Clarendon Press, 2003.

Vincent, Thomas. *God's Terrible Voice in the City of London.* 5th ed. London, 1667.

Walker, Williston, ed. *The Creeds and Platforms of Congregationalism.* Philadelphia: Pilgrim Press, 1960.

Whitaker, William. *A Disputation on Holy Scripture.* Trans. and ed. William Fitzgerald. Cambridge, 1849.

Wilkins, John. *Ecclesiastes, Or, A Discourse Concerning the Gift of Preaching as it Falls Under the Rules of Art.* London, 1647.

Williams, Roger. *The Bloody Tenent of Persecution.* London, 1644.

———. *The Hireling Ministry None of Christs.* London, 1652.

Wilson, Thomas. *The Arte of Rhetorique.* Facsimile edn. Gainesville, Florida: Scholars' Facsimiles and Reprints, 1962.

———. *A Christian Dictionarie.* London, 1611.

Wing, Vincent. *An Almanack and Prognostication for the Year of Our Lord, 1670.* London, 1670.

Wolleb, John. *The Abridgement of Christian Divinitie.* Trans. Alexander Ross. London, 1650.

Woodhouse, A. S. P., ed. *Puritanism and Liberty*. 3d ed. London: Dent and Sons, 1986.

Zwingli, Ulrich. *Of the Clarity and Certainty of the Word of God*, in *Zwingli and Bullinger*. Ed. and trans. G. W. Bromiley. Philadelphia: Westminster Press, 1953.

———. *On the Lord's Supper*. In *Zwingli and Bullinger*. Ed. and trans. G. W. Bromiley. Philadelphia: Westminster Press, 1953.

Secondary Sources

Achinstein, Sharon. *Literature and Dissent in Milton's England*. Cambridge: Cambridge University Press, 2003.

Auerbach, Erich. *Mimesis: The Representation of Reality in Western Literature*. Trans. W. R. Trask. Princeton: University of Princeton Press, 1968.

Avis, P. D. L. *The Church in the Theology of the Reformers*. London: Marshall, Morgan and Scott, 1981.

Baker, C. D. "Certain Religious Elements in the English Doctrine of the Inspired Poet During the Renaissance." *English Literary History* 6 (1939): 300–23.

Ball, Bryan W. *A Great Expectation: Eschatological Thought in English Protestantism to 1660*. Leiden: Brill, 1975.

Balthasar, Hans Urs von. *Word and Revelation*. Trans. A. V. Littledale. Montreal: Palm Press, 1964.

Barker, Arthur E. *Milton and the Puritan Dilemma*. Toronto: University of Toronto Press, 1942.

Bauman, Richard. *Let Your Words Be Few: Symbolism of Speaking and Silence Among Seventeenth-Century Quakers*. Cambridge: Cambridge University Press, 1983.

Bell, Catherine. *Ritual Theory, Ritual Practice*. Oxford: Oxford University Press, 1992.

Bennett, Joan S. *Reviving Liberty: Radical Christian Humanism in Milton's Great Poems*. Cambridge: Harvard University Press, 1989.

Bentley, J. *Humanists and Holy Writ*. Princeton: Princeton University Press, 1983.

Bicknell, E. J. *A Theological Introduction to the Thirty-Nine Articles of the Church of England*. Rev. H. J. Carpenter. 3d ed. London: Longmans, 1955.

Bolam, C. G., and Jeremy Goring. *The English Presbyterians*. London: Allen and Unwin, 1968.

Bond, Ronald B. "God's 'Back Parts': Silence and the Accommodating Word." In *Silence, the Word and the Sacred*, ed. E. D. Blodgett and H. G. Coward, 169–87. Waterloo: Wilfrid Laurier University Press, 1989.

Bossy, John. "Blood and Baptism: Kinship, Community and Christianity in Western Europe from the Fourteenth to the Seventeenth Centuries." In *Sanctity and Secularity: The Church and the World*, ed. D. Baker, 129–43. Oxford: Blackwell, 1973.

———. *Christianity in the West, 1400–1700*. Oxford: Oxford University Press, 1985.

Botterweck, G. Johannes, and Helmer Ringgren, eds. *Theological Dictionary of the Old Testament*. Trans. J. T. Willis et al. 6 vols. Grand Rapids: Eerdmans, 1978.

Bouwsma, William J. *Calvinism as Theologia Rhetorica*. Berkeley: The Center For Hermeneutical Studies in Hellenistic and Modern Culture, 1987.

Brachlow, Stephen. *The Communion of Saints: Radical Puritan and Separatist Ecclesiology, 1570–1625*. Oxford: Oxford University Press, 1988.

Burke, Peter. "The Repudiation of Ritual in Early Modern Europe." In *The Historical Anthropology of Early Modern Italy: Essays on Perception and Communication*, 223–38. Cambridge: Cambridge University Press, 1987.

Cable, Lana. *Carnal Rhetoric: Milton's Iconoclasm and the Poetics of Desire*. Durham: Duke University Press, 1998.

———. "Shuffling Up Such a God: The Rhetorical Agon of Milton's Antiprelatical Tracts." *Milton Studies* 21(1985): 3–33.

Campbell, Gordon. "*De Doctrina Christiana*: Its Structural Principles and its Unfinished State." *Milton Studies* 9 (1976): 243–60.

———. and Thomas N. Corns, John K. Hale, David I. Holmes and Fiona J. Tweedie. "The Provenance of *De Doctrina Christiana*." *Milton Quarterly* 31, no. 3 (1997): 67–121.

Capp, Bernard. *Astrology and the Popular Press*. London: Faber and Faber, 1979.

———. "The Political Dimension of Apocalyptic Thought." In *The Apocalypse in English Renaissance Faith*, ed. C. A. Patrides and Joseph Wittreich, 93–124. Manchester: Manchester University Press, 1984.

Chambers, A. B. *Transfigured Rites in Seventeenth-Century English Poetry*. Columbia: University of Missouri Press, 1994.

Chartier, Roger. *Passions of the Renaissance*. Vol. 3 of *A History of Private Life*. Trans. Arthur Goldhammer. Cambridge: The Belknap Press of Harvard University Press, 1989.

Christianson, Paul. *Reformers and Babylon: English Apocalyptic Visions from the Reformation to the Eve of the Civil War*. Toronto: University of Toronto Press, 1978.

Christopher, Georgia B. *Milton and the Science of the Saints*. Princeton: Princeton University Press, 1982.

———. "The Secret Agent in *Paradise Regained.*" *Modern Language Quarterly* 41 (1980): 131–50.

Clark, Donald. *John Milton at St. Paul's School.* New York: Columbia University Press, 1948.

Coggan, Donald. *The Sacrament of the Word.* London: Fount Paperbacks, 1987.

Cohn, Norman. *Cosmos, Chaos and the World to Come: the Ancient Roots of Apocalyptic Faith.* New Haven: Yale University Press, 1993.

Collinson, Patrick. *From Iconoclasm to Iconophobia: The Cultural Impact of the Second English Reformation.* Reading: University of Reading Press, 1986.

———. *The Religion of Protestants.* Oxford: Clarendon Press, 1982.

———. "With a small 'r'." In *The Times Literary Supplement.* 22 October 1993, 14–15.

Coolidge, John S. *The Pauline Renaissance in England: Puritanism and the Bible.* Oxford: Clarendon Press, 1970.

Cope, Jackson. "*Paradise Regained*: Inner Ritual." *Milton Studies* 1 (1969): 62–79.

Corns, Thomas. *The Development of Milton's Prose Style.* New Haven: Yale University Press, 1975.

———. *John Milton: The Prose Works.* New York: Twayne, 1998.

———. *Uncloistered Virtue: English Political Literature, 1640–1660.* Oxford: Oxford University Press, 1982.

Cox, Lee Sheridan. "Food-Word Imagery in *Paradise Regained.*" *English Literary History* 28 (1961): 225–43.

Cressy, David. *Birth, Marriage, and Death: Ritual, Religion, and the Life-Cycle in Tudor and Stuart England.* Oxford: Oxford University Press, 1997.

———. *Literacy and the Social Order: Reading and Writing in Tudor and Stuart England.* Cambridge: Cambridge University Press, 1980.

Crockett, William R. *Eucharist: Symbol of Transformation.* New York: Pueblo, 1989.

Cuming, G. J. *A History of Anglican Liturgy.* 2d ed. London: Macmillan, 1982.

Cummings, Brian. *The Literary Culture of the Reformation: Grammar and Grace.* Oxford: Oxford University Press, 2002.

Curtis, M. H. *Oxford and Cambridge in Transition, 1558–1642.* Oxford: Clarendon Press, 1959.

Darbishire, Helen, ed. *The Early Lives of Milton.* London: Constable, 1932.

Davies, Horton. *The English Free Churches.* 2d ed. New York: Oxford University Press, 1963.

———. *Worship and Theology in England: From Andrewes to Baxter and Fox, 1603–1690.* Princeton: Princeton University Press, 1975.

————. *The Worship of the English Puritans*. Westminster: Dacre Press, 1948.

De Krey, Gary. "Rethinking the Restoration: Dissenting Cases for Conscience, 1667–1672." *Historical Journal* 38, no. 1 (1995): 53–83.

Derrida, Jacques. "How to Avoid Speaking: Denials." In *Languages of the Unsayable: The Play of Negativity in Literature and Literary Theory*, ed. Sanford Budick and Wolfgang Iser, 3–70. New York: Columbia University Press, 1989.

Dix, Dom Gregory. *The Shape of the Liturgy*. Westminster: Dacre Press, 1945.

Dodd, C. H. *The Parables of the Kingdom*. Rev. ed. New York: Scribner's Sons, 1961.

Dowling, Paul M. "*Areopagitica* and *Areopagiticus*: The Significance of the Isocratic Precedent." *Milton Studies* 21(1986): 64–78.

Ebeling, Gerhard. *Introduction to a Theological Theory of Language*. Trans. R. A. Wilson. London: Collins, 1973.

Eisenstein, Elizabeth L. *The Printing Revolution in Early Modern Europe*. 2 vols. Cambridge: Cambridge University Press, 1979.

Eliade, Mircea. *The Myth of the Eternal Return*. Trans. W. R. Trask. Princeton: Princeton University Press, 1954.

————. *Patterns in Comparative Religion*. Trans. Rosemary Sheed. New York: Harper and Row, 1958.

————. *The Sacred and the Profane*. Trans. W. R. Trask. San Diego: Harcourt Brace, 1959.

Entzminger, R. L. *Divine Word: Milton and the Redemption of Language*. Pittsburgh: Duquesne University Press, 1985.

Fallon, Stephen F. "Milton's Arminianism and the Authorship of *De Doctrina Christiana*." *Texas Studies in Literature and Language* 41 (1999): 103–27.

Febvre, Lucien, and Henri-Jean Martin. *The Coming of the Book: The Impact of Printing 1450–1800*. Trans. D. Gerard and ed. Geoffrey Nowell-Smith and David Wootton. London: N. L. B., 1976.

Finnis, J. M. *Natural Law and Natural Rights*. Oxford: Clarendon Press, 1980.

Firth, Katharine R. *The Apocalyptic Tradition in Reformation Britain, 1530–1645*. Oxford: Oxford University Press, 1979.

Fish, Stanley. "Driving From the Letter: Truth and Indeterminacy in Milton's *Areopagitica*." In *Re-membering Milton: Essays on the Texts and Traditions*, ed. Mary Nyquist and Margaret W. Ferguson, 234–54. New York: Methuen, 1988.

————. "Inaction and Silence: the Reader in *Paradise Regained*." In *Calm of Mind*, ed. Joseph Wittreich Jr., 25–47. Cleveland: The Press of Case Western Reserve University, 1971.

————. *Self-Consuming Artifacts: The Experience of Seventeenth-Century Literature*. Berkeley: University of California Press, 1972.

———. "Wanting a Supplement: the Question of Interpretation in Milton's Early Prose." In *Politics, Poetics and Hermeneutics in Milton's Prose*, ed. David Loewenstein and James Grantham Turner, 41–68. Cambridge: Cambridge University Press, 1990.

Fixler, Michael. "Ecclesiology." In vol. 2 of *A Milton Encyclopedia*. Ed. W. B. Hunter et al. Lewisburg: Bucknell University Press, 1978.

———. *Milton and the Kingdoms of God*. London: Faber and Faber, 1964.

———. "The Unclean Meats of the Mosaic Law and the Banquet Scene in *Paradise Regained*." *Modern Language Notes* 70 (1955): 135–51.

Forstman, H. Jackson. *Word and Spirit: Calvin's Doctrine of Biblical Authority*. Stanford: Stanford University Press, 1962.

Frye, Northrop. *The Anatomy of Criticism*. Princeton: Princeton University Press, 1957.

———. "The Typology of *Paradise Regained*." *Modern Philology* 80 (1956): 227–38.

Funk, Robert. *Language, Hermeneutic, and Word of God*. New York: Harper and Row, 966.

Gadamer, Hans-Georg. *Truth and Method*. Trans. and ed. Garrett Barden and John Cumming. New York: Seabury Press, 1975.

Gardiner, S. R. *The History of the Commonwealth and Protectorate*. 4 vols. London: Longmans, Green and Co., 1903.

———. *The History of the Great Civil War, 1642–1649*. 4 vols. London: Longmans, Green and Co., 1901.

Gay, David. "Astrology and Iconoclasm in Milton's *Paradise Regained*." *Studies in English Literature* 41, no. 1 (2001): 175–90.

Geneva, Ann. *Astrology and the Seventeenth-Century Mind: William Lily and the Language of the Stars*. Manchester: Manchester University Press, 1995.

Gennep, Arnold van. *The Rites of Passage*. Trans. Monika B. Vizedom and Gabrielle L. Caffee. Chicago: University of Chicago Press, 1960.

Gilman, Ernest B. *Iconoclasm and Poetry in the English Reformation: Down Went Dagon*. Chicago: University of Chicago Press, 1986.

Goekjian, G. "Deference and Silence: Milton's 'Nativity Ode.'" *Milton Studies* 21 (1986): 119–35.

Goldie, Mark. "The Theory of Religious Intolerance in Restoration England." In *From Persecution to Toleration*, ed. O. P. Grell, J. I. Israel, and N. Tyacke, 331–68. Oxford: Oxford University Press, 1991.

Goldsmith, Steven. "The Muting of Satan: Language and Redemption in *Paradise Regained*." *Studies in English Literature* 27 (1987): 125–40.

Greaves, Richard L. *Deliver Us From Evil: The Radical Underground in Britain, 1660–1663*. New York: Oxford University Press, 1986.

———. *Enemies Under his Feet: Radicals and Nonconformists in Britain, 1664–1677*. Stanford: Stanford University Press, 1990.

———. *Glimpses of Glory: John Bunyan and English Dissent*. Stanford: Stanford University Press, 2002.

Greene, Thomas. "Ritual and Text in the Renaissance." *Canadian Review of Comparative Literature* (June–September, 1992): 192–207.

Grimes, Ronald L. *Beginnings in Ritual Studies*. Columbia: University of South Carolina Press, 1995.

———. *Ritual Criticism: Case Studies in Its Practice, Essays on Its Theory*. Columbia: University of Columbia Press, 1990.

Haller, William. *The Rise of Puritanism*. New York: Columbia University Press, 1938.

Hamilton, G. D. "*Paradise Regained* and the Private Houses." In *Of Poetry and Politics: New Essays on Milton and his World*, ed. P. G. Stanwood, 239–48. Binghamton, N. Y.: Medieval and Renaissance Texts and Studies, 1994.

Harper, John. *The Forms and Orders of Western Liturgy from the Tenth to the Eighteenth Century*. Oxford: Oxford University Press, 1991.

Helgerson, Richard. *Self-Crown'd Laureates: Spenser, Jonson, Milton, and the Literary System*. Berkeley: University of California Press, 1983.

Hendry, G. S. *The Holy Spirit in Christian Theology*. London: SCM Press, 1965.

Heron, Alasdair I. C. *The Holy Spirit*. Philadelphia: The Westminister Press, 1983.

Hexter, J. H. *On Historians*. Cambridge: Harvard University Press, 1979.

Hill, Christopher. *Antichrist in Seventeenth-Century England*. London: Oxford University Press, 1971.

———. *The English Bible and the Seventeenth-Century Revolution*. Harmondsworth: Penguin, 1993.

———. *The Experience of Defeat: Milton and Some Contemporaries*. London: Faber and Faber, 1984.

———. *Milton and the English Revolution*. London: Faber and Faber, 1977.

———. "Professor William B. Hunter, Bishop Burgess, and John Milton." *Studies in English Literature* 34 (1994): 165–93.

———. *The World Turned Upside Down: Radical Ideas During the English Revolution*. Harmondsworth: Penguin, 1975.

Hill, John S. *John Milton: Poet, Priest and Prophet*. London: Macmillan, 1979.

Hirst, Derek. *Authority and Conflict: England, 1603–1658*. Cambridge: Harvard University Press, 1986.

Hoffman, Manfred. *Rhetoric and Theology*. Toronto: University of Toronto Press, 1994.

Holifield, E. Brooks. *The Covenant Sealed: The Development of*

Puritan Sacramental Theology In Old and New England, 1570–1720. New Haven: Yale University Press, 1974.

Honeygosky, Stephen R. *Milton's House of God: The Invisible and Visible Church.* Columbia: University of Missouri Press, 1993.

Howell, Wilbur S. *Logic and Rhetoric in England, 1500–1700.* New York: Russell and Russell, 1961.

Hughes, Merritt. "The Christ of *Paradise Regained* and the Renaissance Heroic Tradition." *Studies in Philology* 35 (1938): 254–77.

Huguelet, Theodore Long. "Milton's Hermeneutics: A Study of Scriptural Interpretation in the Divorce Tracts and in *De Doctrina Christiana.*" Ph. D. diss., University of North Carolina, 1959.

Hunter, Willam B. "Animadversions upon the Remonstrants' Defences against Burgess and Hunter." *Studies in English Literature* 34 (1994): 195–203.

———. *The Descent of Urania.* London and Toronto: Associated University Presses, 1989.

———. "Forum: Milton's *Christian Doctrine.*" *Studies in English Literature* 32 (1992): 163–66.

———. "Milton Translates the Psalms." *Philological Quarterly* 28 (1949): 125–44.

———. "The Provenance of the *Christian Doctrine.*" *Studies in English Literature* 32 (1992): 129–42.

———. "The Provenance of the *Christian Doctrine*: Addenda from the Bishop of Salisbury." *Studies in English Literature* 33 (1993): 191–207.

———. "Responses." *Milton Quaterly* 33 (1999): 31–37.

———. *Visitation Unimplor'd: Milton and the Authorship of "De Doctrina Christiana."* Pittsburgh: Duquesne University Press, 1998.

———, C. A. Patrides, and J. H. Adamson, eds. *Bright Essence: Studies in Milton's Theology.* Salt Lake City: University of Utah Press, 1971.

Hutton, Ronald. *The Restoration.* Oxford: Oxford University Press, 1985.

Jameson, Fredric. "Religion and Ideology: A Political Reading of *Paradise Lost.*" In *Literature, Politics, and Theory,* ed. Francis Barker et al., 36–57. London: Methuen, 1986.

Jarrott, C. A. L. "Erasmus' *In Principio Erat Sermo*: A Controversial Translation." *Studies in Philology* 61 (1964): 35–40.

Keeble, N. H. *The Literary Culture of Nonconformity in Later Seventeenth-Century England.* Athens: University of Georgia Press, 1987.

Kelley, Maurice. "Milton's Debt to Wolleb's *Compendium Theologicae Christianae.*" *PMLA* 55 (1940): 156–65.

———. "The Provenance of John Milton's *Christian Doctrine*: A Reply to William B. Hunter." *Studies in English Literature* 34 (1994): 153–63.

———. *This Great Argument: A Study of Milton's "De Doctrina Christiana" as a Gloss upon "Paradise Lost."* Princeton: Princeton University Press, 1941.

Kelly, J. N. D. *Early Christian Creeds.* London: Longmans, 1960.

———. *Early Christian Doctrines.* 3d ed. London: Adam and Charles Black, 1965.

Kendall, R. T. *Calvin and English Calvinism to 1649.* Oxford: Clarendon Press, 1979.

Kennedy, George A. *Classical Rhetoric and Its Christian and Secular Tradition from Ancient to Modern Times.* Chapel Hill: University of North Carolina Press, 1980.

Kerrigan, William. *The Prophetic Milton.* Charlottesville: University Press of Virginia 1974.

Kertzer, David I. *Ritual, Politics, and Power.* New Haven: Yale University Press, 1988.

King, John N. *English Reformation Literature: The Tudor Origins of the Protestant Tradition.* Princeton: Princeton University Press, 1982.

———. *Milton and Religious Controversy.* Cambridge: Cambridge University Press, 2001.

Kirby, W. J. Torrance. *Richard Hooker's Doctrine of the Royal Supremacy.* Leiden: Brill, 1990.

Kittel, G. et al., eds. *Theological Dictionary of the New Testament.* Trans. G. W. Bromiley. 10 vols. Grand Rapids: Eerdmans, 1964–76.

Knoppers, Laura. *Historicizing Milton.* Athens: University of Georgia Press, 1994.

Knott, John R. "'Suffering for Truth's Sake': Milton and Martyrdom." In *Politics, Poetics, and Hermeneutics in Milton's Prose,* ed. David Loewenstein and James Grantham Turner, 153–70. Cambridge: Cambridge University Press, 1990.

———. *The Sword of the Spirit: Puritan Responses to the Bible.* Chicago: University of Chicago Press, 1980.

Kranidas, Thomas. *The Fierce Equation: A Study of Milton's Decorum.* The Hague: Mouton Press, 1965.

———. "Words, Words, Words, and the Word: Milton's *Of Prelatical Episcopacy.*" *Milton Studies* 16 (1982): 153–66.

Lake, Peter. *Puritan and Anglican? Presbyterianism and English Conformist Thought from Whitgift to Hooker.* London: Allen and Unwin, 1988.

Lakoff, George and Mark Johnson. *Metaphors We Live By.* Chicago: University of Chicago Press, 1980.

Lamont, William M. *Godly Rule: Politics and Religion, 1603–1660*. London: Macmillan, 1969.

Lanham, Richard A. *The Motives of Eloquence*. New Haven: Yale University Press, 1976.

Lanier, Douglas. "'Unmarkt, unknown': *Paradise Regained* and the Return of the Expressed." *Criticism* 33 (Spring, 1995]: 187–212.

Lewalski, Barbara K. "Forum: Milton's *Christian Doctrine*." *Studies in English Literature* 32 (1992]: 143–54.

———. *The Life of John Milton*. Rev. ed. Oxford: Blackwell, 2003.

———. "Milton: Political Beliefs and Polemical Methods,1659–1660." *PMLA* 74 (1959]: 191–202.

———. "Milton and *De Doctrina Christiana*: Evidences of Authorship." *Milton Studies* 36 (1998]: 203–28.

———. "Milton on Learning and the Learned-Ministry Controversy." *Huntington Library Quarterly* 24 (1961]: 267–81.

———. *Milton's Brief Epic*. Providence: Brown University Press, 1966.

———. *Protestant Poetics and the Seventeenth-Century Religious Lyric*. Princeton: Princeton University Press, 1979.

Lieb, Michael. "Milton and the Organicist Polemic." *Milton Studies* 4 (1972]: 79–94.

———. "Milton's *Of Reformation* and the Dynamics of Controversy." In *Achievements of the Left Hand: Essays on the Prose of John Milton*, ed. Michael Lieb and John Shawcross, 55–82. Amherst: University of Massachusetts Press, 1974.

———. "Reading God: Milton and the Anthropopathetic Tradition." *Milton Studies* 25 (1989]: 213–43.

Lindenbaum, Peter. "John Milton and the Republican Mode of Literary Production." *The Yearbook of Literary Studies* 21 (1991]: 121–36.

Loewenstein, David. *Representing Revolution in Milton and his Contemporaries*. Cambridge: Cambridge University Press, 2001.

Louth, Andrew. *The Origins of the Christian Mystical Tradition*. Oxford: Clarendon Press, 1981.

Low, Anthony. "Milton and the Georgic Ideal." In *The Georgic Revolution*. Princeton: Princeton University Press, 1985, 296–352.

MacCallum, Hugh. "Jesus as Teacher in *Paradise Regained*." *English Studies in Canada* 14 (1988]: 135–51.

———. "Milton and Figurative Interpretation of the Bible." *University of Toronto Quarterly* 31 (1962]: 397–415.

———. *Milton and the Sons of God: The Divine Image in Milton's Epic Poetry*. Toronto: University of Toronto Press, 1972.

Martz, Louis. "Milton's Prophetic Voice: Moving Toward Paradise." In *Of Poetry and Politics: New Essays on Milton and his World*, ed. P. G. Stanwood, 1–16. Binghamton, N. Y.: Medieval and Renaissance Texts and Studies, 1994.

————. *Poet of Exile*. New Haven: Yale University Press, 1980.

Masson, David. *The Life of John Milton*. 7 vols. 1881–1894. Reprint, New York: Smith, 1946.

Matheson, Peter. "Humanism and Reform Movements." In *The Impact of Humanism on Western Europe*, ed. A. Goodman and A. McKay, 32–43. London: Longmans, 1990.

Mayor, Stephen. *The Lord's Supper in Early English Dissent*. London: Epworth Press, 1972.

Mazzeo, Joseph Anthony. "St. Augustine's Rhetoric of Silence: Truth Versus Eloquence and Things Versus Signs." *Journal of the History of Ideas* 23, no. 2 (1962): 175–96.

McColley, Diane. *Poetry and Music in Seventeenth-Century England*. Cambridge: Cambridge University Press, 1997.

McGann, Jerome. *The Textual Condition*. Princeton: Princeton University Press, 1991.

McKenzie, D. F. "Milton's Printers: Matthew, Mary, and Samuel Simmons." *Milton Quarterly* 14 (1980): 87–91.

McKenzie, John L., S. J. *Dictionary of the Bible*. New York: Macmillan, 1965.

McLachlan, H. J. *Socinianism in Seventeenth-Century England*. Oxford: Oxford University Press, 1951.

McLoone, George. *Milton's Poetry of Independence*. Lewisburg: Bucknell University Press; Associated University Presses, 1999.

McLuhan, Herbert Marshall. *The Gutenberg Galaxy*. Toronto: University of Toronto Press, 1962.

McNeill, John. *The History and Character of Calvinism*. New York: Oxford University Press, 1954.

————. "Natural Law in the Teaching of the Reformers." *The Journal of Religion* 26 (1946): 168–82.

Menanger, Daniel. "Calvin et D'Aubigne: vocation prophetique et vocation poetique." *Renaissance and Reformation* n. s. 11 (1987): 15–27.

Miller, Timothy C. "Milton's Religion of the Spirit and 'the State of the Church' in Book XII of *Paridise Lost*." *Restoration: Studies in English Literary Culture, 1660–1700* 13 (1985): 7–16.

Milner, Andrew. *John Milton and the English Revolution*. London: Macmillan, 1981.

Montrose, Louis. "Renaissance Literary Studies and the Subject of History." *English Literary Renaissance* 16 (1986): 5–12.

Morgan, J. *Godly Learning: Puritan Attitudes towards Reason, Learning, and Education, 1560–1640*. Cambridge: Cambridge University Press, 1986.

Morrill, J. *The Nature of the English Revolution*. New York: Longman, 1993.

Mowinckel, S. "Postscript." *Journal of Biblical Literature* 56 (1937): 261–65.

———. "The Spirit and 'The Word' in the Pre-Exilic Reforming Prophets." *Journal of Biblical Literature* 53 (1934): 199–227.

Mueller, Janel. "Embodying Glory: The Apocalyptic Strain in Milton's *Of Reformation.*" In *Politics, Poetics, and Hermeneutics in Milton's Prose,* ed. David Loewenstein and James Grantham Turner, 9–35. Cambridge: Cambridge University Press, 1990.

Muir, Edward. *Ritual in Early Modern Europe.* Cambridge: Cambridge University Press, 1997.

Mustazza, Leonard. "Language as Weapon in *Paradise Regained.*" *Milton Studies* 18 (1983): 195–216.

———. *"Such Prompt Eloquence": Language as Agency and Character in Milton's Epics.* Lewisburg: Bucknell University Press, 1988.

Newbiggin, James E. Leslie. *The Household of God.* 2d ed. London: SCM, 1964.

Norbrook, David. *Writing the English Republic: Poetry, Rhetoric, and Politics, 1627–1660.* Cambridge: Cambridge University Press, 1999.

Nuttall, Anthony David. *Overheard by God: Fiction and Prayer in Herbert, Milton, Dante and St. John.* London: Methuen, 1980.

Nuttall, Geoffrey. *The Holy Spirit in Puritan Faith and Experience.* Oxford: Basil Blackwell, 1946.

———. "Milton's Churchmanship in 1659: His Letter to Jean de Labadie." *Milton Quarterly* 35, no. 4 (2001): 227–31.

Ong, Walter J., S. J. *The Presence of the Word.* New Haven: Yale University Press, 1967.

O'Rourke Boyle, Marjorie. *Erasmus on Language and Method in Theology.* Toronto: University of Toronto Press, 1977.

Parker, William R. *Milton: A Biography.* 2 vols. Oxford: Clarendon Press, 1968.

Patrides, C. A. *Milton and the Christian Tradition.* Oxford: Clarendon Press, 1966.

———. "*Paradise Lost* and the Theory of Accommodation." *Texas Studies in Literature and Language* 5 (1963): 58–63.

Patterson, Annabel. *Censorship and Interpretation: The Conditions of Writing and Reading in Early Modern England.* Madison: University of Wisconsin Press, 1984.

Pauck, Wilhelm. Introduction to *The Kingdom of Christ.* In *Melanchthon and Bucer.* Ed. and trans. W. Pauck. Philadelphia: Westminster Press, 1969.

Pearce, James M. "The Theology of Representation: The Meta-Argument of *Paradise Regained.*" *Milton Studies* 24 (1988): 277–96.

Pelikan, Jaroslav. *The Emergence of the Catholic Tradition (100–600).* Vol. 1 of *The Christian Tradition: A History of the Development of Doctrine.* Chicago: University of Chicago Press, 1971.

———. *The Growth of Medieval Theology (600–1300)*. Vol. 2 of *The Christian Tradition: A History of the Development of Doctrine*. Chicago: University of Chicago Press, 1978.

Pope, Elizabeth. *"Paradise Regained": The Tradition and the Poem*. Baltimore: Johns Hopkins University Press, 1947.

Radzinowicz, Mary Ann. *Milton's Epics and the Book of Psalms*. Princeton: Princeton University Press, 1989.

———. *"Paradise Regained* as Hermeneutic Combat." *University of Hartford Studies in Literature* 16, no. 1 (1984): 99–107.

Ramsey, Michael. *Holy Spirit*. Grand Rapids: Eerdmans, 1977.

Revard, Stella. "Milton and Millenarianism: From the Nativity Ode to *Paradise Regained.*" In *Milton and the Ends of Time*, ed. Juliet Cummins, 42–81. Cambridge: Cambridge University Press, 2003.

Richardson, Alan, ed. and trans. *Creeds in the Making: A Short Introduction to the History of Christian Doctrine*. Philadelphia: Fortress Press, 1981.

Richey, Esther Gilman. *The Politics of Revelation in the English Renaissance*. Columbia: University of Missouri Press, 1998.

Ricoeur, Paul. *The Rule of Metaphor*. Toronto: University of Toronto Press, 1975.

Ross, Malcolm Mackenzie. *Poetry and Dogma: The Transformation of Eucharistic Symbols in Seventeenth-Century English Poetry*. New Brunswick, N. J.: Rutgers University Press, 1954.

Rummel, Erika. *Erasmus and His Catholic Critics*. 2 vols. Nieuwkoop: De Graaf, 1989.

———. *Erasmus' Annotations on the New Testament*. Toronto: University of Toronto Press, 1986.

Rumrich, John P. *Milton Unbound*. Cambridge: Cambridge University Press, 1996.

Rushdy, Ashraf. *The Empty Garden: The Subject of Late Milton*. Pittsburgh: University of Pittsburgh Press, 1992.

———. "Standing Alone on the Pinnacle: Milton in 1752." *Milton Studies* 26 (1990): 193–218.

Russell, Conrad. *The Causes of the English Civil War*. Oxford: Clarendon Press, 1990.

———. *Unrevolutionary England, 1603–1642*. London: The Hambledon Press, 1990.

Sanchez, Reuben. *Persona and Decorum in Milton's Prose*. London: Associated University Presses, 1997.

———. "From Polemic to Prophecy: Milton's Uses of Jeremiah in *The Reason of Church Government* and *The Readie and Easie Way.*" *Milton Studies* 30 (1993): 27–44.

Saunders, J. W. *The Profession of English Letters*. London: Routledge and Kegan Paul, 1964.

————. "The Stigma of Print: A Note on the Social Bases of Tudor Poetry." *Essays in Criticism* 1 (1951): 139–64.

Schmemann, Alexander. *The Eucharist: Sacrament of the Kingdom.* Trans. P. Kachur. Crestwood, N.Y.: St. Vladimir's Seminary Press, 1988.

Schultz, Howard. "Christ and Antichrist in *Paradise Regained.*" *PMLA* 67 (1952): 790–808.

————. *Milton and Forbidden Knowledge.* New York: MLA, 1955. Reprint, New York: Kraus Reprint Co., 1970.

Schwartz, Regina M. *Remembering and Repeating: Biblical Creation in "Paradise Lost."* Cambridge: Cambridge University Press, 1988.

Schwartz, Werner. *Principles of Biblical Translation: Some Reformation Controversies and their Background.* Cambridge: Cambridge University Press, 1955.

Scribner, R. W. *Popular Culture and Popular Movements in Reformation Germany.* London: Hambleton, 1987.

Seasoltz, R. Kevin. "Justice and the Eucharist." *Worship* 58 (1984): 507–25.

Sellin, Paul. "John Milton's *Paradise Lost* and *De Doctrina Christiana* on Predestination." *Milton Studies* 34 (1996): 32–61.

————. "Further Responses." *Milton Quarterly* 33 (1999): 38–51.

Sharon-Zisser, Shirley. "Silence and Darkness in *Paradise Lost.*" *Milton Studies* 25 (1989): 191–211.

Sharpe, Kevin. *Politics and Ideas in Early Stuart England.* London: Pinter Publishers, 1989.

————. and Stephen N. Zwicker, eds. *Politics of Discourse: The Literature and History of Seventeenth-Century England.* Berkeley: University of California Press, 1987.

Shawcross, John T. "Bibles." In vol. 1 of *A Milton Encyclopedia.* Gen. ed. W. Hunter. Lewisburg: Bucknell University Press, 1978.

————. "Confusion: the apocalypse, the millenium." In *Milton and the Ends of Time,* ed. Juliet Cummins, 106–19. Cambridge: Cambridge University Press, 2003.

————. "Forum: Milton's *Christian Doctrine.*" *Studies in English Literature* 32 (1992): 155–62.

————. "Milton's Decision to Become a Poet." *Modern Language Quarterly* 24 (1963): 21–30.

Shuger, Debora K. *The Renaissance Bible.* Berkeley: University of California Press, 1998.

————. *Sacred Rhetoric: the Christian Grand Style in the English Renaissance.* Princeton: Princeton University Press, 1988.

Shullenberger, William. "Linguistic and Poetic Theory in Milton's *De Doctrina Christiana.*" *English Language Notes* 19 (1982): 262–78.

———. "The Omnific Word: Language in Milton." Ph. D. diss., University of Massachusetts, 1982.

Sims, James H. "Jesus and Satan as Readers of Scripture in *Paradise Regained.*" *Milton Studies* 33 (1995): 190–204.

Sirluck, Ernest. Introduction to vol. 2 of *The Complete Prose Works of John Milton.* New Haven: Yale University Press, 1959.

———. "Milton's Idle Right Hand." *Journal of English and Germanic Philology* 60 (1961): 749–85.

Smith, G. W. "Iterative Rhetoric in *Paradise Lost.*" *Modern Philology* 74 (1976): 1–19.

Smith, Nigel. *Literature and Revolution in England, 1640–1660.* New Haven: Yale University Press, 1994.

Smith, Samuel. "'Christs Victorie Over the Dragon': The Apocalypse in *Paradise Regained.*" *Milton Studies* 29 (1993): 59–82.

Somerville, J. P. *Politics and Ideology in England, 1603–1640.* London: Longman, 1986.

Spinks, Bryan D. *Freedom or Order? The Eucharistic Liturgy in English Congregationalism, 1645–1980.* Pittsburgh Theological Monographs, n.s., no. 8. Allison Park, Pa.: Pickwick Publications, 1984.

———. *From the Lord and "The Best Reformed Churches": A Study of the Eucharistic Liturgy in the English Puritan And Separatist Traditions, 1550–1633.* Bibliotheca "Ephemerides Liturgicae" Subsidia, no. 33. Rome: C.L.V. – Edizioni Liturgiche, 1984.

Spitz, Lewis J. *Luther and German Humanism.* Aldershot: Variorum, 1996.

Spurr, John. *The Restoration Church of England, 1646–1687.* New Haven: Yale University Press, 1991.

Stanwood, P. G. "Liturgy, Worship, and the Sons of Light." In *New Perspectives on the Seventeenth-Century English Religious Lyric,* ed. John R. Roberts, 105–23. Columbia: University of Missouri Press, 1993.

———. "Of Prelacy and Polity in Milton and Hooker." In *Heirs of Fame: Milton and Writers of the English Renaissance,* ed. David A. Kent and Margo Swiss, 66–84. Lewisburg, Pa.: Bucknell University Press, 1994.

———. *The Sempiternal Season: Studies in Seventeenth-Century Devotional Writing.* New York: Peter Lang, 1992.

Stavely, Keith. *The Politics of Milton's Prose Style.* New Haven: Yale University Press, 1975.

———. Preface to *Of True Religion.* In vol. 8 of *The Complete Prose Works of John Milton.* Ed. Maurice Kelley. New Haven: Yale University Press, 1982.

Steadman, John M. *The Hill and the Labyrinth: Discourse and Certitude in Milton and His Near-Contemporaries.* Berkeley: University of California Press, 1986.

Stein, A. *Heroic Knowledge*. Minneapolis: University of Minnesota Press, 1957.

Stephan, H. "Word of God." In vol. 6 of *Sacramentum Mundi*. Gen. ed. Karl Rahner, S. J. Montreal: Palm Publishers, 1970.

Stock, Brian. *The Implications of Literacy: Written Language and Models of Interpretation in the Eleventh and Twelfth Centuries*. Princeton: Princeton University Press, 1983.

———. *Listening for the Text: On the Uses of the Past*. Baltimore: Johns Hopkins University Press, 1990.

Stroup, Thomas B. *Religious Rite and Ceremony in Milton's Poetry*. Lexington: University of Kentucky Press, 1968.

Talley, Thomas. "The Literary Structure of the Eucharistic Prayer." *Worship* 58 (1984): 404–20.

Thompson, W. D. J. Cargill. "The Philosopher of the Politic Society: Richard Hooker as a Political Thinker." In *Studies in Richard Hooker: Essays Preliminary to an Edition of His Works*, ed. W. Speed Hill, 3–76. Cleveland: Press of Case Western Reserve University, 1972.

Todd, M. *Christian Humanism and the Puritan Social Order*. Cambridge: Cambridge University Press, 1987.

Tolmie, Murray. *The Triumph of the Saints: The Separate Churches in London, 1616–1649*. Cambridge: Cambridge University Press, 1977.

Torrance, T. F. "The Eschatology of the Reformation." *Scottish Journal of Theology*. Occasional Papers, no. 2 (1952): 36–62.

———. *God and Rationality*. London: Oxford University Press, 1971.

———. *Kingdom and Church: A Study in the Theology of the Reformation*. Edinburgh: Oliver and Boyd, 1956.

Trevor-Roper, Hugh. *Catholics, Anglicans, and Puritans*. London: Fontana, 1987.

Trinkaus, Charles. *In Our Image and Likeness: Humanity and Divinity in Italian Humanist Thought*. 2 vols. London: Constable Press, 1970.

Tuck, Richard. *Natural Rights Theories: Their Origin and Development*. New York: Cambridge University Press, 1979.

Turner, Victor. *The Ritual Process: Structure and Anti-Structure*. Chicago: Aldine Press, 1969.

Tyacke, Nicholas. *Anti-Calvinists: the Rise of English Arminianism, c. 1590–1640*. Oxford: Clarendon Press, 1987.

———. "Puritanism, Arminianism and Counter-Revolution." In *The Origins of the English Civil War*, ed. Conrad Russell, 119–43. London: Macmillan, 1973.

Wainwright, Geoffrey. *Eucharist and Eschatology*. London: Epworth, 1971.

Wall, John M. *Transformations of the Word: Spenser, Herbert, Vaughan*. Athens: University of Georgia Press, 1989.

Wallace, Ronald S. *Calvin's Doctrine of the Word and Sacrament.* Edinburgh: Oliver and Boyd, 1953.

Watkin-Jones, H. *The Holy Spirit from Arminius to Wesley.* London: Epworth Press, 1928.

Webster, John B. *Eberhard Jungel: An Introduction to his Theology.* Cambridge: Cambridge University Press, 1986.

Weinberg, Bernard. *The History of Literary Criticism in the Italian Renaissance.* 2 vols. Chicago: University of Chicago Press, 1961.

White, B. R. *The English Separatist Tradition.* Oxford: Oxford University Press, 1975.

White, J. F. *Protestant Worship: Traditions in Transition.* Louisville: Westminster / John Knox Press, 1989.

Wiener, Aharon. *The Prophet Elijah in the Development of Judaism.* London: Routledge and Kegan Paul, 1978.

Wilding, Michael. *Dragons Teeth: Literature in the English Revolution.* Oxford: Oxford University Press, 1987.

Williams, G. H. *The Radical Reformation.* London: Weidenfeld and Nicolson, 1962.

Wittreich, Joseph Anthony., Jr. "The Crown of Eloquence: The Figure of the Orator in Milton's Prose." In *Achievements of the Left Hand: Essays on the Prose of John Milton,* ed. Michael Lieb and John T. Shawcross, 3–54. Amherst: University of Massachusetts Press, 1974.

———. *Visionary Poetics: Milton's Tradition and his Legacy.* San Marino: Huntington Library, 1979.

Wolfe, D. M. *Milton in the Puritan Revolution.* New York: Thomas Nelson and Sons, 1941.

Wolfson, H. A. *The Philosophy of the Church Fathers.* 2d ed. Cambridge: Harvard University Press, 1964.

Wolterstorff, Nicholas. *Reason Within the Bounds of Religion.* Grand Rapids: Eerdmans, 1976.

Woodhouse, A. S. P. *The Poet and His Faith.* Chicago: University of Chicago Press, 1965.

———. "Theme and Pattern in *Paradise Regained.*" *University of Toronto Quarterly* 25 (1956): 167–82.

Woolrych, Austin. *Commonwealth to Protectorate.* Oxford: Clarendon Press, 1982.

———. Introduction to vol. 7 of *The Complete Prose Works of John Milton.* Ed. Robert W. Ayers. Rev. ed. New Haven: Yale University Press, 1980.

Worden, Blair. *The Rump Parliament, 1648–1653.* Cambridge: Cambridge University Press, 1977.

———. "Milton, *Samson Agonistes,* and the Restoration." In *Culture and Society in the Stuart Restoration: Literature, Drama, and*

History, ed. Gerald MacLean, 111–36. Cambridge: Cambridge University Press, 1994.

Yule, George. *The Independents in the English Civil War.* Cambridge: Cambridge University Press, 1958.

INDEX

Act of 1641, 164
Act of Uniformity, 164
Acts, book of, 17, 19
Admonition to Parliament, 97
Alsted, Johann Heinrich, 157
Ames, William, 122
Anabaptists, 60
Andrewes, Lancelot, 1, 47
Anglicans: as Antichrist, 156–57; and antitoleration, 165–66; and church discipline, 95, 204n53; and church-state relations, 149; communion service of, 129; liturgy of, 113; Milton and, 30; and theology of ministry, 60–61
Animadversions (Milton), 73–74, 113, 116, 118–19, 163
Annotations Upon the Books of the New and Old Testament, 48
ante-communion service, 108, 128–29
Antichrist: astrology and, 179–81; church as, 143, 156–58, 161–64, 167, 174
antiepiscopal tracts, 2–4, 96–97
antitrinitarianism, 10
Apocalypse, 142
apocalypticism: astrology and, 178–85; church conflicts and, 160–64; Milton and, 155–58, 163, 168, 184–85, 211n5; in *Paradise Regained*, 158–60; reformers and, 156–57; and Satan's fall, 178; scriptural basis of, 211n5

Apologetical Narration (Goodwin et al.), 112
Apology against a Pamphlet, An (Milton), 69, 75, 113, 115, 116
apostolic church, 21
Arcadia (Sidney), 114
Archer, Henry, 149
Areopagitica (Milton): body in, 23; Christian liberty doctrine in, 6, 17; on church-state relations, 151–52; ecclesiology in, 18; purpose of, 17–19; toleration in, 4; on truth, 79; Word as spiritual food in, 32
Arianism, 16
Aristotle, 62, 67, 99
astrology, 178–85
Athanasius, 194n28
Auerbach, Erich, 38
Augustine, Saint, 40, 139–40, 144

Bainbridge, John, 179
Baker, C. D., 64
Bale, John, 160
baptism, 124, 126–28
Barclay, Robert, 41
Barker, Arthur E., 3, 97
Bartas, Guillaume de Salluste, Seigneur du, 63, 180
Bastwick, John, 73
Baxter, Richard, 108, 112, 129
Bennett, Joan, xi
Bible. *See* Scripture

247

153–54, 171–77; Reformed view of, 148; state and, 145–48; visible church and, 144–48; Word of God and, 147. *See also* church-state relations
kingship, 172
Knoppers, Laura, xi
Knox, John, 129

Labadie, Jean de, 209n25
laity, and ministry, 55–56, 87–88, 124. *See also* priesthood of believers
Laud, William, 60, 96, 108, 157, 169
Laudian church, 72, 73, 96
L'Estrange, Roger, 5, 181
"Letter to a Friend" (Milton), 70
Lewalski, Barbara, xi, 41, 168, 174, 213n37
Licensing Act (1662), 164–65, 180–81
Licensing Order (1643), 17–18, 24
Lilly, William, 179, 181
Lingua (Erasmus), 10
literary practice: ecclesiology and, ix–xii, 25–26, 32, 103–04, 141–42; liturgy and, 141, 208n18; religious role of, 84–85; and rituals, 109; style in, 115–18; and Word of God, 118; and worship, 111. *See also* rhetoric
liturgy: definition of, 206n1; literary practice and, 141, 208n18; Milton and, 112–16, 120–21; Westminster Assembly and, 111–12; of the Word, 129. *See also* rituals; worship
logos, 8–9, 11, 13, 22, 194n28
Lords Loud Call to England, The (Jessey), 180
Luther, Martin, 9, 27, 58, 60, 107, 148
Lycidas (Milton), 1, 70, 72, 73

MacCallum, H. R., 91
Marshall, Charles, 41
Martz, Louis, 75
Marvell, Andrew, 166
Marxism, 188n6
Mask, A (Comus) (Milton), 1–2, 22, 99–100, 199n40
material world, versus sacred world, 107
Matthew, Gospel of, 89, 183
Mede, Joseph, 157
millenarianism, 149, 157

Milner, Andrew, x
Milton, John: *Animadversions*, 73–74, 113, 116, 118–19, 163; and Antichrist, 157–58; antiepiscopal tracts of, 2–4, 96–97; apocalypticism of, 155–58, 163, 168, 184–85, 211n5; *An Apology against a Pamphlet*, 69, 75, 113, 115, 116; *Areopagitica*, 4, 6, 17–21, 23, 32, 79, 151–52; Bibles used by, 191n10; "Brief Notes Upon a Late Sermon," 153; Christology of, 41–42, 45; on church discipline, 95–99, 102–03; on church-state relations, 141–42, 150–58; *Considerations Touching the Likeliest Means to Remove Hirelings Out of the Church*, 4, 88–90, 152, 153; *De Doctrina Christiana*, 2, 4–6, 9–11, 17, 45, 80, 82, 101, 115, 116, 119–20, 123, 127, 136–37, 143, 153, 158, 163, 191n8; denominational approach to, x; *The Doctrine and Discipline of Divorce*, 18, 78, 151; ecclesiology of, ix–x, 1–26, 58–59, 83, 95, 106, 154–55, 209n25; *Eikonoklastes*, 81, 113, 115–16, 166, 208n19; "Elegy 5," 73; "Elegy VI," 68; and English reformation, 2–5; and inspiration, 71, 82–83, 85; on kingdom of Christ, 151–56, 167–68; "Letter to a Friend," 70; and liturgy, 112–16, 120–21; *Lycidas*, 1, 70, 72, 73; *A Mask (Comus)*, 1–2, 22, 99–100, 199n40; and ministry, 1–2, 56–57, 67–84, 91, 203n36; and mysticism, 207n12; Nativity ode, 1, 72, 73, 77, 82; *Of Civil Power*, 154, 171; *Of Education*, 171; *Of Reformation*, 4, 21, 95, 118, 151, 157–58, 169; *Of True Religion*, 5, 167; *Paradise Lost*, 22, 43–44, 110, 122–23; *Paradise Regained*, x–xi, 6, 32–38, 40–52, 59, 62, 85, 99–102, 106, 110, 126–38, 142–43, 153–54, 158–60, 166, 168–77, 183–86, 187n1; "Il Penseroso," 72; and poetry, 62, 67, 71–72; and politics, 151–53, 155–56, 213n37; and prayer, 118–20, 124–25; and Presbyterianism, 4, 18, 23, 30, 83, 96–97, 168, 205n57; "The